2-8-93   7   38.45

HANDBOOK OF INTERNATIONAL BUSINESS
AND MANAGEMENT

Handbook of International Business and Management

S. J. Gray, M. C. McDermott
and E. J. Walsh

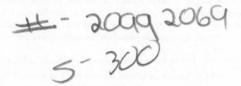

Basil Blackwell

Copyright © S. J. Gray, M. C. McDermott and E. J. Walsh 1990

First published 1990

Basil Blackwell Ltd
108 Cowley Road, Oxford, OX4 1JF, UK

Basil Blackwell Inc.
3 Cambridge Center
Cambridge, Massachusetts 02142, USA

British Library Cataloguing in Publication Data
A CIP catalogue record for this book is available from
the British Library.

Library of Congress Cataloging in Publication Data
Gray, S. J.
Handbook of international business and management / S. J. Gray,
M. C. McDermott, and E. J. Walsh.
p. cm.
Includes bibliographical references.
ISBN 0-631-15024-2
1. International business enterprises – Dictionaries.
I. McDermott, Michael C. II. Walsh, E. J. III. Title.
HD2755.5.G73 1990
658'.049'03 – dc20   89-77224 CIP

Typeset in 9½ on 11½ pt Palatino
by Joshua Associates Ltd, Oxford
Printed in Great Britain by
T. J. Press Ltd, Padstow, Cornwall

CONTENTS

CONTENTS

LIST OF ENTRIES

A

Academy of International Business [USA]
Accounting Standards Board (ASB) [UK]
adjustable bond
ad valorem duty [tax]
advertising agencies
affiliated company [associated company]
agency theory
agreement corporation
Allied–Lyons [UK]
American depository receipt (ADR)
Amstel Club [Switzerland]
anti-dumping duty
anti-trust legislation [merger policy]
arbitrage
Asea Brown Boveri [Switzerland]
Asiacurrency market
Asia–Pacific Economic Cooperation
  Conference (APECC)
Association of South East Asian Nations
  (ASEAN)
AT&T (American Telephone & Telegraph)
  [USA]

B

back-to-back financing [parallel financing]
balance of payments
bank draft [bill of exchange]
barrier to entry
barrier to exit
BASF [Germany]
Bass [UK]
B.A.T. Industries [UK]
Bayer [Germany]
bearer bond
Bhopal [India]
bid–ask spread
bill of lading
blocked funds
BMW [Germany]
Boeing [USA]
Boston Consulting Group (BCG) [USA]
boycott
BP (British Petroleum) [UK]
Brady Plan
brands
Bretton Woods agreement
bribes

Bridgestone [Japan]
BSN–Gervais Danone [France]
BTR [UK]

C

cabotage
capital asset pricing model (CAPM)
capital budgeting
capital structure
CARICOM (Caribbean Community)
  [Guyana]
Caterpillar [USA]
chartism [momentum analysis, technical
  analysis]
Chicago International Money Market
  [USA]
Chrysler [USA]
Ciba–Geigy [Switzerland]
CMEA, *see* COMECON
CoCom (Coordinating Committee for
  Multilateral Export Controls) [France]
codes of conduct
cola wars
collateral
COMECON [CMEA] (Council for Mutual
  Economic Assistance) [USSR]
commercial paper
commodity agreement
Common Agricultural Policy (CAP)
Commonwealth [British Commonwealth]
Compaq [USA]
comparative advantage
competitive advantage
competitive strategy
compressibility ratio
concentration, industrial
concession agreement
consignment
consolidation accounting
containerization
contract manufacturing
controlled foreign corporation (CFC)
convertible bond
corporate diversification
corporate raider
corporate strategy
correspondent banks
counterfeiting

H

Hanson Trust [UK]
Hecksher–Ohlin Theorem
Hirsch Method
Hoffman La Roche [Switzerland]
home country
host country
hot money
human resource management (HRM)
Hyundai [South Korea]

I

IBM (International Business Machines)
   [USA]
ICI (Imperial Chemical Industries) [UK]
industrial espionage
infant industry
Interest Rate Parity Theorem (IRPT)
internalization theory
international accounting standards
international auditing
international cash management
International Chamber of Commerce
   (ICC)
International Federation of Accountants
   (IFAC) [USA]
International Finance Corporation (IFC)
   [USA]
international Fisher Effect
International Labour Office (ILO)
   [Switzerland]
international mergers
International Monetary Fund (IMF) [USA]
International Organisation of Securities
   Commissions (IOSCO) [Canada]
international taxation
international trade unions
ITT Corporation [USA]

J

J-curve
Japanese-style management
joint venture
junk bond
just-in-time inventory management

K

keiretsu
Komatsu [Japan]

L

Latin American Integration Association
   (LAIA) [Uruguay]
Law of the Sea Convention
leading and lagging
letter of credit
licensing
lifestyle research
Lomé Convention
London Interbank Offered Rate (LIBOR)
London International Financial Futures
   Exchange (LIFFE)
Lucky–Goldstar (South Korea)

M

management buy-out
management contract
market segmentation
marketing mix
Matsushita Electric [Japan]
mercantilism
Merck [USA]
merger accounting
Michelin [France]
Minnesota Mining & Manufacturing (3M)
   [USA]
Monopolies and Mergers Commission
   (MMC) [UK]
multinational [transnational] corporation

N

NEC (Nippon Electric Company) [Japan]
Nestlé [Switzerland]
netting
new international economic order
NIC (newly industrializing country)
nineteen-ninety-two (1992)
Nippon Telegraph & Telephone [Japan]
Nissan [Japan]
Nokia [Finland]
non-tariff barrier

O

offshore production
OPEC (Organisation of Petroleum
   Exporting Companies) [Austria]
OPIC (Overseas Private Investment
   Corporation) [USA]
option

PREFACE

The purpose of this book is to provide an interesting, useful, reliable, succinct and readable guide to the rapidly growing field of international business and management. A selection of key terms and concepts in this area is provided, together with information and analysis relating to major international companies and organizations worldwide. The selection of entries reflects the authors' perceptions of what is important, subject to the usual limitations of time and space.

The book is intended for a broad audience but is directed in particular to corporate executives, government officials and business students. It is hoped that the book will be useful both to the busy executive or official and to the business student who wishes to obtain a quick grasp of key issues and information, as well as serving as a valuable reference work.

While the authors have been involved individually in drafting specific entries they accept responsibility collectively for the scope of the book, the selection of entries and the final version of the text.

S. J. GRAY
M. C. MCDERMOTT
E. J. WALSH

ACKNOWLEDGEMENTS

The authors are grateful to the many companies and organizations who have cooperated in providing information for this handbook. The research assistance of Aleksandar Tojagic is also gratefully acknowledged. Mary W. Mowat, the librarian of the Wards Research Library in the University of Glasgow, deserves a special mention and thanks for preparing the bibliography of business information sources and for her help and advice throughout.

S. J. GRAY
M. C. MCDERMOTT
E. J. WALSH

LIST OF ABBREVIATIONS

ABB	Asea Brown Boveri
ADR	American depository receipt
ADS	American depository share
APECC	Asia–Pacific Economic Cooperation Conference
ASB	Accounting Standards Board
ASEAN	Association of South East Asian Nations
BCG	Boston Consulting Group
BMW	Bayerische Motoren Werken
BP	British Petroleum
CAP	Common Agricultural Policy
CAPM	capital asset pricing model
CARICOM	Caribbean Community
CFC	controlled foreign corporation
CMEA	Council for Mutual Economic Assistance
CoCom	Coordinating Committee for Multilateral Export Controls
COMECON	Council for Mutual Economic Assistance
DEC	Digital Equipment Corporation
DM	Deutschmark
EB	Elektriska Bureau
EC	European Community
ECGD	export credit guarantee department
ECOWAS	Economic Community of West African States
ECU	European currency unit
EEC	European Economic Community
EEIG	European Economic Interest Grouping
EFTA	European Free Trade Association
EIB	European Investment Bank
EMS	European Monetary System
EPA	Environmental Protection Agency
EPOS	electronic point-of-sale
EPZ	export processing zone
ETUC	European Trade Union Confederation

FASB	Financial Accounting Standards Board
FCIA	Foreign Credit Insurance Association
FDI	foreign direct investment
FF	French franc
FMS	flexible manufacturing system
FRN	floating rate note
FTC	Federal Trade Commission
G5	Group of Five
G7	Group of Seven
G10	Group of Ten
G77	Group of Seventy-Seven
GATT	General Agreement on Tariffs and Trade
GE	General Electric
GEC	General Electric Company
GM	General Motors
GNP	gross national product
GTC	general trading company
HDTV	high definition television
HRM	human resource management
IASC	International Accounting Standards Committee
IBM	International Business Machines
IBRD	International Bank for Reconstruction and Development
ICC	International Chamber of Commerce
ICFTU	International Confederation of Free Trade Unions
ICI	Imperial Chemical Industries
IDA	International Development Association
IFAC	International Federation of Accountants
IFC	International Finance Corporation
ILO	International Labour Office
IMF	International Monetary Fund
IMM	international money market
IOSCO	International Organisation of Securities Commissions
IRPT	Interest Rate Parity Theorem
JIT	just-in-time
LAFTA	Latin American Free Trade Association
LAIA	Latin American Integration Association
LDC	less developed country

LIBOR	London Interbank Offered Rate
LIFFE	London International Financial Futures Exchange
3M	Minnesota Mining & Manufacturing
MBB	Messerschmitt–Bolkow–Blohm
MMC	Monopolies and Mergers Commission
MNC	multinational company
NATO	North Atlantic Treaty Organisation
NEC	Nippon Electric Company
NIC	newly industrializing country
NPV	net present value
NTT	Nippon Telegraph & Telephone
OECD	Organisation for Economic Co-operation and Development
OEM	original equipment manufacturing
OFT	Office of Fair Trading
O&M	organization and methods
OPEC	Organisation of Petroleum Exporting Countries
OPIC	Overseas Private Investment Corporation
OTC	over the counter
PC	personal computer
P&G	Procter & Gamble
R&D	research and development
SBU	strategic business unit
SDA	Scottish Development Agency
SDR	special drawing right
SEC	Securities and Exchange Commission
SEL	Standard Elektrik Lorenz
SF	Swiss franc
SITC	Standard International Trade Classification
SSAP	Statement of Standard Accounting Practice
SWIFT	Security for Worldwide Interbank Financial Telecommunications
TCE	Thomson Consumer Electronics
UN	United Nations

UNCTAD	United Nations Conference on Trade and Development
UNCTC	United Nations Commission on Transnational Corporations
UNICE	Union of Industries of the European Community
USM	unlisted securities market
VAT	value added tax
VCR	video cassette recorder
WCL	World Confederation of Labour
WHO	World Health Organisation

NOTE ON THE USE OF THE BOOK

The entries in the *Handbook* are ordered alphabetically; numerals are ordered before letters.

Companies and bodies known equally by the spelled-out and abbreviated forms of their names are entered under the spelled-out form. Only companies and bodies known almost exclusively by an acronym are entered under the abbreviated form of their names. In all cases where it is deemed useful, cross-reference entries lead readers from one form to the other.

Alternative forms of name for companies and bodies are given in parentheses following the bold heading. Other kinds of alternative heading are given in brackets following the bold heading.

For all entries on companies, bodies, etc., a country is given in brackets in the heading: this identifies the home country of a multinational corporation or government body, the country of the headquarters of an international body or association of nations.

There are a number of cross-reference entries on general subjects (e.g. **accounting** and **banks**, **banking**) leading the reader to individual entries. There are, in addition, cross-references at the ends of some entries (introduced by 'see' or 'see also' in italic type), to lead the reader to related entries. In all cross-references the entry referred to appears in small capital letters.

No cross-reference entries are included in the List of Entries at the beginning of the book.

As far as possible, information is up-to-date as of 1989.

HANDBOOK OF INTERNATIONAL BUSINESS AND MANAGEMENT
A–Z

A

Academy of International Business [USA]. An association of persons interested in fostering education in international business and advancing professional standards in the field. Based in the USA, but with membership from around the world and branches at regional level, the Academy fosters the exchange of information and ideas among professionals in academic, business and government organizations who are concerned with international business education. The Academy encourages research that advances knowledge pertinent to international business and aims to augment the available body of research and teaching materials.

accounting, see ACCOUNTING STANDARDS BOARD, CONSOLIDATION ACCOUNTING, CREATIVE ACCOUNTING, FINANCIAL ACCOUNTING STANDARDS BOARD, FOREIGN CURRENCY TRANSLATION, GOODWILL, INTERNATIONAL ACCOUNTING STANDARDS, MERGER ACCOUNTING, SEGMENTAL REPORTING.

Accounting Standards Board (ASB) [UK]. In the United Kingdom, the need to improve accounting practice was recognized initially with the setting up of the Accounting Standards Committee (ASC) in 1970 by the professional accountancy bodies. This followed criticism of the lack of comparability between corporate financial statements and a tendency towards 'creative accounting' arising from the variety of acceptable accounting methods. The prime objective of the ASC, a sub-committee of the Consultative Committee of Accountancy Bodies in the UK and Ireland, was to narrow the areas of difference and variety in accounting practice. It did this by recommending Statements of Standard Accounting Practice (SSAPs) for adoption by the accountancy bodies. The ASC was preoccupied in recent years with an unsuccessful experiment to introduce 'current cost accounting' as a means of accounting for inflation. There are now attempts to recover some of its authority and status in a political environment where the advantages of self-regulation are becoming increasingly questioned. Thus, with effect from August 1990, the ASC has been replaced by the Accounting Standards Board (ASB) with the independent right to issue accounting standards. A Financial Reporting Council has also been established to guide the ASB on work programmes and issues of public concern. A Review Panel will examine any contentious departures from accounting standards. A limited form of statutory support has also been introduced, including the power to require revision of accounts which do not give a true and fair view.

adjustable bond. In countries with relatively high inflation rates, inflation-adjustable bonds may be available. The bond's principal amount is adjusted on a periodic basis according to changes in the inflation rate. They are of relevance to MNCs attempting to minimize their exposure to foreign exchange risk, when there is a forward market available in the local currency.

ADR, see AMERICAN DEPOSITORY RECEIPT.

ad valorem duty [tax]. A duty levied as a percentage of the value of a product rather than as a fixed amount. For example, value added tax in Europe is an *ad valorem* tax. Tax is levied at a fixed rate (15 per cent for example) of the value of the goods. A country wishing to discourage the importation of automobiles might introduce a duty of 10 per cent to be levied upon the value of each automobile. Such a duty is an *ad valorem* duty. It may be contrasted with a duty of $100 per automobile.

advertising agencies. The internationalization drive of advertising agencies reflects the globalization of their clients, the major multinationals. New York was once the capital of the advertising world, but today many of America's leading advertising agencies have been acquired by UK companies. Madison Avenue is adapting to the British invasion. In 1986, Saatchi & Saatchi paid $450m for Ted Bates, and the combined worldwide gross income of both made the UK company the world's largest agency. In 1987 the legendary J. Walter Thompson was acquired for $566m by Britain's WPP, led by Martin Sorrell. More recently, WPP paid $864m to acquire the Ogilvy Group. These deals transformed WPP from an obscure producer of supermarket trolleys into one of the world's top marketing services companies. Table 1 shows details of advertising income for the world's top five agencies.

1992 may make it easier to ship goods but harder to sell them, and this will act as a further stimulus to advertising agencies in Western Europe, the world's fastest-growing advertising market worth almost $50bn in 1988. The market leader in Europe is Young & Rubicam. Europe now accounts for almost 40 per cent of total revenues (see table 2).

Table 1 Advertising gross income, 1988

Rank	Group	1988 worldwide gross income ($m)
1	Saatchi & Saatchi	1,990
2	Interpublic Group of Companies	1,260
3	WPP Group	1,173
4	Omnicom Group	986
5	Ogilvy Group	865

Source: Advertising Age

Table 2 Europe rankings by income, 1988

Company	$m	European income as per cent of total
Young & Rubicam	296.6	39.1
Saatchi & Saatchi	276.4	37.4
Ogilvy & Mather[a]	269.6	42.5
McCann[b]	253.7	38.6
BSB/Bates[c]	245.8	n.a.
Lintas[d]	215.0[e]	40.0
Grey	203.1	46.9
JWT[f]	197.2	35.3
BBDO[g]	188.2	32.1
DMB&B	174.4	n.a.

[a] Part of WPP [UK]
[b] Part of Interpublic [USA]
[c] Part of Saatchi & Saatchi [UK]
[d] Part of Interpublic [USA]
[e] Approximation
[f] Part of WPP [UK]
[g] Part of Omnicom [USA]
Source: Financial Times

affiliated company [associated company]. A company linked to another company, usually, but not necessarily, by share ownership. An affiliated company is not considered to be owned or controlled as in the case of a subsidiary company. However, a significant influence may be exercised over an affiliated company's affairs – which is usually reflected for reporting purposes by incorporating an appropriate share of profits in the consolidated accounts of the MNC.

agency theory. A theory that aims to deal with the possibility that the agent (or manager) may act in ways contrary to the interests of the principal (or shareholder) of a company. It states that the problem may be solved – assuming a self-interest motivation – by (1) providing incentives to the manager so that there is a mutuality of interest, or (2) by investing in monitoring devices including accounting, disclosure and audit. Management may be encouraged to act in ways that will be consistent with shareholder interests by incentives in the form of compensation linked to company profits or share prices. Such compensation may take the form of bonuses and/or options to buy shares in the company at an attractive price. At the same time, it will be in the interests of management to inform shareholders about their performance in the context of the compensation contracts involved.

agreement corporation. A subsidiary of a US bank which engages in international or foreign banking. Under US banking rules, local banks are not allowed to engage in international business. The Federal Reserve Act was amended in 1916 to permit larger banks to reach an 'agreement' with the Federal Reserve to engage in international banking.

Allied-Lyons [UK]. One of Britain's top 20 companies with sales in excess of £3bn. Allied-Lyons consists of three divisions – beer, wines and spirits, and food – and it has an attractive range of successful brands in each division, which include Skol and Double Diamond beer, Babycham, Harvey's sherry, Teacher's whisky, Lyons cakes, Lyons Maid ice cream and Tetley Tea. With such a strong brand portfolio, the company remains a likely takeover target, but at the same time it too is acquiring in order to enhance its competitive position in the global drinks industry. Its largest purchases have been the spirits divisions of Hiram Walker and Britain's Whitbread. It has also formed a strategic alliance with Japan's Suntory.

A brief review of the company's history testifies to the crucial role of acquisitions. In 1961 three breweries merged to form Allied Breweries, and in 1968 Showerings, famous for its Babycham drink, was acquired. In 1975, Sir Keith Showering became chairman, and three years later he masterminded the merger with J. Lyons, the food company. In the autumn of 1985, though, Allied-Lyons was a takeover target, when the Australian company, Elders, mounted a hostile bid for a then record £1.8bn, as it attempted to become a global brewing giant. The bid was referred to Britain's Monopolies and Mergers Commission which cleared the bid, but by which time circumstances had changed and Elders decided not to pursue the bid.

Like many British companies (e.g. Hanson Trust, ICI, and Pilkington), Allied-Lyons has learned that it must consolidate its reputation with the financial institutions which, regulation aside, determine the outcome of takeover battles. Thus it now promotes its brands and the company simultaneously, whereas in the past the emphasis was purely on brand promotion.

American depository receipt (ADR). A popular method of obtaining a quotation on the US stock exchanges for overseas companies. Unlike a normal stock exchange quotation, the issuing firm must arrange to have its shares held by a US bank or trust company. The US bank or trust company then issues a new security (an American depository share or ADS) against the ordinary shares which it holds. US investors may then purchase the ADS and trade them in secondary markets in the USA, as well as obtaining their dividends in dollars rather than foreign currency.

The ADR is attractive to US investors since it decreases the transaction costs associated with the purchase of foreign stocks. The device is also beneficial to foreign corporations, since US capital markets may be tapped, without the need to comply with US regulatory requirements. Moreover, the ADR is an obligatory first step for overseas firms seeking a full quotation on US stock exchanges.

American Telephone & Telegraph, *see* AT&T.

Amstel Club [Switzerland]. A confederation of European finance houses with reciprocal trade finance arrangements facilitating a clearing-house operation between them. Its official title is Amstel Finance International AG and it is based in Switzerland.

anti-dumping duty. In recent years, the EC has imposed tariffs on products from various countries, but the measures against Japanese firms have attracted most attention. However, western industrialists have argued that these penalties are being evaded, as Japanese firms establish 'screwdriver' plants (basic assembly plants) in the EC, dependent on cheap imported components. The EC has thus imposed duties on the components of items subject to anti-dumping measures. More recently the EC has focused on imports from Korea and has levied duties on video cassette recorders and videotapes. This has undoubtedly led a number of Korean firms (e.g. Daewoo, Samsung, Lucky–Goldstar) to establish a manufacturing presence in 'Fortress Europe'. *See also* DUMPING.

anti-trust legislation [merger policy]. With the recent boom in mega-mergers, anti-trust legislation or merger policy has become a major political issue on both sides of the Atlantic. The United States has a long tradition of anti-trust dating back to the last century, and the Sherman Anti-trust Act of 1890 which aimed to prohibit mergers leading to private monopolies. This act was not renowned for its success, and in 1914 the Federal Trade Commission was established by the Act of that name, and the Clayton Act was passed, Section 7 of which prohibits takeovers which 'lessen competition, or tend to create a monopoly'. Since 1914, a number of other acts have been passed. Current US merger policy is outlined in the Justice Department's 1984 Anti-Trust Merger Guidelines. The Reagan administration's merger policy was strongly influenced by a brand of *laissez-faire* economics whose basic tenet was that mergers improve efficiency which benefits business and consumers, and thus they are inherently good. The protection of consumers' welfare is now seen as the sole objective of anti-trust law by US policy enforcers. However, long before the calamitous worldwide share price crash of 'Black Monday', 19 October 1987, there were many critics of US policy of allowing merger-mania to go unchecked. On the other hand, the adoption in 1982 of the Herfindahl–Hirschman Index as a guide to industrial concentration has ensured that the response of US policy-enforcers is now predictable.

In Europe merger control is a recent development. Prior to 1973, the UK was the only country with such a policy, but Germany (1973), France (1977), Ireland (1978) and Sweden (1982) all introduced merger controls. British policy is based 'primarily but not exclusively on competition grounds', and as such it can be unpredictable. However, in recent years the only bids referred to the Monopolies and Mergers Commission (MMC) on non-competition grounds have been leveraged bids. At present, policy is enforced by the Office of Fair Trading (OFT), the MMC, and the Secretary of State for Trade and Industry. Some observers believe that the implementation of UK policy is unnecessarily time-consuming and that one body should be responsible for enforcing policy, just as the Federal Cartel Office does in Germany.

The absence of, or differences in, merger policy among EC countries has resulted in the European Commission issuing a stern warning that it will use all its powers to prohibit anti-competitive mergers. In December 1989, a Council regulation to control EC mega-mergers was approved.

APECC, *see* ASIA–PACIFIC ECONOMIC COOPERATION CONFERENCE.

arbitrage. A trading technique brought into play when identical financial instruments or goods are traded at different prices in different markets. The arbitrageur buys in the cheaper market and sells in the more expensive market to earn arbitrage profits. Clearly, transaction costs must be relatively low and deals must be capable of being implemented quickly in order to earn substantial profits. In modern financial markets, arbitrage opportunities within markets are difficult to find, since they disappear extremely quickly. For example, the price of gold or the dollar is likely to be the same in most financial markets. Opportunities do, however, arise when instruments purchased in one market are used to replicate the pay-off of instruments purchased in other markets.

Covered-interest arbitrage is one of the simplest arbitrage techniques. It consists of substituting foreign investment for domestic investment in order to exploit international interest rate differentials, without incurring foreign exchange risk.

Assume that:

US interest rate	= 20% p.a.
UK interest rate	= 10% p.a.
Spot exchange rate	= $1 per £1
Forward exchange rate	= $0.95 per £1 (12-month contract)

An investor could earn arbitrage profits by using the following strategy.

1 Borrow £1,000 stg and convert to dollars at the spot rate.
2 Enter a forward contract to sell $1,200 in 12 months time at a rate of $0.95 per pound.
3 Deposit $1,000 in a bank account and receive $1,200 at the end of 12 months.
4 Complete the forward contract by selling $1,200 for £1,263 stg (i.e. 1,200/0.95).

It may be seen from table 1 that it is profitable:

Table 1   Covered-interest arbitrage

	Cash flow in $t = 0$	Cash flow in $t = 1$
Borrow sterling	1,000 stg	−1,100 stg
Convert sterling to dollars	−1,000 stg	
	+1,000 $	
Invest dollars	−1,000 $	+1,200 $
Sell dollars forward		−1,200 $
		+1,263 stg
Total pay-off:	0	163 stg

Table 1 shows the ultimate free lunch! Invest nothing, incur no risk and earn money for doing so. Opportunities like this rarely occur in financial markets. One would expect that these arbitrage opportunities would disappear extremely quickly. Interest rates and forward rates will adjust to ensure that these opportunities do not persist. For example, if the forward rate were $1.091 per pound, then one would earn zero return on the strategy.

Arbitrage opportunities do arise in modern financial markets. However, the techniques are beyond the scope of this book. The interested reader might consult any of the published works on options and futures trading. The prerequisites for taking advantage of these opportunities are access to real-time information from financial markets, substantial lines of credit or cash, and the ability to execute transactions quickly. *See also* BID–ASK SPREAD.

ASB, *see* ACCOUNTING STANDARDS BOARD.

Asea Brown Boveri [Switzerland]. This $18bn world leader in electrical engineering was formed in 1988, when Sweden's Asea and Switzerland's Brown Boveri came together in one of Europe's largest ever cross-border mergers which created one of the world's 50 largest industrial corporations. ABB's principal activities are related to the production, distribution and application of electricity. The group relies on western Europe for two-thirds of its turnover, where Germany, Sweden and Italy are its largest markets. It is intent though on achieving geographical diversification, and increasing its presence in North America and Asia. It has 170,000 employees and 2,500 manufacturing plants – probably more than any other industrial company.

ABB employs a matrix structure with eight business segments, each reporting to a member of the executive board for a product group or geographical region. It has 50 product-based business areas, 800 companies and 3,500 decentralized profit centres. Each segment bears responsibility for global strategies, business plans, allocation of manufacturing responsibilities and product development.

The merger in 1988 was a highpoint in the career of Percy Barnevik, chief executive of Asea since 1980. Under Barnevik sales and profits grew impressively as the company was transformed through acquisitions from a Swedish-centred into a pan-Nordic multinational. Costs were slashed too. For example, he reduced headquarters staff from 1,700 to just 200. Brown Boveri, in contrast, had suffered poor financial results and was considered out of touch with its market. Nevertheless, Boveri was strong where Asea was weak (i.e. central and southern Europe) and vice versa (i.e. northern Europe). The merger was thus highly complementary. Barnevik himself readily admits his eagerness to marry the two parties. The deal was put together in just six weeks and it 'violated every page in the takeover manual'.

With Barnevik at the helm, ABB is one of many MNCs pursuing a strategy of product consolidation and geographical diversification. ABB aims to stay the most efficient producer in a mature industry dogged by overcapacity. In another era (e.g. the 1960s) this would have been considered industrial suicide, and rapid product diversification would have been considered paramount.

The ABB merger has led to a restructuring of the power equipment industry internationally, but particularly in Europe where Siemens, the traditional market leader, now lags behind ABB and GEC–Alsthom (UK/France). The other major players are America's General Electric and from Japan, Mitsubishi, Toshiba and Hitachi.

ASEAN, see ASSOCIATION OF SOUTH-EAST ASIAN NATIONS.

Asiacurrency market. This market emerged in the late 1960s in Singapore and is similar to the Eurocurrency market. It consists mostly of dollar-denominated transactions and is a source of funds for south-east Asian countries. As well as serving the local countries, it also has the advantage of being an offshore dollar market in an Asian time zone.

Asia–Pacific Economic Cooperation Conference (APECC). A new group of ten Pacific nations formed in 1989 comprising Australia, New Zealand, Japan, South Korea, Thailand, Singapore, Philippines, Malaysia, Indonesia and Brunei. This organization has been described as a kind of Pacific OECD. However, unlike the OECD, the Pacific countries are at very different levels of development. On the other hand, the intention of this new grouping is that it should promote mutual discussion and cooperation.

associated company, see AFFILIATED COMPANY.

Association of South-East Asian Nations (ASEAN). The association was formed by the governments of Indonesia, Malaysia, Singapore, Philippines and Thailand at the Bangkok declaration – 8 August 1967. In 1984, Brunei joined the association.

Like other country associations, its aim is to accelerate economic growth by mutual assistance and to enhance social and cultural development by cooperating with similar international organizations.

Priorities are the intensification of inter-ASEAN trade and the association's trade with the rest of the world. The member countries are also involved in joint research programmes, promotion of tourism, improving communications and transport and other cultural Asian studies.

Annual meetings are held in each country on a rotational basis, each country represented by its foreign minister. This is known as the Annual Ministerial Meeting and is the highest policy-making body. Other groups include two economic and three non-economic committees responsible for the implementation and running of projects.

AT&T (American Telephone and Telegraph) [USA]. No longer classified by *Fortune* as an industrial company, it ranks as America's largest diversified services corporation with annual sales in excess of $35bn. It is nevertheless the world's leading manufacturer of telecommunications equipment, though rivals are narrowing the gap by acquisition (e.g. France's CGE bought ITT's telecoms business Alcatel) or merger (e.g. GEC and Plessey merged their telecoms business).

The second half of the 1980s was traumatic for AT&T, as it adjusted to the US government's 1984 decision to break up the AT&T telephone network on anti-trust grounds. In recent years, sales have exceeded $30bn, but profits have been erratic. In 1986, restructuring was necessary and AT&T took a $3.2bn write-off, and net income fell to a paltry $139m. In 1987 net income was $1.4bn – more than the turnover of Compaq in the same year – but in 1988 it reported its first annual loss in its 103-year history, after making probably the biggest write-off in corporate history, $6.7bn for outdated equipment.

AT&T has decided to focus on its core businesses, but to diversify geographically. Foreign sales accounted for just 10 per cent of total revenues in 1988, but by the end of the century AT&T hopes this will have risen to 25 per cent. In order to rapidly penetrate foreign markets, it has formed numerous strategic alliances. For example, in 1984 it paid $260m for a 25 per cent stake in Italy's Olivetti, Europe's largest computer company, but this alliance failed to meet both parties' expectations and AT&T sold its stake for $850m in 1989. AT&T also has alliances with Philips, Italy's Italtel and Spain's Telefonica. In Japan it has alliances with NTT, Ricoh and Toshiba.

B

back-to-back financing [parallel financing]. A back-to-back loan or parallel loan is an agreement between two companies to borrow currency from one another. For example, suppose that MNC Ltd, a UK company, has a subsidiary in Nigeria, and that the Nigerian authorities have forbidden all dividend payments to overseas companies. Another company, Tiger PLC, is considering expanding its Nigerian subsidiary, and investing sterling in Nigeria. MNC Ltd could overcome its repatriation problems by lending Nigerian currency to Tiger, in return for an equivalent loan in sterling. This technique is illustrated in figure 1.

The parallel loan is a useful technique for overcoming blocked funds or foreign exchange risk in the absence of forward markets. It may also be an opportunity for corporations to share transaction costs that they may have otherwise paid to banks. Unfortunately, it can be difficult to locate a company with which to transact, but multinational banks or investment houses may help locate suitors. The basic deal is also of interest since it was a forerunner to the swap. *See also* CREDIT SWAP.

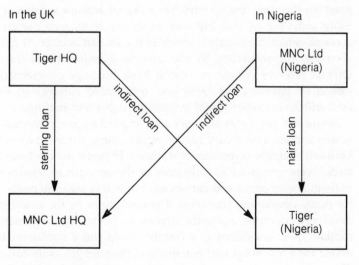

1   A back-to-back loan

balance of payments. In theory, the net amount of all economic transactions between the residents of one country and the residents of all
other countries. In practice, 'black holes' may occur due to the failure
of local authorities to record all transactions, and the failure of
residents to report all transactions (e.g. the importation of narcotic
substances).

In figure 1, a hypothetical balance of payments is illustrated. There
are three major components within the balance of payments: the
capital account, the current account and the official reserves account.

The current account contains the balance of trade (exports and
imports of goods), the balance of services and investments or in-
visibles, and the balance of unilateral payments which would include
emigrants' remittances and development aid to third world countries.
In this particular example, there is a deficit on the balances of goods
and services (the country imports more than it exports) and a surplus
on the unilateral transfers account. This surplus might arise from
grant-aid received from other countries. Summing these items, there
is a current account deficit of 190. Since it is necessary to pay
foreigners for goods imported in foreign currency, it is necessary to
finance the current account imbalance.

The other two components of the balance of payments tell us how
the deficit was financed. In this particular example, financial assets
were sold to overseas residents which exceeded the investment in
foreign assets by home residents. This sale of financial assets implies
that this country will have a liability to foreign residents. It would
include raising overseas debt which is treated as the sale of a financial
asset. In this case, the country has a capital account surplus of 240.
Since only 190 of this 240 was necessary to finance the current
account deficit, 50 remains, which is the overall balance. It may be
seen that the remaining 50 was used to increase official reserves.
Official reserves consist of central bank holdings of international
means of payment (i.e. gold and convertible currencies). Freely
convertible currencies would include the dollar and sterling.

Balance-of-payments statistics are compiled by government statis-
ticians and are a necessary part of any economic survey of a country.
Formerly, balance-of-payments statistics, in particular the balance of
trade, were perceived as indicators of the strength or weakness of
individual economies and currencies. While this may still be the case
for many developing countries, it is unlikely to be the case for the
developed countries, due to the increased significance of international
capital flows. For example, a country could run a significant trade
deficit for a few years without affecting the strength of its currency.
This is due to overseas confidence in the economy, which is reflected

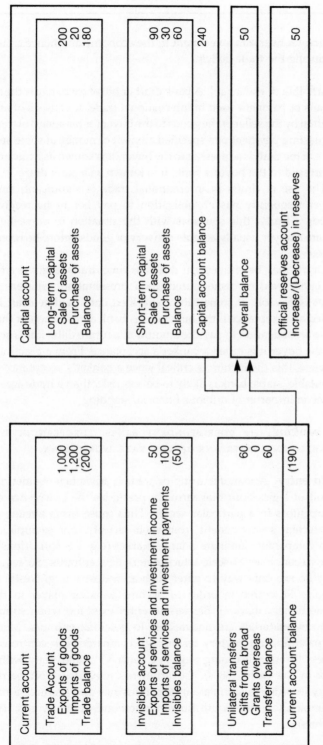

1 Balance of payments

in greater overseas investment in the economy and hence a means of
financing the trade deficit.

bank draft [bill of exchange]. A bank draft or bill of exchange is the normal
   means of payment used in international trade. It consists of an order
   written by the seller of the goods to the buyer (or his agent) of the goods
   requesting payment of a specified amount of money at some specified
   date. If the draft is addressed to the buyer, it is known as a trade draft; if
   addressed to the buyer's bank, it is known as a bank draft.
      The use of drafts in international trade is significant, since the
   buyer frequently has an obligation to pay before he receives the
   goods. Clearly, this contrasts with the situation in domestic trade,
   where a buyer usually accepts delivery of goods before he receives an
   invoice.
      Drafts may be either sight drafts or time drafts. Sight drafts must
   be either paid or dishonoured upon presentation, whereas a time
   draft is payable at some future specified date. A time draft is then
   called an acceptance if the buyer or his bank agree to accept that they
   have an obligation to pay the amount at a future date. If it is accepted
   by the buyer it is called a banker's acceptance. From a practical point
   of view, this distinction is critical since a banker's acceptance from a
   reputable, stable bank is likely to be less risky than a trade acceptance
   from an importer of dubious financial standing.

banks, banking, *see* CORRESPONDENT BANKS, EUROPEAN INVESTMENT
   BANK, LONDON INTERBANK OFFERED RATE, WORLD BANK.

barrier to entry. A manufacturing or trading advantage (sometimes the
   result of legislation) that virtually precludes the emergence of new
   competitors in a particular sector. Thus those firms already in this
   'protected' sector benefit from such security. For example, if just
   two companies dominate a large market (e.g. US soft drinks), they
   enjoy economies of scale which deters new entrants. So acquisition
   may be the only way to enter such an industry (e.g. Nestlé had to
   acquire Rowntree in order to become a major player in the UK
   confectionery market). Barriers to entry exist too when supplies of
   key raw materials are unavailable to potential entrants. Moreover,
   by patenting proprietory technology companies can control market
   access through licensing (e.g. JVC with VHS and Sony with Betamax in the early 1980s). Governments may also erect barriers to
   entry in order to stimulate infant industries and promote a national
   champion (e.g. the South Korean automobile industry and Hyundai
   Motors).

barrier to exit. Any factor that prevents or deters divestment. A company may wish to withdraw from a certain business or close a particular plant, but barriers to exit may exist which must be overcome before divestment can occur. There may be specialized assets which will be difficult to sell, heavy termination costs arising from compensation settlements and pensions, strategic costs such as damaging the company's image and access to capital markets, information barriers to exercising appropriate judgement, emotional reluctance and pride, and finally governmental and social pressure not to sell or close down.

BASF [Germany]. The largest of Germany's 'big three' chemical companies, and one of the world's 30 largest industrial corporations with sales of around $25bn, the vertically integrated BASF has diversified to higher value-added products (e.g. plastics and composites) which now account for 60 per cent of annual sales. It has some 130,000 employees, and production plants in almost 40 countries. It sells in 160 countries and foreign sales now account for 65 per cent of group sales compared with just 52 per cent at the end of the 1970s. This reflects its recent acquisition strategy which has concentrated on expanding US business. Nevertheless BASF remains one of Germany's largest exporters, with exports accounting for more than a third of its total sales.

BASF made three major US acquisitions in 1985: the high-performance composite materials division of Celanese Corporation for $135m; the Inmont car paint and printing ink operation, a subsidiary of United Technologies, for $1bn; and American Enka's fibre activities for an undisclosed sum.

The Inmont acquisition gave BASF, which was already the biggest paint supplier to Volkswagen, Daimler–Benz and BMW in West Germany, a leading position in supplying paint to the US automobile industry. Japan is obviously the missing link, but BASF has an agreement with a small, privately owned Japanese company which manufactures paint as a BASF licensee. Executives at BASF's headquarters at Ludwigshafen hope that this relationship might be used as a base for expansion in Japan. Thus BASF would have a stake in supplying paint to the world's three biggest car-producing nations. However, developing BASF's position in the North American market remains a priority.

Bass [UK]. Britain's leading brewer has 20 per cent of the UK market, its main brands being Carling Black Label and Tennent's. In the UK it owns 7,400 pubs, 650 off-licences (including the Augustus Barnett chain) and 850 Coral betting offices. It also owned Horizon Travel, Britain's second-largest tour operator, until it sold the business to Thomson, the number one, in 1988. Unlike some other leading UK brewers (e.g. Allied–Lyons, Whitbread, and Scottish and Newcastle), Bass makes no political donations, while the other three contribute to the Conservative Party each year. Critics of multinationals contend that political donations by large corporations ensure that governments look favourably upon their interests.

As of 1988, Bass had 85,000 employees and sales amounted to $5.5bn, placing it in the 150 largest non-US industrial corporations. In the late 1980s, the company was transformed. Three major acquisitions between 1987 and 1989 saw it become the owner of the Holiday Inn hotel chain worldwide, and thus the world's leading hotelier.

The hotel industry is in the throes of a major transformation, as table 1 shows.

Table 1 Major acquisitions in the hotel industry

Year	Hotel/hotel chain	Seller (country)	Buyer (country)	Price
1987	Holiday Inn (all except N. America and Mexico)	Holiday Corporation (USA)	Bass (UK)	£290m
1987	Hilton International	Hilton (USA)	Ladbroke (UK)	£645m
1987	Westin Hotels & Resorts	Westin Hotels & Resorts	Aoki (Japan)	$750m
1988	Inter-Continental	Grand Metropolitan (UK)	Seibu Saison (Japan)	$2bn
	Intercontinental (40 per cent stake)	Seibu Saison (Japan)	Scandinavian Airline Systems (Scandinavia)	$500m
1989	Holiday Inn (Canada)	Holiday Corporation (USA)	Bass (UK)	£142
1989	Holiday Inn (USA & Mexico)	Holiday Corporation (USA)	Bass (UK)	£1.28bn
	Ramada	Ramada (USA)	New World Development (Hong Kong)	$540m
1989	Hilton (USA)	Hilton (USA)		offers of $3.06bn invited

Source: Press reports; *Acquisitions Monthly*

B.A.T. Industries [UK]. Britain's second-largest manufacturing company with sales of more than $14bn, like other large tobacco companies it has spent heavily to diversify away from its original base.

The initial goal of Patrick Sheehy, who became chairman in 1982, was to find a fourth product line to add to its other two businesses, paper-making (Wiggins-Teape) and retailing (Saks Fifth Avenue, Marshall Fields, Argos). Financial services was eventually the sector chosen, and in 1984, B.A.T. paid a then record £946m for Eagle Star, one of Britain's largest insurance companies, and in the following year it acquired Allied Dunbar. Nevertheless, this giant company with more than 300,000 employees and 20 per cent of the global tobacco market, still relied on tobacco for 50 per cent of its operating profit. In 1988, however, B.A.T. paid $4.2bn for Farmers Union, one of America's largest insurance companies. The majority of company profits will now come from non-tobacco business.

Having achieved product diversification, B.A.T. is likely to concentrate on geographical diversification, as sales remain heavily concentrated in Europe and the USA. However, in July 1989 the company received a hostile takeover bid of £13.5bn from Hoylake, a consortium of financiers including Sir James Goldsmith, Kerry Packer, Jacob Rothschild, Giovanni Agnelli, whose aim was to break up B.A.T. and to sell off all but the tobacco business. In response, B.A.T. decided to 'unbundle' itself and, in so doing, remove the rationale for the bid. Hoylake subsequently withdrew in April 1990.

Bayer [Germany]. Among the world's top 40 companies, its sales of $23bn are focused on consumer-related and sophisticated products, namely pharmaceuticals, agrochemicals and photographic equipment, made by subsidiary company Agfa–Gevaert. Bayer is the most international of the large German chemical companies, with foreign sales accounting for almost 80 per cent of total sales, though almost 60 per cent are still derived from Europe. It has recently concentrated on expanding its US business, and in 1989 paid $500m to acquire Cooper Technicon, making Bayer's $1bn diagnostic business second in size only to that of Abbott Laboratories.

Bayer has 81 subsidiaries and other affiliated companies in 28 countries, and 166,000 employees. Around 40 per cent of total sales are accounted for by its overseas production plants.

A brief history of Bayer highlights the impact political events can have on the international firm. In 1863 Frederich Bayer was established as a dyestuffs company; during the First World War, the Bayer name and the US rights to aspirin, which had been discovered in 1899, were taken over by the US Alien Property Custodian and subsequently sold to Sterling Drug. In January 1986, it sold them back again for $25m. During this period Bayer traded in the US under the name of Rhine–Chem Corporation. In 1925, Bayer, Hoeschst and

BASF were merged to form the gigantic chemicals combine I. G. Farben Industrie. After the Second World War, in 1951, the conglomerate was split up and the individual companies were reestablished.

Traditionally, Germany's chemical companies were headed by scientists, but in 1984, Bayer appointed Hermann-Josef Strenger, whose background was in marketing. This move was indicative of the company's shifting emphasis, and part of a broader trend at many of Europe's other leading companies (e.g. Philips). Since 1984 management has been streamlined to accelerate decision-making, debt has been halved, and record profits achieved. Bayer is not planning any 'spectacular' acquisitions, but it aims to consolidate its position and diversify into new but related areas.

In common with other European chemical giants, Bayer spends heavily (i.e. almost £500m a year) on environmental protection, but it may have to increase this expenditure due to the growth in support for green politics, which is especially prominent in Germany itself. Moreover, there has been a decline in public confidence in the chemical industry since the major fire in 1986 at the Basle plant of Sandoz, Switzerland's second-largest chemical company with sales of $7bn. This accident resulted in serious pollution of the Rhine. Europe's chemical companies fear that the introduction of tougher pollution controls, and the resulting extra cost of adhering to more stringent regulation could place them at a disadvantage in an increasingly competitive global industry. To remain competitive, research and development is essential. Thus Bayer spent £720m on R&D in 1987 or 6 per cent of total sales, and has 12,000 scientists engaged in this activity. Details on the R&D activities of Europe's four largest chemical companies are provided in table 1.

BCG, see BOSTON CONSULTING GROUP.

bearer bond. A bond which does not have its owner's name registered by the issuer. This feature may be extremely convenient for individuals wishing to avoid paying tax on the interest payable from the bond, since revenue authorities will be unable to trace the ownership of the bond. When an interest payment is due, the holder simply removes an interest coupon from the bond and pays it in at a bank. Eurobonds are normally issued as bearer bonds.

Bhopal [India]. This Indian industrial city was the victim of the world's worst ever industrial disaster in which almost 2,000 people were killed and tens of thousands were injured when, in December 1984,

Table 1   Big four R&D in 1987 (chemicals)

Company	Amount	% of sales	No. of employees	Areas of R&D
Bayer	£720m	6	12,000	25% health care 25% agrochemicals 19% information technology 17% polymers
Hoechst	£680m	6	14,000	56% biological sciences, 17% materials
BASF	£500m	4	12,000	biological sciences specialist materials polymers
ICI	£460m	4	10,000	52% biological sciences 22% materials

Source: Financial Times

the Union Carbide plant leaked a deadly chemical – methyl soiyanate. Since the disaster, Union Carbide has been forced to restructure its operations radically, and to sell off chunks of the company, such as its agricultural equipment division (with the exception of the Bhopal plant). In 1989 it agreed to pay $480m in compensation to India.

bid–ask spread. The difference between the buying price and the selling price of a commodity or financial instrument. For example, the following exchange rates might appear in a newspaper:

pesetas/stg: 200
dollars/stg: 2
pesetas/$:   90

This would appear to be a relatively painless way of earning money. Buy pesetas with pounds, use the proceeds to purchase dollars, and then convert the dollars into pounds (see table 1).

The arbitrage strategy in table 1 is called triangular arbitrage. Now, suppose that our enterprising investor visits his local bank, and finds that bank is offering the rates shown in table 2. The strategy becomes considerably less profitable (see table 3).

Frequently, arbitrage opportunities which may seem profitable, may become extremely unprofitable when bid–ask spreads are taken into account. Bid–ask spreads are critical to an understanding of foreign-exchange risk management activities in corporations. A variety of strategies may be used to ensure that purchases and sales in each foreign currency are matched with one another. This matching strategy ensures that bid–ask spreads are minimized. It is also

Table 1   Triangular arbitrage

	Cash flow
Borrow 1,000 pounds	+1,000 stg
Buy 200,000 ptas	−1,000 stg
	+200,000 ptas
Buy $2,222 for 200,000 ptas	−200,000 ptas
	+2,222 $
Sell $2,222 for 1,111	−2,222 $
	+1,111 stg
Repay loan	−1,000 stg
Profit	111

Table 2   Triangular arbitrage

	Buy/bid	Sell/ask
Pesetas/stg:	190	210
Dollars/stg:	1.85	2.15
Pesetas/$:	80	100

Table 3   Triangular arbitrage

	Cash flow
Buy 190,000 ptas	−1,000 stg
Buy $1900 for 190,000 ptas	
Sell $1,900	+883
Profit	−117

possible that spreads and transaction costs are related to the size of the transaction. If this is the case, then centralized mechanisms which result in the aggregation of deals may be employed. *See also* ARBITRAGE.

bill of exchange, *see* BANK DRAFT.

bill of lading. When goods are sold to a customer in a foreign country, the carrier responsible for transporting the goods issues a bill of lading to the shipper. The bill of lading serves a number of purposes, since it implies that:

1 The carrier has agreed to transport the goods.
2 The carrier has received the goods.
3 The exporter has title to the goods for insurance purposes and as security against a bank loan.

The third point is critical. Transportation may take many months, and it may be desirable to have some means of financing this portion of the exporter's working capital.

blocked funds. If a country has insufficient foreign exchange or expects to have a shortage of foreign exchange, then restrictions may be introduced on the uses to which foreign exchange is put. The extent of the restrictions may be seen along a continuum. At one end, measures might include simply requiring official approval for all transactions, at the other end, the central bank may not allow any domestic currency to be converted to foreign currency. Half-way measures might include simply requiring official approval for all trade-related transactions, and forbidding all forms of capital transaction. The nature of this continuum and the possible managerial responses are illustrated in figure 1. The managerial responses are discussed below.

Restrictions	Freely convertible	Trade-related permitted and capital forbidden	Non-convertible
Management tactics	None necessary	Transfer pricing Unbundling services Fronting loans Export creation Government dispensation Bribery	Countertrade

1 Blocked funds

Management responses to restrictions on capital transactions might include the use of transfer pricing and the use of leading and lagging. Other responses might include:

Unbundling services

One could claim that dividends represent both a charge for services provided by the HQ and a return on the capital invested by the HQ. By unbundling the services, e.g. management charges, service fees, royalty payments, it may be possible to ameliorate the impact of restrictions. Rather than pay a dividend of 10 million foreign currency units, the subsidiary might pay a 2-million management charge, a 3-million royalty payment, and a service fee of 3 million.

The dividend would then be reduced to 2 million foreign currency units. This treatment might also have tax implications, since payments of a different form may be subject to differing tax rates. Many companies attempt to unbundle services immediately upon entering a new country, since it avoids accusations of opportunism or exploitation in later years, if the host government introduces more stringent controls. Moreover, tax authorities are not impressed by companies which are quite clearly altering the treatment of items from year to year in order to minimize tax liabilities.

Link financing/fronting loans

If there is considerable political turmoil in a host country, it is more likely that host governments will restrict the repayment of loans to the parent company than an overseas bank. In order to take advantage of this bias, some MNCs arrange loans to affiliates to appear as if they are loans from a commercial bank. They do so by depositing the amount they wish to lend in a branch of a bank in their home country and then the bank lends the same amount of money to the affiliate through its local branch. From the bank's point of view, the loan is risk free since the loan is secured on a deposit made by the parent. In principle, this strategy is similar to a back-to-back loan.

Creation of exports

Export creation involves altering the sourcing policies of the MNC in order to use blocked funds in a productive way. For example, a US film company displays its films in Spain and the Spanish authorities have restrictions on the transfer of royalty and rental fees overseas. This restriction gives rise to blocked funds; the company is unable to use the pesetas. Export creation to utilize the pesetas could include purchasing equipment in Spain for export, arranging conferences and premieres in Spain, shooting films in Spain or appointing the Spanish national airline as the company's official carrier.

Dispensation/bribery

Rather than altering the financial or operational characteristics of the local affiliate, the affiliate may attempt to obtain a special dispensation from the local government by arguing that their industry is a special case, or threatening to make local employees redundant. However, best practice may be to reach agreement with a host government before entering a country, rather than after the investment has taken place. Alternatively, corrupt local officials may be found and persuaded to accommodate the MNC. Needless to say, this latter practice is both unethical and may be illegal. US corporations may be in breach of the US Foreign Corrupt Practices Act and MNCs from other countries may be subject to adverse publicity.

BMW [Germany]. With annual sales of $12bn and 66,000 employees, it is among the world's top 100 industrial corporations. Its prestigious cars are sold worldwide, but Europe accounts for 70 per cent of total sales. This niche producer would clearly be a most attractive acquisition for any of the leading mass-producers, but the Quandt family, which controls BMW, is believed to have spurned foreign suitors.

Large companies are sometimes accused of being secretive. Until recently BMW's profit-and-loss account did not portray the company's real strength, because it did not consolidate worldwide results, similar to many German companies. In 1988 it produced a consolidated balance sheet for the first time, a year in advance of the legal requirement to do so, which arose from the EC's Seventh Directive. It reported net profits of $216m.

BMW is also at the heart of a major tangle between I. G. Metall, the 2.5m-strong metalworkers union and the Metal Employers Federation. In 1987 BMW persuaded the local works council at its newly opened Regensburg plant to accept a nine-hour day, four-day week, including working two Saturdays in three. This allowed it to raise factory operating time from 40 to 54 hours a week. German trades unions are fearful that Regensburg-type agreements may become the norm.

Boeing [USA]. With 55 per cent of the market – 10 per cent down on 1979 – this $17bn corporation is still the world's top manufacturer of commercial aircraft, ahead of Europe's Airbus Industrie and America's McDonnell Douglas. During 1988 Boeing sold a record 636 aircraft for $30bn, but in the first half of 1989 it sold 603 aircraft worth $33bn. This boom in sales coincided, however, with Boeing's reputation reaching its lowest ebb. Every $2\frac{1}{2}$ seconds a Boeing plane is either landing or taking off somewhere in the world. But in 1989, customers (e.g. British Airways and Japan Air Lines) criticized the quality of aircraft being delivered; national aviation authorities said that the new 747–700 failed to meet their safety standards. An investigation of the wiring on all Boeing aircraft discovered 94 cases of faulty wiring. This led to accusations that Boeing's quality-control standards had fallen.

The unexpected surge in demand also resulted in a shortage of manpower. In just 18 months Boeing recruited an extra 5,000 employees in its home city, Seattle, bringing the total workforce there to 103,000. Moreover, 650 workers were taken on six months loan from Lockheed.

bond, *see* ADJUSTABLE BOND, BEARER BOND, CONVERTIBLE BOND, DEEP DISCOUNT BOND.

Boston Consulting Group (BCG) [USA]. The Boston Consulting Group (BCG) is famous for designing in the 1970s a popular method of corporate strategy analysis known as the 'portfolio matrix approach'. By 1980 about half of the 500 largest US corporations were using a version of this approach. The BCG matrix focuses on the contributions that various businesses bring to corporate cash flows by relating corporate market share, on the horizontal axis, to market growth of the industry on the vertical axis (see figure 1). The four cells of the matrix define products or business units that are either 'cash cows' with a large market share and a stable market growth, 'dogs' with a low market share and slow growth, 'stars' with a large market share and anticipated rapid growth, or 'question marks' with small market share but possible rapid growth. The BCG matrix emphasizes market share and growth due to the underlying assumptions that there are experience curve effects and associated scale economies arising from production. The BCG matrix must, therefore, be treated with some caution. It was also designed for domestic firms. In the international context, the foreign subsidiaries of multinationals are often viewed as cash cows. This oversimplifies the situation since the nature of international markets may help to turn a cash cow in one market into a dog or star in others. Thus product lines must be analysed across markets internationally. Another international implication is that competition may be such that a multinational may retain a business with slow market growth to defend its interests and pre-empt entry

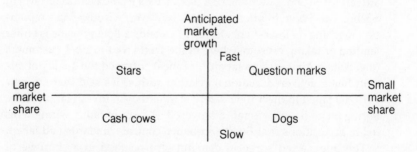

1   Boston Consulting Group matrix

by rivals. Other factors also need to be introduced into the matrix, e.g. profitability and growth of business units, synergy effects and diversification effects.

boycott. During the 1970s, the Swiss multinational Nestlé had to contend with pressure groups encouraging a boycott of its products in the US especially. This was because of its policy of marketing powdered baby milk in developing countries, where poor sanitation and uneducated mothers often rendered it unsuitable. Similarly, in the 1980s, other major companies have also faced orchestrated boycotts. For example, in the UK, the National Union of Students urged its members to avoid banking with Barclays because of its close ties with South Africa. Barclays eventually withdrew from South Africa. Another case involved Eli Lilly, the US pharmaceutical company, the manufacturer of 'Opren', the anti-arthritis drug. In 1988, it faced a British-based campaign to boycott the company's products worldwide. The action arose after a UK court settlement in December 1987 in which Eli Lilly offered £2.2m as compensation to the 2,000 cases in the UK of ill health linked to 'Opren'. Campaigners in Britain are trying to force the Indianapolis-based firm to match the compensation offered to US claimants.

More recently the French drug maker Roussel-Uclaf withdrew its abortion-inducing drug RU486 after street demonstrations in France. Roussel, whose main shareholders are the French government and Hoechst, was ordered to return RU486 to the market. The company will now probably face a boycott for all its products, precisely what Roussel hoped to avoid when it withdrew the drug.

However, the Arab–Israeli boycott has had greatest impact on international trade. Arab nations have a blacklist of companies that deal with Israel, and Arab customers often refuse to purchase goods from companies selling their goods to Israel. The Export Administration Act prohibits US companies from complying with the Arab boycott, and fines companies which comply (e.g. Japanese-owned Daiichi Jitsugyu (America)). Until recently, Japanese companies tended to avoid direct trade with Israel, but in 1989 Honda decided to export its US-made cars to Israel, a move described by the American Jewish Congress as a 'breakthrough' in Israeli–Japanese trade.

BP (British Petroleum) [UK]. Operating in 70 countries with 126,000 employees, and an annual turnover in excess of $40bn, BP is Britain's largest company, and one of the ten largest in the world. It consists of ten separate divisions each with its own chief executive. Its main activities are oil and gas exploration and production, supply and marketing of chemicals and technology. For example, with the purchase of America's Purina Mills in 1986 it became one of the world's leading manufacturers of animal foodstuffs. Oil though remains the hub of the business. Its exploration activities are based in 25 countries, and it supplies 6 per cent of the non-community world's oil supplies. It is the world's third-largest company and has boosted its size by major acquisitions, including the largest ever international takeover, the $7.5bn purchase of the outstanding stake in Standard Oil (formerly Sohio) in 1987. In 1988 its R&D budget was $266m. *See also* SEVEN SISTERS.

Brady Plan. In March 1989, Nicholas Brady, the US Treasury Secretary, launched an initiative to ease the debt crisis of third world countries. His debt reduction plan recognized the huge problems these debtors face in meeting their obligations, but the plan is seen by some as 'too little, too late', while leading bankers have been equally critical. Table 1 provides details on the world's main third world debtors.

Table 1   LDCs: the largest debtors

	Debt outstanding ($bn)	Interest payments as % of exports
Brazil	112.7	36.1
Mexico	102.6	27.3
Argentina	61.9	27.5
Poland	40.1	5.6
Venezuela	34.1	24.1
Philippines	28.5	18.6
Morocco	20.8	15.3
Peru	19.9	5.6
Chile	18.5	15.1
Hungary	17.9	10.1

Source: World Bank

brands. Multinationals in pursuit of global market leadership appreciate the value of established brand names associated with consumer and household products. So much so that many mergers of the 1980s were inspired by the desire to acquire leading brands, e.g. Nestlé and Rowntree, Unilever and Chesebrough-Pond's, Grand Metropolitan and Pillsbury.

Some companies have even gone so far as to put brands, usually purchased but sometimes internally generated as well, on their balance sheets albeit at subjective and questionable amounts in an attempt to beef-up their reported equity and loan potential. More questionable still is the practice of some service companies, e.g. WPP, which have also included acquired company names as brands. This is a matter of controversy in the accounting profession where intangible assets are usually treated on a very conservative basis.

A brand's profitability is determined not by its market share but by market rank. Thus, whether a brand leader has 60 per cent or just 6 per cent of a particular market is irrelevant, the fact that it is number one is critical. It has been suggested that the top two brands will be profitable, while the number three is vulnerable, but the fourth best-selling brand is unlikely to prove profitable.

This rather simplistic notion appears to have convinced many executives, hence the clamour to acquire companies with leading brands. Other firms with best-selling brands can expect rumours to persist that they too will be acquired. See table 1 for some examples of brand acquisitions.

Table 1 Brand acquisitions (some examples)

Acquired		Purchaser	
Automobiles			
Aston Martin	(UK)	Ford	(US)
Lamborghini	(Italy)	Chrysler	(US)
Lotus	(UK)	General Motors	(US)
Ferarri	(Italy)	Fiat	(Italy)
Jaguar	(UK)	Ford	(US)
Drinks			
Martell	(France)	Seagrams	(Canada)
Rémy-Martin	(France)	Martini-Rosso	(Italy)
Metaxa	(Greece)	Grand Metropolitan	(UK)
Cosmetics			
Calvin Klein	(US)	Unilever	(UK–Netherlands)
Fabergé	(US)	Unilever	(UK–Netherlands)
Helena Rubinstein	(US)	L'Oréal	(France)
Yves Saint Laurent	(US)	Yves Saint Laurent	(France)
(Squibb Corp)		Carlo de Benedetti	(Italy)
Gucci	(Italy)	Investcorp	(Bahrain)
Giorgio	(US)	Avon Products	(US)

Source: Press reports; *Acquisitions Monthly*

Bretton Woods agreement. In 1944 the Allied Powers met in Bretton Woods, New Hampshire, and decided to adopt a gold exchange standard. The countries agreed to fix the value of their currency in terms of gold. Since the dollar was to be the only currency convertible into gold, it was tantamount to all exchange rates being fixed vis-à-vis the dollar. The countries also agreed to try to maintain their currencies within 1 per cent of this value by buying and selling foreign currencies or gold.

The agreement was adhered to until 1971, and gave rise to an intervening period of stable exchange rates with sporadic revaluations and devaluations. It may be seen in figure 1 that exchange rates have been considerably more volatile in recent years.

bribes. In the 1970s, a major bribes scandal involved the US aircraft manufacturer Lockheed, which had made payments to Japanese politicians in order to secure lucrative contracts. This led the US to pass the Foreign Corrupt Practices Act outlawing bribes. More recently Bofors, the Swedish arms supplier, admitted paying large sums to three consultancy companies to secure a $1.4bn howitzer contract from the Indian government.

Bridgestone [Japan]. The largest Japanese tyre producer with 50 per cent of its domestic market, saw its sales grow six-fold during the 1970s and by 1987 it was the world's third-largest tyre company. In 1988 it paid $2.6bn to acquire Firestone, America's second-largest tyre company, in the largest ever US acquisition by a Japanese company. Prior to the Firestone deal, Bridgestone had sales in excess of $9bn, a worldwide labour force of 35,000, five overseas manufacturing plants (i.e. four in Asia, one in the USA), and foreign sales accounted for approximately 30 per cent of total sales. The Firestone acquisition has given Bridgestone the stronger international base which it required to compete on an equal footing with industry leaders, Michelin and Goodyear. Firestone had five plants in North America that were major suppliers to General Motors and Ford. Moreover, Firestone had four plants in southern Europe and three in South America.

The Firestone takeover may eventually prove successful, but Bridgestone has admitted that rehabilitating the US company has proven more difficult than expected. Initially, the Japanese company appeared reluctant to introduce major changes, but by the end of 1989 senior management and hundreds of engineers had been sent to the USA to accelerate Firestone's recovery.

Bridgestone's difficulties were compounded by high interest costs arising from the $1.4bn debt used to finance the deal.

British Commonwealth, see COMMONWEALTH.

British Petroleum, see BP.

1 Currency movements, effective exchange rate (IMF data 1985 = 100)

BSN–Gervais Danone [France]. Europe's third-largest food company and second-largest brewer has sales of almost $8bn, of which more than 80 per cent is derived from Europe, and it has almost 50,000 employees. Its brands include the world's best-selling mineral water and yoghurt, Evian and Danone, respectively, Lea and Perrins sauce and Kronenbourg beer. It comprises four divisions: beverages, dairy products, grocery products and containers. It is a master of growth through successful diversification. Since failing to acquire the French glass giant, Saint Gobain in 1968, it has been transformed under chairman Antoine Ribaud, from a glass company into France's leading food company and the world's leading producer of dairy products. The group was formed in 1972 when BSN merged with Gervais Danone. By 1982 the group had completed its three-year programme of withdrawal from the flat-glass sector.

Its principal strategic objectives have been the internationalization of its activities, and the achievement of a better balance in its operations through diversification and a wider geographic market. It has followed this corporate philosophy by developing or acquiring top brand names in the expanding food and beverage market. Moreover, it has looked overseas for managerial expertise, forming an International Advisory Committee which includes the chairmen of Pilkington, the UK glass company, and Japan's Sony.

Its 1989 acquisitions included five European biscuit and crisp companies from RJR–Nabisco for $2.5bn, and Henninger Hellas, Greece's second-largest brewer, with 35 per cent of its domestic market. It also teamed up with Italy's Ifil, the Agnelli family holding, to acquire Galbani, Italy's leading producer of cheeses and salt meats. It has a 35 per cent stake in this £1bn investment. The deal with RJR–Nabisco made BSN Europe's joint leading biscuit manufacturer, alongside United Biscuits of the UK. Shortly after completing this deal it recouped more than half of the $2.5bn paid for RJR–Nabisco's European biscuit and snack operations by selling two leading UK crisp brands, Walkers and Smiths, for $1.35bn to PepsiCo, the world's leading crisp maker. In beer, it has formed strategic alliances with other brewers to develop its European network.

BTR [UK]. This $10bn conglomerate owes its growth largely to an acquisition programme which has developed dominant market positions in the company's core businesses and skills. Its core businesses are rubber, plastics and metal manufacturing, and industrial marketing is its forte. Strong market shares in new areas have been developed through sequential, related acquisitions.

BTR has invariably mounted a bid when the target company has

been at its most vulnerable. For example, Thomas Tilling's profits
peaked at £81.1m in 1979, but in 1982 they had fallen to less than
£44m. The time was ripe to strike, and in a narrow victory in 1983,
BTR acquired Tilling, which itself had been a very acquisitive
industrial company. Before the bid, BTR had a market capitalization
of £1.05bn and Tilling's stood at £358m. Ten days after the acquisition, the enlarged BTR was worth £1.87bn. This represented an
increase of £507m on the sum of the market capitalization's of the two
firms before the bid.

In late November 1986, BTR launched its largest ever bid. Its target
was Pilkington, the world's leading flat-glass company. However,
shortly after the billion-pound-plus bid was launched, the Guinness
scandal broke. The timing of the bid was thus unfortunate, and
Pilkington had the support of employees, and many politicians from
the major parties. In early 1987, BTR withdrew its bid, following an
unexpectedly high profits forecast from Pilkington, the effect of
which was to raise the value of Pilkington beyond what BTR was
prepared to pay.

In 1989 BTR bid $1.6bn for Norton, the Massachusetts-based
abrasives manufacturer. Its hostile and bitterly opposed bid failed
when France's Saint Gobain emerged in early 1990 as a 'white knight'
with a $2.0bn agreed bid.

C

cabotage. The practice of reserving domestic trade for domestic transport services, e.g. shipping, trucking. This is now a controversial issue in the European Community context where all non-tariff barriers are to be eliminated by 1992 in accordance with the Single European Act of 1987.

CAP, *see* COMMON AGRICULTURAL POLICY.

capital asset pricing model (CAPM). A theoretical model for measuring the riskiness of the shares of a public company. Under a number of restrictive assumptions, it may be shown that all investors will hold a combination of a risk-free security (for example, short-dated gilts and treasury bills) and a portfolio of all the stocks available. Should these assumptions hold, then the expected return k on security j will be a function of the risk-free rate R_f, the return k on the portfolio of all shares in the market m, and the statistical relationship between km and kj which is known as Beta, β. We may express the expected return on security j in the following way:

$$k_j = R_f + (k_m - R_f)\beta$$

In practice, one finds that the model is a poor explanation of security price movements, and that less than 50 per cent of individual security price movements is explained by changes in the market index. A number of agencies publish the Beta for individual securities, both in the UK and the USA. The model is frequently used by institutional investors. In principle, it is also applicable to corporations seeking to evaluate the discounted cash flows of a proposed investment, since it may give some guidance as to an appropriate risk-adjusted discount rate.

capital budgeting. Once a company has identified a number of prospective investments, it must then select the combination of projects that will maximize the company's value to its shareholders. Capital budgeting comprises the set of rules and decision criteria which in theory help managers to determine whether to accept or reject an investment proposal. It is generally accepted that the criterion of net present value is the most appropriate as it is consistent with the objective of creating shareholder value. Net present value (NPV) is defined as the discounted value of the expected future cash flows less the initial cash outlays on the project. Those projects with a positive NPV should be accepted. If two projects are mutually exclusive, the one with the higher NPV should be accepted. The discount rate, also known as the cost of capital, is the expected rate of return on projects of similar risk.

capital structure. The relative proportions of share capital and loan capital employed in financing the firm. The share and loan capital represent the long-term capital available, and bank overdrafts. The ratio of share capital to loan capital (or of equity to debt) is known as gearing and has important implications for financial management purposes. The higher the proportion of debt to equity, the more highly geared the company. In an ideal world with no taxes and no market imperfections, capital structure would be irrelevant. However, in the real world, as a company increases its debt it can take advantage of tax benefits, e.g. the net cost of debenture interest may be less than the net cost of dividends on a further issue of ordinary shares and fixed-dividend preference shares may cost less than issuing ordinary shares. But at the same time it may increase the chances of bankruptcy. The stability of the share price can also be affected by the firm's capital structure as fluctuations in net income may have disproportionate effects on the returns accruing to ordinary share-holders in a highly geared company, and hence on the price of ordinary shares.

CAPM, see CAPITAL ASSET PRICING MODEL.

CARICOM (Caribbean Community) [Guyana]. A relatively small grouping of Caribbean nations, including Trinidad and Tobago, formed in 1973 to promote the coordination of development policies, planning and trade relations with third countries. It is based in Georgetown, Guyana.

Caterpillar [USA]. This $10.5bn corporation is the world's largest producer of earth-moving equipment with 15 plants in the United States, Brazil, Canada, France, the United Kingdom, Australia, Belgium, Indonesia and Mexico. It faced unprecedented problems in the first half of the 1980s. After reporting then record sales of $9.1bn and profits of $549m in 1981, the following year Caterpillar reported its first loss (of $180m) in 50 years, as demand slumped and sales shrank to $6.5bn. The company faced a catalogue of problems. Major construction projects in the third world were postponed due to the debt crisis, while in the developed world, record high interest rates had the same effect. Between 1980 and 1985, the dollar appreciated by almost 50 per cent against the yen, making imports from Japan very attractive, and arch-rival Komatsu increased its share of the US market from 15 to 25 per cent. Moreover, the company lost a major order to supply equipment for the Trans-Siberian pipeline project because of the Reagan administration's trade embargo with the Soviet Union following the invasion of Afghanistan. Between 1982–5, Caterpillar lost almost $1bn as it chased a shrinking market. Under such circumstances, excess capacity became a major problem. Rationalization was essential and plants were closed and jobs lost both in the US and overseas. In the UK, Caterpillar failed to ensure that it was first to inform employees at Newcastle, England, that their plant was to close. The British Trades Union Congress was so incensed that it formally accused the company of breach of the OECD's Guidelines for Multinational Enterprises, as well as its own code of conduct Caterpillar had issued in 1974.

In 1987 Caterpillar was once again embroiled in controversy. Its Glasgow, Scotland, plant was included in its Plant with a Future Programme, and local management announced a £60m investment to upgrade the plant. Sixteen weeks after this announcement, the same management told the workforce that the plant was to close. In Scotland, the US company was vociferously denounced by all political parties, including the Scottish Secretary of State. What could have caused such a dramatic reverse of policy? Perhaps the company saw further rationalization as a means of discouraging a hostile take-over bid. Other world market leaders, such as Gillette and Goodyear, were being beseiged by corporate raiders at the time, so Caterpillar could have felt vulnerable. It certainly did not rule out the possibility of such a bid, and the company was reincorporated in Delaware, the state which affords US companies most protection from corporate raiders.

CFC, see CONTROLLED FOREIGN CORPORATION.

chartism [momentum analysis, technical analysis]. A series of techniques for forecasting movements in the prices of financial instruments, foreign currencies or commodities by examining price movements in earlier periods. The aim of chartism is to identify patterns in past price movements, with a view to making some prediction about future movements. There is no underlying theory of chartism and it is contrary to the weak form of the efficient market hypothesis. An example of one type of pattern a chartist might examine is called a

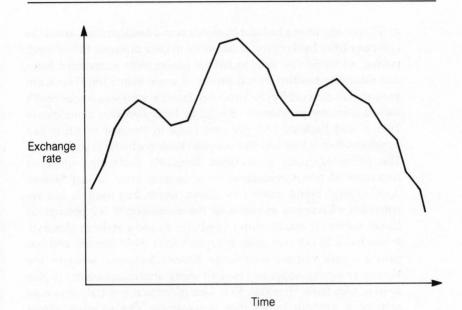

1 'Head and shoulders' diagram

'head and shoulders' and it is depicted in figure 1. A chartist would attempt to spot a head-and-shoulders pattern as it emerged, and if the chartist were correct, substantial profits might accrue if one had this information at the top of the right shoulder.

Chicago International Money Market [USA]. A Chicago-based international money market where foreign currency futures are traded. It was set up in 1972 as part of the Chicago Mercantile Exchange.

Chrysler [USA]. With sales of some $35.5bn, America's third-largest car company is among the world's 15 largest companies. It has four divisions: Automotive Operations (known as Chrysler Motors); Chrysler Financial Corporation; Gulfstream Aerospace Corporation; and Chrysler Technologies, which takes a prominent role in seeking future acquisitions in high-technology fields such as control components and other military equipment. Gulfstream Aerospace was acquired in August 1985, and is a major producer of jet aircraft for corporate, personal and governmental use. Chrysler Financial Corporation provides opportunities for growth in the financial services market.

During the 1980s Chrysler was on the verge of bankruptcy, but retrenched, recovered and expanded. In 1980 Chrysler suffered a loss of \$1.7bn, and only a bail-out by the Reagan administration saved the company from bankruptcy. It has since made a dramatic turnaround, paying off its \$1.2bn debt in federal government guaranteed loans and returning healthy annual profits of more than \$1bn. This turn-around was directed by chairman Lee Iacocca, who was sensationally sacked from the presidency of Ford in 1978. Recovery complete, in 1986 it sold back its 12.5 per cent stake in Peugeot which it had acquired when it had sold its European business to the French group. The following year, it acquired Renault's controlling stake in American Motors Corporation for a bargain price of just \$600m. AMC's 'Jeep' brand name was almost worth that itself. It has re-entered the European market with the acquisition of the prestigious Italian sports car manufacturer Lamborghini and a stake in Maserati. It also has a 24 per cent stake in Japan's Mitsubishi Motors, and has agreed a joint venture with South Korea's Samsung, whereby the Korean company supplies low-cost parts and components. It also sources cars from Hyundai. This lack of vertical integration is now seen as a strength rather than a weakness. Out-sourcing allows greater flexibility, crucial in recession.

Ciba–Geigy [Switzerland]. With sales in excess of \$12bn, this is the largest of Switzerland's 'big three' chemical companies, ahead of Sandoz and Hoffman La Roche. It has eight divisions, but the three largest account for more than 70 per cent of total sales: pharma-ceuticals (30 per cent), agricultural (21 per cent) and dyestuffs and chemicals (20 per cent). Similarly its two main markets account for almost 75 per cent of sales (Europe, 45 per cent; North America, 30 per cent).

Ciba–Geigy has 137 companies in 60 countries and a workforce of almost 89,000 of which fewer than 25,000 are employed in Switzer-land. R&D accounts for more than 10 per cent of total sales.

In 1988, Ciba sold its Ilford Group division, renowned for its photographic products, to International Paper Corporation of the USA. During the year, it acquired the contact lens care business of Cooper Companies outside the USA, but the US Federal Trade Commission vetoed the takeover of the US business.

CMEA, see COMECON.

CoCom (Coordinating Committee for Multilateral Export Controls) [France]. Founded in 1950, CoCom (which is based in Paris) consists of members of the North Atlantic Treaty Organisation (NATO) and Japan. The aim of this exclusive and secretive club is to vet strategic trade with communist countries in order to stop the export of high-tech and militarily sensitive products to proscribed countries. There is, however, likely to be some relaxation of restrictions following the recent improvement of relations between East and West.

CoCom members

US	Norway
UK	Greece
Germany	Spain
Italy	Turkey
Luxembourg	Portugal
Belgium	Japan
Netherlands	Canada
Denmark	

Proscribed destinations

Soviet Union	China
Poland	Vietnam
East Germany	Mongolia
Czechoslovakia	North Korea
Hungary	Albania
Bulgaria	Afghanistan
Romania	

codes of conduct. Most of the major codes of conduct for multinationals were introduced in the course of the 1970s. At the international level, the main codes are the OECD's Guidelines (1976), the ILO Declaration of Principles (1977) and the UNCTAD Code on Restrictive Business Practices (1980). The UN's General Code has been under negotiation since 1977. At the regional level, there was the Andean Pact Code (1970) and the EEC Lange–Gibbons Code (1977). Codes have also been formulated to deal with specific issues: the US 'Sullivan Principles' on investment by US firms in South Africa (1977), the EEC 'Code of Conduct for companies with subsidiaries, branches or representation in South Africa' (1977), ICC Code on Illicit Payments (1977) and the WHO's 'International Code of Marketing of Breast Milk Substitutes' (1981). Some multinationals themselves have also produced their own codes (e.g. Caterpillar and Coca-Cola).

Codes of conduct are nothing more than guidelines which because of their status carry no legal sanctions. Thus, for example, the OECD's Guidelines are in fact of little value as the crucial Employment and Industrial Relations section merely invites MNCs to abide by the national legislation of the countries in which they operate.

Similarly, codes issued by the companies themselves do not seem to have had any bearing on corporate behaviour. Caterpillar's alleged deviance from its own code was highlighted in the European Parliament in 1983 when the firm closed its Newcastle (UK) plant. However, the effectiveness of such codes was not a burning issue by the late 1980s. Society's perceptions of MNCs have apparently improved judging by the deregulation of controls on MNCs. Countries which once sought to restrict inward investment (e.g. Canada and Portugal) now compete vigorously to attract investment.

cola wars. The US soft drinks market is a $40bn industry dominated by Coca-Cola (38.6 per cent) and PepsiCo (27.4 per cent). Both companies rely heavily on promotion to boost sales. At least two of Coca-Cola's jingles have topped the UK music charts, while Pepsi relies on international celebrities such as actor Michael Fox and singers Madonna and Michael Jackson to promote its product. At major media events (e.g. sporting events and rock concerts) both companies compete to obtain exclusive promotion rights.

Promotion is not the sole means of securing market share. PepsiCo reached agreement with Philip Morris to pay $380m for Seven-Up, the industry's number three with a 7.1 per cent market share. Coke retaliated with a $470m bid for Dr. Pepper with 6.3 per cent of the market share. The deals would have seen Coke and PepsiCo increase their combined market share from 67 to 81 per cent. This was too much for even the US Federal Trade Commission which during the Reagan Administration has been criticized for its failure to restrict mega-mergers. An internal Coca-Cola document suggested that the company's bid for Dr. Pepper was an elaborate ruse to scuttle PepsiCo's bid for Seven-Up.

The two rivals have sought to boost their position by launching an array of different brands and also by gaining control of their previously independent bottlers. Coca-Cola spent $2.4bn buying two bottlers (JTL for $1.4bn and Coke's bottling operation from Beatrice for $1bn). It now controls 20 per cent of its US bottling network. PepsiCo paid $590m for MEI Corporation to raise its share of its bottling network to about 33 per cent.

collateral. Security for a loan, which reverts to the owner when the loan is repaid. Household mortgages are one example of a secured loan, and the borrower's home is collateral for the loan. One hopes that by providing collateral to the lender, a lower interest rate will be charged.

COMECON [CMEA] (Council for Mutual Economic Assistance) [USSR]. Each European socialist country is a member of a system based on cooperation and mutual assistance and determined by the predominance of socialist ownership of the means of production. This system is operated through the Moscow-based Council for Mutual Economic Assistance or COMECON. Collaboration between the states allows resources to be transferred from member to member at minimum cost. Thus COMECON stands for a collaborative network of socialist states which relies on the specialization of industry within the member countries in order to form a stable environment in which socialism can thrive.

Events in eastern Europe during 1989 are likely to precipitate radical changes in COMECON.

commercial paper. Short-term (30–170 days) unsecured corporate borrowings which may be traded in secondary markets. Issuers of commercial paper are normally large corporations with impeccable credit ratings. It is a useful instrument for raising short-term finance at money-market rates as part of a working capital management programme, particularly since some larger corporations may have credit ratings superior to their bankers. Usually, commercial paper is issued at a discount, but it may also be interest bearing. Traditionally, it has been a source of finance in the USA. However, opportunities are now available to issue commercial paper in Europe. There is also a growing Euromarket for commercial paper. The availability of a Euromarket ensures that there is a secondary market for the paper.

commodity agreement. The prices of commodities often fluctuate wildly due to natural forces, business cycles and speculation. A commodity agreement is an attempt by consumer and producer alike to stabilize prices and facilitate planning. The most common types of commodity agreement are those involving buffer stocks and export/import quotas. In the case of buffer stocks, floor and ceiling prices are set by agreement and a special fund is established to cover the operating costs involved. When the price falls below the floor price, the stock is added to, and when prices go above the ceiling, sales are made from the stock. In this way, prices are stabilized. In the case of quotas the aim is to keep up or stabilize prices by limiting supply.

Attempts to stabilize prices in these ways have tended to be inefficient and unsuccessful particularly in the cases of tin, wheat, sugar, coffee, cocoa, olive oil and textiles. Producers and consumers often disagree about the appropriate floor and ceiling prices and the financial contribution for buffer stocks. Exporters often fail to agree on the basis for sharing quotas.

An alternative approach to helping developing countries in this area is for the developed countries to provide financial assistance when commodity prices fall to very low levels.

Common Agricultural Policy (CAP). The CAP of the European Community (EC) is an attempt to stabilize the prices of agricultural products within the EC for the benefit of consumers and producers alike. The two main instruments of this policy are a system of levies and intervention purchases. Levies ensure that imports from outside the EC are priced at levels similar to the prices fixed within the EC. Intervention purchases ensure that producers receive a guaranteed price for their products by purchasing produce which is surplus to requirements at the guaranteed price. Unfortunately, a considerable amount of produce has been purchased which has not been consumed, giving rise to butter mountains, wine lakes and other surpluses. More recently quotas and levies have been introduced in order to curtail production of certain foodstuffs, for example, milk.

The CAP is of particular relevance to MNCs involved in the food industry, since the CAP will determine the market conditions for raw materials. The CAP can also have implications for the hedging of foreign exchange risk since monetary compensatory amounts will affect the cash flows from importing and exporting foodstuffs. Essentially, the system of monetary compensatory amounts is a system of tariffs and subsidies which ensures that market conditions will be stable, even if there are deviations from purchasing power parity.

Common Market, see EUROPEAN COMMUNITY.

Commonwealth [British Commonwealth]. A voluntary association of independent nations comprising the UK and most of its former colonies including Australia, New Zealand, Canada, Ghana, India, Kenya, Malaysia, Nigeria and Singapore. The Commonwealth is not a federation and there are no obligations or commitments between its members. It is not a contractual association like the United Nations and it has no written constitution. But all of its members have a broad community of interests and they share a common interest in peace, freedom and security. The queen has a special relationship with each of the member nations and is the symbolic head of the Commonwealth.

Compaq [USA]. This personal computer manufacturer was founded in 1982 by Rod Canion and Bill Murto, former employees of Texas

Instruments. Canion originally intended producing storage disks, but venture capitalist Ben Rosen, now Compaq's non-executive chairman, rejected the proposal. He asked the co-founders to re-submit with a different product. In his second application, Canion identified the portable niche in IBM's PC range, and received $30m in venture funding, a record at the time.

Within three years of its foundation, Compaq had become one of the 500 largest US industrial corporations, setting a record for the shortest time to reach the *Fortune 500*, and within six years just missed being in the top 200.

Foreign sales account for almost half of total sales of over $2bn, and in the European personal computer market Compaq is second only to IBM. This success overseas has led to the establishment of overseas manufacturing operations in Singapore and Scotland. Both countries won the Compaq investment in the face of strong competition from neighbouring countries. Worldwide, the battle for inward investment has intensified, but the spin-off benefits to the host country can be limited if key components are imported. Most of the key components used for the Compaq Deskpro 386, which is manufactured at the Scottish plant, are in fact imported.

comparative advantage. By specializing in the production of the goods which it manufactures most efficiently a country can benefit from international trade. The general principle is that there are gains from trade whenever the relative price ratios of two goods differ under international exchange from what they would be solely in the domestic context. Trade ensures higher economic output and consumption to the trading countries jointly as a result of their specialization in production – exporting the good where they have a comparative advantage and importing the good where they have a comparative disadvantage. The theory of comparative advantage shows that countries jointly benefit from trade even if one country has an absolute advantage in the production of both goods. While no country will lose under free trade it is possible, in theory at least, that most or all of the gains could accrue to one of the trading countries.

competitive advantage. According to Michael Porter, a professor at the Harvard Business School, competitive advantage arises from the value that a company is able to create for its buyers in excess of the cost of creating it:

Value is what buyers are willing to pay and superior value stems from offering lower prices than competitors for equivalent benefits or providing unique benefits that more than offset a higher price (*Competitive Advantage*, Free Press, 1985, p. 3).

competitive strategy. A strategy designed to achieve competitive advantage in each of the lines of business in which a company operates. This should be distinguished from corporate strategy, which is concerned with the company's performance as a whole. In formulating a competitive strategy, Michael Porter of the Harvard Business School identifies five types of competitive force to be incorporated into the analysis: industry competitors, potential entrants, substitutes, suppliers and buyers. In order to be successful, a company must be able to define its goals, current strategy, assumptions used and its capabilities in the process of seeking to match the internal strength of the company to its external environment.

compressibility ratio. The ratio of a country's debt service payments and imports to exports and other capital inflows. In many respects, it is similar to the quick ratio for individual firms, and gives some indication of the likelihood of a country being able to meet its international debt commitments, and borrow further tranches of foreign currency.

concentration, industrial. An industry's concentration level is determined by the number of competitors and their respective market share. High concentration exists when a small number of producers account for a large proportion of the total market. On the other hand, a low concentration means there are many producers, each with a small share of the market. The automobile industry is an interesting example. Perverse as it may seem, although national markets are increasingly concentrated (e.g. UK, France, Italy), on a worldwide basis the industry is less concentrated because of the increasing number of national champions which are increasing their global market share at the expense of traditional industry leaders, General Motors and Ford.

concession agreement. An agreement between sovereign states and individual companies. Up until the twentieth century in Britain, Royal Charters were frequently granted to companies which effectively gave the company a monopoly, or a protected market, in return for undertaking certain duties which were considered of national importance.

More recently, concession agreements have been drawn up between MNCs and host countries. The agreements consist of a series of mutual rights and obligations and may well include clauses dealing with taxation, international trade, international capital flows, social responsibilities and local participation in the subsidiary. Unfortunately, the countries where an MNC is most likely to favour a concession agreement (where there are political upheavals and risks are likely to be high), is also likely to be a country where the probability that host government commitments may be renounced is highest.

Confederation of Industries of the European Community, *see* UNICE.

consignment. An arrangement whereby an exporter retains title to goods until the importer has sold the goods to a third party. As such, it is similar to a 'sale or return' arrangement in domestic business. In practice, it may be an extremely risky transaction from the exporter's point of view, since implementing retention of title under a foreign legal system may be extremely costly, and there will be far greater time lags between the despatch of goods and the return of the goods.

consolidation accounting. A method of accounting for groups of related companies whereby the financial statements of the individual entities are added together to provide the worldwide set of financial statements for the multinational as a single economic entity. In the process of consolidation, transactions between members of the group are eliminated so that the statements reflect transactions with external parties only. While consolidated financial statements have been common practice amongst US and UK MNCs they are a relatively recent phenomenon in continental Europe and Japan. Given the growing complexity of international business there is a strong case not only for comprehensive reporting (consolidation) but also disaggregated or segmental information disclosures by MNCs.

containerization. The use of a large outer package or container within which is stored numbers of smaller items, which are thus easily handled and transferred between different modes of transportation such as sea, rail and road.

contract manufacturing. A manufacturing agreement (the reverse of a franchise) in which a multinational pays the licensing fee. Where foreign direct investment is not warranted the multinational may contract out production to a low-cost producer (e.g. Reebok in South Korea) and continue to market the product under its own brand name. However, quality control is essential if the multinational's reputation is to be protected.

controlled foreign corporation (CFC). A concept used by revenue authorities (both in the UK and the USA) to minimize tax avoidance via tax havens. Similar rules apply in Germany, France, Japan and Canada. Essentially, if an overseas subsidiary in a low tax country is defined as a CFC, then certain profits of the CFC will be subject to home country taxation. While these regulations may remove the most blatant abuses of the home country tax system, there are still considerable opportunities for the innovative tax expert to take advantage of low tax countries. However, the advent of CFC legislation highlights the need to analyse the tax implications of international investments. Otherwise, the unsuspecting company may be subjected to high rates of home country taxation.

convertible bond. A long-term debenture with an option to convert the bond into shares at certain times, or throughout the life of the bond. For example, a company might issue a bond in $1,000 units with a 9 per cent coupon, redeemable in 2009, and convertible into 100 shares at any time. Clearly, if the company is extremely successful, and the share price increases to $20 per share in the first year, then the investor is holding a valuable financial instrument. For all intents and purposes, a convertible is simply a call option combined with a long-term bond, where the exercise price of the call is equal to the value of the bond.

corporate diversification. The management of a variety of operations, by product, line-of-business or geographical region, in order to reduce the variability of returns. Diversification reduces risk where the cash flows from different operations are imperfectly correlated. It has been suggested that investors in shares can diversify more effectively than companies by holding portfolios and that it is therefore inefficient for companies to diversify unless there are synergistic benefits. However, company managements are often concerned to protect their own and their employees' interests as well as investors' and may therefore diversify irrespective of whether this adds to shareholder value.

corporate raider. A term first applied to the small number of individuals or companies in the USA who mounted hostile bids for companies, often much larger than themselves. Those individuals described as raiders object to this label. According to T. Boone-Pickens, the management of many large corporations have forgotten their prime duty, namely to maximize shareholders' wealth. He claims that executives often pursue their own interests and objectives, at the expense of shareholders. The most notorious case in the 1980s involved Allegheny Corporation which spent lavishly on luxuries such as private jets and corporate entertainment. At the same time, Allegheny's performance was at best mediocre and the chief executive was forced to resign in August 1986 when details of corporate expenditure were disclosed.

'Active investors', as the raiders prefer to be called, argue that they have had a major positive impact on corporate America. Firms such as Borg–Warner, Goodyear, Gillette and Union Carbide, to name but a few, have, they claim, all benefited from the threat of a hostile take-over bid. Many company chairmen bitterly resent such claims. They argue that greedy investors with short-term perspectives have forced them to abandon long-range planning and cut down on the various costs, such as R&D, which are essential for a prosperous future.

corporate strategy. The overall plan for a company. It is long-term planning, basically qualitative in nature, which integrates and directs the individual business activities and functions of a company into a unified whole which adds up to more than the sum of its parts. It concerns the fundamental questions of what businesses the company should be in and how to manage those businesses as a group. However, it is a matter of some controversy as to the importance of corporate strategy and also how to formulate it.

If companies are to be successful then corporate strategy must result in a company's individual businesses adding value to the whole beyond what they could achieve individually and the best way to do this is by developing synergy between those businesses which will enhance competitive advantage.

correspondent banks. Banks in different countries which have close working relationships with each other. Neither bank in such a relationship will have employees or a branch in the other bank's country, but each bank will have a deposit in the other. For the international manager, sympathetic banking facilities will be available in countries where his own bank has no branches. This may be convenient if finance is being sought in a foreign country, and for services connected with international trade, including accepting bank drafts, letters of credit and so on.

counterfeiting. Said to be perhaps the second-oldest profession of mankind, it is now a major industry worth an estimated $60bn a year, or 3 per cent of world trade. The UK Anti-Counterfeiting Group defines a counterfeit product as one 'which so closely imitates the appearance of the product of another as to appear to be the product of another'. Indonesia, South Korea and Taiwan are regarded as the capitals of the counterfeit industry, selling fake Rolex watches, Louis Vuitton luggage, Lacoste shirts, Chanel handbags, Yves Saint Laurent accessories, not to mention pirate music and video tapes.

In order to combat counterfeiting, producers of luxury goods are pursuing counterfeiters. Cartier and Gucci spend an estimated $1m a year, while Christian Dior spends almost $500m policing its 313 trademarks.

The good news for western producers of luxury goods is that because Taiwan and Korea have large trade surpluses with the USA and EC, their key markets, both the US Bush administration and the EC's European Commission can leverage concessions from such far-eastern producers including a clamp down on counterfeiting.

Of course it is not just luxury goods manufacturers that suffer the effects of counterfeiting. Within weeks of its launch, *Batman* looked set to break all cinema box-office records, and Warner concluded some 100 licensing agreements for 300 items in the USA alone, allowing licencees to produce *Batman* merchandise (i.e. T-shirts, etc.). However, licensees found their products were competing with cheap illegal copies, and worse still counterfeiters had sometimes snapped up the necessary raw materials (e.g. black T-shirts). Nevertheless, royalty payments for *Batman* paraphernalia could exceed the $2.5bn which *Star Wars* netted.

countertrade. An increasingly popular technique for international trade, essentially a barter transaction. At its simplest, a UK car manufacturer might have an opportunity to export 10,000 cars to a COMECON country. The COMECON country has very little hard foreign currency, but an excess supply of dining chairs. The car manufacturer can either reject the order or exchange 10,000 cars for 1,000,000 dining chairs. It is a difficult choice, since the car manufacturer might ask itself why the COMECON country will not sell the chairs for hard currency and pay for the cars in sterling or dollars. However, there may be sound economic reasons for this deal. The UK government may be more receptive to a UK company attempting to sell 1,000,000 dining chairs, than an enterprise from a COMECON country. Also, a UK company may be in a better position to market chairs in Britain than a COMECON state agency. Therefore, it is possible that both parties may gain from a countertrade deal.

In practice, countertrade deals may be considerably more complex than the scheme outlined above. For example, the 1,000,000 chairs may be scheduled for production over a ten-year period, and the cars may be for immediate delivery. The deal may include some transfer of cash (either hard currency, or non-convertible local currency) from one party to the other, and the deal might include a range of merchandise, rather than chairs alone. Other variations on the theme include supplying plant, in return for a proportion of the output of the plant.

Whilst countertrade was originally associated with the COMECON countries, it then became associated with some oil exporting countries attempting to evade production quotas. More recently, it has been used by third world countries which have limited access to credit facilities.

Due to the complexity of countertrade deals, and the need to know of potential markets for countertraded goods, there are now a number of consultancies and departments within international banks specializing in countertrade.

creative accounting. A legitimate means of reporting profit results which flatter management performance. The creative use of generally accepted accounting principles is endemic in the USA and UK and is largely in response to pressures from the stock market for steady growth and ever-increasing profits. In his recent best-seller entitled *Creative Accounting* (Sidgwick & Jackson Ltd, 1986, p. 1), Ian Griffiths asserts that:

> Every company in the country is fiddling its profits. Every set of published accounts is based on books which have been gently cooked or completely roasted. The figures which are fed twice a year to the investing public have all been changed in order to protect the guilty. It is the biggest con trick since the Trojan horse.

credit swap. A form of financing similar in many respects to a back-to-back loan, save that the parties to the transaction are a multinational firm and a bank (frequently the central bank) in the host country. The nature of the transaction is illustrated in figure 1.

The transaction is useful for the MNC, since it circumvents some of the risks attached to converting hard currency into local currency with a view to converting the local currency back into hard currency at some future date. While a swap transaction may minimize the risks connected with the principal of the loan, it is possible that local interest rates may have to be paid on the foreign currency loan, while the hard currency deposit may earn little or no interest. Another critical aspect of the transaction, is the exchange rate used in determining the amount of currency to be swapped, since it may be more or less favourable than the spot exchange rate. Credit swaps can be a

In the UK   In Nigeria

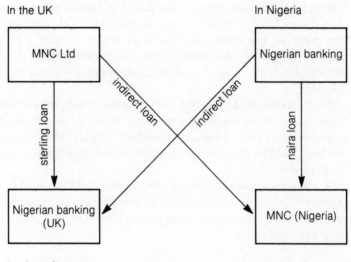

1 A credit swap

useful tool for foreign exchange risk management. *See also* BACK-TO-
BACK FINANCING.

crisis management. The ability to cope with a crisis is exemplified by
cases such as the Bhopal chemical disaster involving Union Carbide
and the contamination of Perrier's mineral water stocks by minute
traces of benzene, a carcinogenic substance. Perrier attempted to limit
the damage to its worldwide business by withdrawing all of its stocks
from the market. At stake were not only its major share of the
booming mineral water sector but also the international market itself
which has been built on an image of purity and quality.

In a crisis situation, it would seem crucial that management acts
decisively to reassure customers and the public. Not only must
management act quickly to ensure that any dangers to health and
safety are removed but they must mount a large-scale information
campaign to keep all concerned fully informed. Given the speed with
which a crisis can occur, an emergency system of crisis management
and communication is best established before rather than after the
event.

cross default provision. A clause within a loan agreement which permits
the lender to call in the loan, should the borrower default on any
payments under any loan agreements, irrespective of whether they
are loans from the lender or third parties. Lenders are then protected

from a company encountering financial difficulty which has not breached the loan agreement in any way. From a corporate viewpoint, it implies that default on any one debt may lead to other lenders invoking cross default provisions. However, MNCs can use cross default clauses as a way to decrease political risk. If an MNC is locating in a politically unstable country, then part of the project might be financed with a World Bank loan. If the host government causes difficulties for the local subsidiary, then the subsidiary may default on its loans, and if there is a cross default clause, the World Bank loan. This would mean that the host country could be held responsible for defaulting on a World Bank loan. The host government is unlikely to risk a default on the World Bank.

cross rate. A method of calculating the exchange rate between two currencies when only exchange rates between each of the two currencies and a third currency are available. For example, suppose that we wish to calculate the peseta–dollar exchange rate from the following data:

pesetas/stg: 200
dollars/stg: 2

Given that a pound may be purchased for 200 ptas or $2, we would expect that a dollar could be purchased for 100 ptas. Therefore, the cross rate is 100 ptas per dollar. One would expect that the cross rate will equal the spot rate, otherwise there would be arbitrage opportunities.

culture. The significance of culture in the business context has been recognized only relatively recently. Culture has been defined by Geert Hofstede in his path-breaking book *Culture's Consequences* (Sage, 1980) as 'the collective programming of the mind which distinguishes the members of one human group from another'. The word 'culture' is reserved for societies as a whole, or nations, whereas 'subculture' is used for the level of an organization, profession or family. While the degree of cultural integration varies between societies, most subcultures within a society share common characteristics with other subcultures. The implication of this is that while a common corporate culture within national boundaries may be promoted relatively easily it will be necessary to adopt a much more sensitive approach internationally where cultural differences may be profound.

currency, *see* ASIACURRENCY MARKET, CURRENCY COCKTAIL, EUROPEAN CURRENCY UNIT, FOREIGN CURRENCY TRANSLATION.

currency cocktail. A bond which is denominated in a basket of currencies, rather than a single currency. Popular baskets include SDRs (special drawing rights) and ECUs (European currency units). From an investor's point of view, they may be attractive since one would expect that the volatility of a basket of currencies would be less than the volatility of a single currency, in other words, a currency diversification effect. A currency-cocktail bond issue may be a useful foreign exchange risk management tool if it is used to finance a project which is likely to have receipts in a number of currencies. Currency-cocktail bonds have not been extremely popular with investors, and may be risky for the issuer, as it is difficult to cover a currency cocktail in the forward market.

currency risk, *see* EXCHANGE RISK.

D

Daewoo [South Korea]. 'Great Universe' was founded in 1967 by Kim Woo-Choong who today is chairman of an $18bn conglomerate with 120,000 employees. It regularly accounts for 10 per cent of South Korean exports, which in 1988 amounted to $67bn, making the country one of the world's top 12 exporters. Daewoo is no longer family controlled, but in 1984 chairman Kim received the International Chamber of Commerce award as the world's best businessman.

Daewoo's main domestic rival is Hyundai, though major differences exist in their organizational culture and strategy. Hyundai, with its autocratic management style, has minimized cooperation with foreign parties, adopted an aggressive export strategy and promoted the Hyundai name. In contrast, Daewoo has decentralized management, 22 of its 55 companies are joint ventures with US and European firms, and the foreign partners' brand names are used in overseas marketing. It has joint ventures with, for example, United Technologies, General Electric, General Motors and Thomson.

Daewoo began as a trader in textiles and diversified its trading activities. In the mid-1970s, it began to focus on heavy industries such as construction and shipbuilding. By 1980, it was operating the world's largest shipbuilding dock.

In addition to joint ventures, Daewoo has developed internationally through contract manufacturing. It has OEM contracts with Caterpillar, supplying forklift trucks, with Leading Edge of the USA, making personal computers, and with British Aerospace, producing wing parts for the European Airbus.

In the early 1980s, Daewoo emerged as South Korea's third major electronics company. Its domestic market share rose from 0.1 per cent in 1981 to 16.5 per cent in 1986. Almost 62 per cent of electronics production is exported. Daewoo has been subject to EC investigations for dumping microwave ovens and video cassette recorders (VCRs). In 1988, the European Commission imposed tough anti-dumping duties of 29.2 per cent on Daewoo's VCRs. Two months later, Daewoo announced it was establishing a VCR plant in Northern Ireland, to add to its microwave oven facility in France.

Daimler–Benz [Germany]. With annual sales in excess of $30bn, this motor conglomerate has a total of 320,000 employees, of whom

263,000 are employed in Germany. It has 11 manufacturing plants in Germany, and 43 plants overseas, of which 25 are assembly operations. It has grown rapidly during the 1980s through domestic acquisitions to become the biggest industrial company in Germany, and one of the 20 largest in the world. In 1985 it acquired major stakes in AEG and Dornier, and outright control of Motoren und Turbinen Union. These purchases represented a major diversification step for the car manufacturer, which is the leading bus producer in Europe and the world's largest manufacturer of diesel lorries. In 1989 the German Cartel Office blocked the proposed merger with Messerschmitt–Bolkow–Blohm (MBB), the country's main aerospace and defence concern, on the grounds that the deal would give the new company a market dominance position in key areas. Daimler–Benz appealed successfully against this ruling to the economics minister. It paid £556m for a 50.01 per cent stake in MBB. The takeover has created one of the world's largest and most diversified engineering, aerospace, defence technology conglomerates.

The 1980s also witnessed significant changes within the company. In 1983, the then chairman, Gerhard Prinz, died from a heart attack on his exercise bicycle. His successor was Werner Breitschwerdt, but in 1987 he was unexpectedly replaced by his deputy and finance director, Edzard Reuter.

debt finance. Raising debt finance in an international context offers potential opportunities to the MNC and considerable pitfalls to the unwary and inexperienced. The MNC has the scope to borrow money in a number of different countries and currencies, and by virtue of its size, access to international markets such as the Eurocurrency and Asiacurrency markets. In a world where covered-interest arbitrage was the order of the day, we would expect that a MNC would be indifferent as to the source or currency of its borrowings, since borrowings in one currency at a given interest rate could be converted into borrowing in a different currency by using spot and forward transactions. Therefore, the main impetus for an international debt policy rests upon imperfections in the market for debt. The sources of these imperfections include transaction costs, corporate taxes, personal taxes, government intervention, information asymmetries and project-specific finance.

1 *Transaction costs*. Transaction costs include bid–ask spreads and differences between the lending rate and the borrowing rate. Bid–ask spreads may be particularly significant if one is considering the purchase of a long-dated forward contract, since such

contracts may be unavailable, or markets may not be sufficiently liquid. This in turn implies that covered interest arbitrage may not apply.

2 *Corporate taxes*. Since interest payments are tax deductible expenses, it may be useful to consider where the debt is issued and the coupon (or interest rate) in order to maximize the tax shields arising from corporate debt.

3 *Personal taxes*. If the tax code requires the corporation to deduct taxes from interest payments to bondholders, then bondholders will require a higher interest rate than a regime which does not require deduction of income tax at source. Many UK MNCs use a Netherlands finance subsidiary in order to circumvent the need to deduct interest at source. Bearer bonds will also be appreciated by investors.

4 *Government intervention*. Governments may restrict access to local debt markets by foreigners. This in turn may lead to a local market becoming segmented from the rest of the world capital market and the failure of covered interest arbitrage to hold. Governments may also restrict borrowing on local markets by the subsidiaries of foreign MNCs.

5 *Information asymmetries*. Information asymmetries may lead to companies being able to raise capital on more favourable terms in their home market than in overseas markets. Moreover, some national markets are more liquid in certain instruments than others. For example, one might find that fixed (interest) rate debt was available more cheaply in one country, while floating-rate debt was cheaper than fixed-rate debt in another. The phenomenon of information asymmetries with respect to credit ratings, and differences in liquidity between different markets, has been one of the reasons for the growth of interest-rate swaps.

6 *Project-specific finance*. Project-specific finance may be available on extremely favourable terms from either host governments or international development agencies. This in turn leads to new opportunities to lower the cost of capital for the project.

When one combines all of these factors, one can identify opportunities for lowering the cost of debt for the multinational firm. However, a failure to identify these factors may lead to expensive mistakes. For example, a number of British companies lost considerable sums of money in the mid-1970s by borrowing Swiss francs as Swiss interest rates were significantly less than UK interest rates. Granted, the firms made considerable savings in interest payments. However, the Swiss franc strengthened significantly against the pound and the UK firms lost out when it came to repaying the Swiss franc principal with sterling. The real sting in the tail came when the Inland Revenue was reluctant to allow the companies to write off the loss against their tax bills, since the loss constituted a loss on a liability.

DEC, see DIGITAL EQUIPMENT CORPORATION.

deep discount bond. A bond issued at a deep discount on its nominal value. For example, suppose that the prevailing interest rate for a one-year bond is 10 per cent, and that a company wishes to raise $1,000. The company could package the bond in a variety of ways, some of which are displayed in table 1.

Table 1   Packaging a deep discount bond: some alternatives

No.	Face value ($)	Interest payment ($)	Issue price ($)
1	1,000	100 (10%)	1,000
2	1,100	0 (0%)	1,000
3	1,080	20 (1.85%)	1,000
4	950	150 (15.8%)	1,000

The issuer and the investor would be expected to be indifferent between all four bonds, since in each case, the investor pays $1,000 now and receives $1,100 at the end of one year. Similarly, the company receives $1,000 now and pays out $1,100 at the year end. Options 2 and 3 are both deep discount bonds, since the face value of the debt is greater than the issue price of the debt. Indeed, option 2 is known as a 'zero coupon bond' since it carries no interest payments whatsoever. In a world of relatively frictionless capital markets and no taxes, it would not matter which option was chosen. However, in a world of differential tax rates, the choice may be critical. For example, assume that corporations are not permitted to deduct interest payments against their tax liabilities, and that investors are taxed at 60 per cent on income and 0 per cent on capital gains. The cash flow received by investors at the year end is shown in table 2.

Under this scenario, investors will prefer a zero coupon (2) or deep discount bond (3) to options 1 and 4. The converse will hold if income tax rates are less than capital gains rates. This in turn implies that the way in which debt is issued (i.e. the split between capital gains and income) may be critical. Corporations may attempt to maximize the issue price of debt by adapting to the tax regimes in individual countries.

Table 2 Investors' year-end cash flow

No.	Face value ($)	Interest payment ($)	Cash flow ($) (investor)
1	1,000	100 (10%)	1,040
2	1,100	0 (0%)	1,100
3	1,080	20 (1.85%)	1,088
4	950	150 (15.8%)	1,010

design. Design, relating to the appearance and effectiveness of a product and its packaging, can have as much impact on profitability as labour costs, stock control and market penetration, etc. New, innovative designs are required to penetrate many world markets. Also the close analogy between design and quality has been recognized. If a company falls behind in design, it may lag in quality and perceived quality, and eventually loses competitive power without which it must fail.

Until recently this function has been neglected by many companies. A minority of others, on the other hand, have excelled in product design (e.g. Bang & Olufsen, Braun (owned by Gillette), Olivetti and Philips). There is ample evidence that consumers do prefer well-designed products. Companies would do well to realize that the design of their products is critical in determining their success in the market place. Thus, companies such as Fiat, Peugeot, Philips and Swatch have all recovered lost ground by concentrating on design. For other companies (e.g. Sony), innovative design is a means of keeping competitors at bay. The logical conclusion is that design should be regarded as essential to product development, rather than a luxury for premium-brand producers.

Design should enter the product development process at the earliest strategic planning stage with the selection of the design resource (in-house or consultant) and the establishment of a design brief. A design development programme will then typically follow five distinct stages:

preliminary discussions between client and designer;

design appraisal, where the designer prepares ideas and options for the first presentation at which an agreed product profile is selected;

design proposal, where the conceptual product profile is developed into a specific design proposal detailing the technical features in drawing and model form;

development, which involves the detailed design of component drawings, prototypes and mechanical and materials testing; and

manufacturing, which includes supervision of components and sub-assemblies to ensure product quality.

development agency. An agency established by the government of a country to further national and regional economic development, area development and environmental renewal. Agencies such as the Scottish Development Agency (SDA) in the UK aim to work in partnership with public- and private-sector institutions, companies and individuals. In Scotland, priority is given to promoting the strategic, research and development, and marketing capacities of small and medium-sized companies; to helping new businesses to start up; to upgrading the industrial infrastructure; and to promoting technology transfer through investment, licensing and joint ventures.

Digital Equipment Corporation (DEC) [USA]. Founded in 1957 by Ken Olsen, it has sales of almost $13bn and is a leading supplier of computer systems. Its strength lies with minicomputers, which it invented. It has 32 plants worldwide, 21 in the USA (including one in Puerto Rico), 9 in the EC, and 1 each in Canada and Taiwan, and 125,000 employees. Its products are sold in 60 countries, and in 1989 for the first time domestic sales were overtaken by foreign sales which accounted for 51 per cent of the total. R&D accounts for almost 11 per cent of total sales and involves almost 8,000 employees.

The 1980s have seen major internal and external developments at DEC. When profits plunged as its PC flopped in 1983, it introduced a more disciplined, centralized, conventional management system to replace the entrepreneurial philosophy that had dominated DEC since its formation. In order to overcome its weakness in the burgeoning market for personal computers, in 1988 DEC joined with Apple, famous for its highly 'user-friendly' PCs, (though not through merger) in order to challenge IBM. However, in 1989 DEC, like many other US computer manufacturers (e.g. Wang), reported disappointing financial results. The 1990s are likely to see a worldwide restructuring and rationalization of the industry.

diversification, *see* CORPORATE DIVERSIFICATION, PORTFOLIO DIVERSIFICATION.

divestment. A reduction of ownership percentage in an investment on either a voluntary or involuntary basis. It is also often used in describing a multinational's decision to close a foreign manufacturing plant. While divestment occurs in domestic operations, foreign divestment merits special consideration. During the 1970s host countries (e.g. India) insisted that local interests should hold the majority stake in investments involving foreign partners. Thus companies were compelled to reduce their stake if they wished to continue operating within such countries. Some firms (e.g. Coca-Cola and IBM) refused to accept this stipulation and were forced to divest completely from India. During the 1980s host nations either lifted or relaxed controls on foreign investors. Now voluntary foreign divestment is more popular. For example, it may occur once a firm recognizes it has made an ill-conceived foreign acquisition, or a company may have purchased an entire company in order to gain control of a particular division, and thus it divests unwanted assets. Some firms may acquire others simply to divest at a profit. Divestment may also occur for political reasons. Many US multinationals have divested from South Africa, reflecting perhaps the political clout of the black population in the USA. The most noteworthy divestment by a European company came when Barclays Bank announced its decision to pull out of South Africa. However, the UK remains the largest foreign investor in South Africa.

dumping. A company can be accused of dumping if its goods are sold in overseas markets for less than in the exporter's domestic market, or below cost price, or both. Accusations of dumping tend to occur when relatively inexpensive imports have a major impact on the foreign market. Recently, Asian manufacturers in numerous industries (e.g. automobiles, ball bearings, consumer electronics, textiles) have faced charges of dumping in either of the North American markets, the EC, or all three. South Korea though has recently accused a French cement manufacturer of dumping, and Japan has accused Korean textile producers of dumping. The increasing frequency of such charges is symptomatic of growing friction in international trade, witness Section 301 of the 1988 US Trade Omnibus Bill.

Du Pont de Nemours [USA]. The world's largest chemical company with sales in excess of $30bn is also among the world's 20 largest industrial corporations. It consists of eight divisions and its main businesses are in oil-related products and man-made fibres; Du Pont is perhaps still best known as the inventor in 1938 of nylon. In 1981 Du Pont paid $7.8bn to acquire Conoco. However, while Conoco accounts for 30 per cent of total sales it contributes only 16 per cent of operating profits. Du Pont is also diversifying into electronics and pharma-ceuticals.

Du Pont manufactures in almost 40 countries and markets in more than 150 with international sales accounting for 40 per cent of total sales. One in four of the group's 140,000 employees works outside the USA.

R&D expenditure in 1987 was $1.2bn and the group has 10,000 staff engaged in R&D. Recent discoveries include 'Stainmaster' to protect carpets against a range of household stains.

E

Eastman Kodak [USA]. Known as the 'Yellow Father', Eastman Kodak is the world's leading manufacturer of still and motion picture films, consumer cameras and films, as well as medical X-ray films. This $17bn corporation consists of five business groups. These are Commercial and Information Systems, bolstered by the acquisition in 1988 of IBM's copier service business; Diversified Technologies/Life Sciences, which includes Verbatim Corporation, acquired in 1985 and one of America's top three manufacturers of floppy disks; Eastman Chemicals, with annual sales of $2.6bn, which if independent would rank among America's top 160 companies in terms of sales; Photographic Products, which has a joint venture with Matsushita to manufacture alkaline camera batteries; and Sterling Drug, acquired for $5.1bn in 1988. Kodak describes the Sterling acquisition as 'the most significant in its history'. Sterling was particularly strong in over-the-counter medicines and had an extensive development, registration, marketing and distribution network – one that would take considerable time and cost for Kodak to develop. Sterling has 21,000 employees, 17 plants in the USA, and 55 in 45 countries overseas, with products sold in 124 countries.

Kodak as a whole has manufacturing and marketing facilities in some 45 countries with sales outlets in more than 150 countries. It has more than 145,000 employees, with almost 88,000 or 61 per cent employed in the USA. Each year Kodak allocates a sizeable proportion of revenues to R&D (see table 1).

Table 1 Kodak: the cost of R&D ($m)

Year	Sales	R&D expenditure	R&D as a percentage of sales
1988	17,034	1,147	6.7
1987	13,305	992	7.4
1986	11,550	1,059	9.2
1985	10,631	976	9.2
1984	10,600	838	7.9
Mean			8.1

Source: Kodak, Annual Reports

In order to gain access to key technology for photocopiers, Kodak established in 1988 a $74m R&D centre in Yokohama, Japan. It also signed an agreement with Canon, under which it will manufacture high-volume copiers for sale in Japan under the Canon name. This licensing agreement gives Kodak improved access to the Japanese market where its sales are approaching the $1bn mark.

After some major marketing blunders, Kodak is beginning to make full use of this function in its competitive armoury. In the early 1980s, Kodak failed to secure official sponsorship status of the 1984 Los Angeles Olympics. Instead arch-rival Fuji of Japan won this contract and with it a marvellous opportunity to promote its products in Kodak's domestic market. In 1988 Kodak reversed this situation, securing sponsorship rights for the Seoul games. Apart from offering global TV coverage Kodak was attracted in particular by the prospect of stalling Fuji in the burgeoning Asian market.

In retrospect, Kodak's decision to withdraw from the fully automatic 35mm camera market appears to have been a major error. By 1988, just two years after re-entry, Kodak had become US market leader. It appears that the company is better equipped than ever to protect its market share.

EC, see EUROPEAN COMMUNITY.

ECGD (Export Credit Guarantee Department) [UK], see EXPORT CREDIT INSURANCE.

eclectic theory. The eclectic approach to the theory of foreign direct investment was developed by Professor John Dunning while at Reading University and provides a consolidation of ideas drawn from approaches to industrial organization, location theory and market imperfections. The eclectic theory specifies three conditions for foreign direct investment to occur. There must be company-specific advantages, largely of an intangible nature, relative to other firms; there must be internalization advantages in that it must be more beneficial for the company to use its specific advantages itself rather than to sell them or lease them to foreign companies; and there must be country-specific advantages in that it must be profitable to locate operations abroad.

Economic Community of West African States (ECOWAS) [Nigeria]. A grouping established in 1975 and comprising Ghana, Liberia, Nigeria, Senegal, Sierra Leone, Togo, Benin, Ivory Coast, Gambia, Niger, Upper Volta and Guinea. The main objectives are to remove trade barriers, adopt common external tariffs, promote the free movement of factors of production, establish a cooperation fund and harmonize agricultural, industrial and monetary policies. The prospects for ECOWAS are bright in that it does seem to have made identifiable progress.

economies of scale. The reductions in average cost made possible by increasing the size of manufacturing plant. The greater the plant size the greater the output; and the greater the output, the smaller the proportion of fixed costs attached to each unit of output. This enables the manufacturer to sell his product at a cheaper price. However, there reaches a point (minimum optimum scale) when economies of scale are totally exhausted and any further increase in size will lead to diseconomies.

Real economies of scale relate to increased efficiency due to larger plant size, i.e. less input for the same output. Pecuniary economies of scale are those savings made when it is cheaper to buy the input in bulk, but with no increase in efficiency. Large-scale plants based on production technologies usually enjoy real economies of scale whereas economies of multi-plant operations are unlikely to be purely pecuniary.

economies of scope. Cost reductions which result from the simultaneous production of several related products, but with the volume of any one product held constant. They arise from the flexibility of new computerized manufacturing technology which permits the sharing or joint use of inputs across a number of product lines so that multiple products can be made in combination rather than separately. Flexible manufacturing systems facilitate the production of custom-ized products closely tied to demand.

ECOWAS, see ECONOMIC COMMUNITY OF WEST AFRICAN STATES.

ECU, see EUROPEAN CURRENCY UNIT.

EEC (European Economic Community), see EUROPEAN COMMUNITY.

EEIG, see EUROPEAN ECONOMIC INTEREST GROUPING.

efficient market hypothesis. A hypothesis stating that security prices (e.g. share prices, foreign exchange rates, etc.) reflect all available information. This in turn would imply that traders cannot hope to make excess returns, as all information is already impounded in market prices. Many studies are consistent with share prices reflecting publicly available information. However, the evidence relating to foreign exchange markets is inconclusive. Usually, three levels of informational efficiency are distinguished:

1 *Weak form efficiency*. Security prices reflect all past price information. This implies that excess returns could not be earned from analysing past price data, or (assuming some technical conditions hold) that security prices behave as if they were a random walk. Forecasts of security prices based upon patterns of past price information (e.g. chartism) are likely to be useless, since this information is already impounded in security prices.

2 *Semi-strong efficiency*. Security prices reflect all publicly available information. By implication, attempts to forecast future security prices using fundamental information (e.g. company accounts, macroeconomic data, balance of payments data) are likely to be unsuccessful, since the information is already impounded in security prices.

3 *Strong form efficiency*. Security prices reflect all information (including private or insider information). Inside information relating to the response of regulatory authorities to takeovers, or government intervention in foreign exchange markets will not yield any excess profits to a trader.

EFTA, see EUROPEAN FREE TRADE ASSOCIATION.

EIB, see EUROPEAN INVESTMENT BANK.

Electrolux [Sweden]. Scandinavia's second-largest company with sales of more than $12bn, it consists of about 500 operating companies in 48 countries, which cover 24 product lines organized into six business areas. It has 280 plants, and sells its products in some 45–50 nations. It has expanded through acquisitions to become one of the world's leading white goods manufacturers, and a leader in vacuum cleaners, chain saws, commercial laundry equipment and car seat belts. Its success is largely due to its rare ability to digest and integrate acquisitions. Over 70 white goods firms have been acquired at 'scratch and dent' prices, and then fully restored. The company has also diversified with notable aplomb. Since 1967, it has acquired more than 300 companies in 40 countries. Two deals stand out. In 1984 it acquired Italy's Zanussi, then unprofitable but one of the joint leaders of the European domestic appliance market. This deal gave Electrolux 25 per cent of the European market, double the share of Philips, its nearest rival. The acquisition was complementary. Zanussi was strong in those products and markets (washing machines, small and medium-sized refrigerators, southern Europe) where Electrolux was weak, and Electrolux was strong (large refrigerators, northern Europe) where Zanussi was weak. The Italian firm was quickly restored to profitability but tensions remain between the hierarchical Italian and informal Swedish business cultures. Since 1988 Italian factory managers have been 'product division managers' with total responsibility for negotiating sales volumes and transfer prices with Electrolux marketing companies in Europe. This led to major disputes when the Italian country manager insisted that rising raw material prices would have to be borne by the UK marketing company rather than Italian plants. Adjudication from Stockholm proved necessary.

In 1986, Electrolux paid $745m to acquire White Consolidated Industries in the largest ever US acquisition by a Swedish company. This purchase gave Electrolux a complete product range of kitchen equipment, so important in the age of designer kitchens where all the appliances must match. Equally importantly, it secured a major presence in the world's single largest market. As Anders Scharp explained: 'There are three principal markets for consumer durables in the world – Western Europe, the USA, and Japan. In order to ensure long run survival, it is . . . necessary . . . to be well established in more than one of these regions.'

embargo. A deliberate act, by a government, prohibiting trade with another country due to some point of principle. It is most commonly used in wartime or to obtain political or economic concessions. One example is the US embargo on trade with the USSR following the Soviet involvement in Afghanistan.

EMS, see EUROPEAN MONETARY SYSTEM.

Environmental Protection Agency (EPA) [USA]. An independent agency of the US government founded in 1970. Existing legislation had been enforced by nine different agencies. The EPA pulled these enforcement powers under one roof, thereby creating the largest agency in the federal government. During the 1970s the EPA met with intense resistance from industry and from some state and local governments. For example, 29 states failed to meet the EPA's 1979 deadline for plans to reduce air pollution to acceptable levels by 1983. However, during the second half of the 1980s, the environment became a priority, and the EPA undoubtedly benefited from both popular support for 'green' issues and personnel changes.

EPA, see ENVIRONMENTAL PROTECTION AGENCY.

EPZ, see EXPORT PROCESSING ZONE.

Ericsson [Sweden]. One of the world's leading players in the $115bn telecommunications market, Ericsson has eight business areas, but public telecommunications alone accounts for almost 50 per cent of its total sales of $5bn. Radio and business communications account for 15 and 11.5 per cent respectively. Geographically, sales are firmly rooted in Europe which accounts for 70 per cent of total sales, Sweden accounting for 20 per cent.

It has 65,000 employees in 80 countries, and 30 widely dispersed manufacturing plants in places such as Australia, Malaysia and Mexico. Rationalization may be necessary to remain competitive, and one cannot underestimate the commitment of a firm which allocates 8 per cent of total sales to R&D.

During the mid-1980s, Ericsson's sales dropped due to costs associated with its then IT business and with its penetrating the US market. Since then sales have exceeded $5bn, and Ericsson now has 40 per cent of the world market for cellular communications equipment.

The company is consolidating its position in communications, divesting peripheral businesses such as its computer business to Finland's Nokia for $217m in 1988. It also acquired Intelsa, the Spanish telecommunications equipment supplier, the telecommunications operations of one of Norway's largest industrial groups, Elektriska Bureau (EB), 60 per cent of which is controlled by Asea Brown Boveri. At the same time, it sold its signalling business to EB.

ethnocentric organization. An inward-looking company that believes that what works at home should work abroad. Ethnocentric companies tend to see the world as one market for their products and usually organize by product line. Within each product division the MNC's activities will be centralized but there will be little, if any, coordination between divisions. The ethnocentric approach can spell disaster in the conduct of foreign operations located in different business and cultural environments.

Euromarkets. The Eurocurrency market and the Eurobond market constitute the Euromarkets. These markets may be distinguished from national financial markets since they consist of currencies or claims on currencies which are issued outside the currency's country of origin. For example, a Eurodollar is a dollar which is deposited in a bank outside the US.

The Eurocurrency market

This market consists of banks which grant loans and accept deposits denominated in foreign currencies. The raison d'être for these markets is government intervention or the fear of government intervention in the currency's country of origin. For example, suppose that a corporation fears that the Ruritanian government may impose exchange controls, or impose a tax upon Ruritanian deposit accounts held by non-nationals. The corporation may wish to maintain a proportion of liquid assets in the Ruritanian currency, and therefore would welcome the opportunity to place its holdings of the currency outside Ruritania. This, however, is an extreme form of intervention, and government intervention may include banking regulations, interest rate restrictions, and exchange controls.

Due to the popularity of these markets, large amounts of money may be raised in these markets with maturities ranging from three to ten years. Loans are on a floating rate basis (i.e. the coupons on the loans are related to trends in interest rates). Usually, the basis for determining the interest rate is the London Interbank Offered Rate (LIBOR). Loans may be raised in a variety of currencies, and may contain provisions to alter the currency of the loan during the life of the loan. In the absence of arbitrage opportunities and government intervention, interest rates in national markets would be expected to be close to Euromarket rates. However, due to government intervention the difference (spread) between lending and borrowing rates is less in Euromarkets than national markets. Nevertheless, owing to the nature of the markets, they are restricted, in the main, to banks.

The Eurobond market

Eurobonds are bonds which are sold outside the countries of the currency of denomination. Unlike the Eurocurrency market, where claims upon banks are traded, Eurobonds are issued by the final borrower. Final borrowers are restricted to entities which have impeccable credit ratings. They would include the larger multinational corporations and governments from developed countries.

The market is not subject to the regulatory and taxation requirements of national bond markets and it permits borrowers to raise money in a speedy, flexible way while investors may avoid the payment of national taxes. The most significant differences between Eurocurrencies and Eurobonds are:

Eurobonds have longer maturities.

Fixed rate issues are possible in the Eurobond market.

European Community (EC) [Belgium]. Founded by the Treaty of Rome in 1957, the European Community (EC), with its headquarters in Brussels, is the world's largest trading bloc. Its founder members are France, West Germany, Italy, the Netherlands, Belgium and Luxembourg. In 1973, the UK, Eire and Denmark joined, followed by Greece in 1981 and Spain and Portugal in 1986.

The objectives of the community are to promote economic development and productive efficiency by removing tariffs and other regulatory barriers and by establishing common policies within the member states on industry and agriculture.

The EC is administered by the European Commission which drafts policies decided upon by the Council of Ministers (one Minister per member country). While the European Parliament does not have much political muscle, even though the ultimate aim of the Community is political as well as economic union, its powers are increasing and likely to continue to do so.

In 1987, the Single European Act was passed, which aimed at removing all non-tariff barriers within the EC by 1992. On a wide range of issues, majority voting by the EC Council of Ministers will be accepted with a view to speeding up the process of integrating and developing a European market of more than 320 million consumers.

European Community directive. The EC Council of Ministers issues the directives which form the basis of Community law. Each directive is issued in pursuance of an objective and each member state must, by whatever means necessary, incorporate these directives into its own domestic law, even if implementation means changing the existing law of a member state. The purpose of this is to harmonize the law of the member countries to achieve international parity within the European Community with a view to promoting equality of competition and economic integration.

European currency unit (ECU). A composite currency comprising a basket of EC currencies. Its value is determined by taking a weighted average of the currencies of the European Community. This weighting is based on each country's share of GNP and EC trade and is usually reviewed every five years.

European Economic Interest Grouping (EEIG). A legal form of corporate organization established by the European Community in 1985 as a means by which companies or persons in different countries of the EC can group together for common commercial purposes.

European Free Trade Association (EFTA) [Switzerland]. An organization of European countries outside the European Community, including Austria, Finland, Norway, Sweden and Switzerland, designed to promote economic integration by abolishing tariffs among its members but with each member maintaining its own external tariffs against non-EFTA countries. Its headquarters are in Geneva.

European Investment Bank (EIB). Founded under the Treaty of Rome in 1957, it is an organization similar to the World Bank group but which deals primarily with the EC countries. It invests in both the private and public sectors and is particularly supportive of the less developed regions of Europe.

European Monetary System (EMS). An arrangement established in 1979 to stabilize exchange rates between a number of EC countries. With the exception of Britain, all of the EC countries participate in a joint float. Each member's currency is expressed as an exchange rate vis-à-vis a basket of currencies called the European currency unit (ECU). The ECU is a composite currency which is based upon all of the EC currencies (including sterling) weighted by GNP and intra-European trade. The members of the system peg their currencies to the ECU and, for most of the currencies, if a currency deviates by more than 2.25 per cent local central banks are expected to intervene to maintain the currency within the trading band.

exchange controls. A series of restrictions and administrative devices which regulates the convertibility of a currency. Frequently, exchange controls are enforced by central banks, and commercial banks may also be involved in the administration of exchange controls. At the extreme, the government may render the currency inconvertible which gives rise to blocked funds. Intermediate treatment will allow all trade-related transactions to take place (provided documentary evidence is supplied), while there will be strict control of all transactions which are not of a trade-related nature. Such strict controls may extend to the use of dual exchange rates (a less favourable rate being applied to capital transactions) or a complete moratorium upon transactions of a capital nature. Additional restrictions may be applied to the use of forward contracts, netting and leading and lagging.

exchange rate. A currency's exchange rate is determined by supply and demand in the foreign exchange market. The foreign exchange market does not have a physical location like a stock exchange or an auction room, but is conducted by telephone, cable and video between the trading rooms of large banks, dealers and foreign exchange brokers. There are two basic types of transaction within the foreign exchange market: spot transactions and forward transactions.

Spot transactions

The actual physical exchange of currency takes place two days after the deal is arranged with a spot transaction. In the case of a forward transaction the physical exchange of currency does not take place until some date in the future.

If an individual had FF15,000 and wished to exchange the francs into sterling, he would find out the current spot rate. There are two types of quotation that he might receive. Firstly, he could be told the number of French francs he would have to pay for £1 or he could be told the number of pounds he would receive for FF1. In the UK, quotations are nearly always expressed as the number of units of foreign currency which one would receive for £1. A similar practice is used in the US for all currencies other than sterling. However, in most other countries, the number of units of local currency payable for one unit of foreign currency is used. For example, if the current exchange rate is FF5 for £1 stg (an indirect quotation), then the individual would expect to receive £3,000 stg for his francs. This exchange rate could also be expressed as £0.2 stg for FF1 (a direct quotation). Needless to say, in a market where transactions are executed on the telephone the existence of two exchange rates could be most confusing. This is the reason why a number of conventions are applied to the quotation of exchange rates. In Britain, rates are expressed as the number of units of foreign currency per pound (e.g. $1.6 per pound).

Inevitably, traders in the foreign exchange market attempt to earn money by buying currencies cheaply, and selling them at a profit. The difference between the price at which they are prepared to buy currency and the price at which they will sell currencies is called the bid–ask spread. The 'bid' price is the price at which they will buy currencies and the 'ask' price is the price at which they will sell currencies.

Forward transactions

The other type of foreign exchange transaction is a forward transaction. This consists of an agreement between two dealers to exchange currencies at a specified exchange rate at a specified date in the future. The rate at which they intend transacting is called the forward rate. Forward rates are expressed as either an outright rate or in terms of a discount or premium on the spot rate. For example, if the current franc exchange rate is FF5/£ and one can buy or sell francs in a month's time at FF4/£, then the outright rate is FF4/£, and the forward rate is at a 'sterling discount' because one will receive fewer francs for £1 in the forward market than in the spot market.

Changes in the forward rate are highly correlated with changes in the spot rate. This arises because of covered interest arbitrage. Given that interest rates are less volatile than exchange rates, most of the variation in forward rates may be attributed to spot rate movements.

Finally, it should be pointed out that if one has exchange rates against one currency, then one can calculate exchange rates against all other currencies. For example, if the exchange rate for the French franc in London is FF5/£ and the dollar exchange rate is $2/£, then one can calculate the dollar–franc exchange rate in the following manner.

$$\frac{FF/£}{\$/£} = \frac{5}{2} = FF2.5/\$$$

This process of finding out the exchange rate between two currencies using their relationship to a third currency is called calculating cross rates.

exchange rate changes. Calculating exchange rate changes depends on whether direct or indirect quotations are used. A direct quotation is the number of units of home currency that one would pay for a single unit of foreign currency. An indirect quotation is the number of units of foreign currency that one would pay for a unit of home currency. For an indirect quotation:

$$\text{percentage change} = \frac{\text{beginning rate} - \text{ending rate}}{\text{ending rate}} \times 100$$

So if the exchange rate changes from FF5/£ to FF4/£ then:

$$\text{percentage change} = \frac{5 - 4}{4} \times 100$$
$$= +25\%$$

If we had used the direct quotations, the exchange rate would have changed from £0.2/FF to £0.25/FF. The formula used for direct quotes is somewhat different. It is:

$$\text{percentage change} = \frac{\text{ending rate} - \text{beginning rate}}{\text{beginning rate}} \times 100$$

$$= \frac{0.2 - 0.25}{0.25} \times 100$$

$$= -20\%$$

A British person cannot get as many francs for a pound at the end of the period. Therefore, the pound has devalued 20 per cent against the franc. However, from the point of view of a Frenchman, he can now obtain more pounds for a franc, therefore the franc has revalued against the pound. Normally, the terms revaluation and devaluation are applied in situations where currencies are pegged. When currencies are floating against one another one speaks in terms of weakening/depreciating currencies and strengthening/appreciating currencies. Currencies which are likely to be weak are described as soft currencies, and currencies which are likely to be strong are referred to as hard currencies.

exchange rate forecasting. The success of exchange rate forecasting is contingent on the extent to which foreign exchange markets are efficient, and the related issue of the exchange rate regime. If exchange rates are floating freely and the market is fully efficient, then one would expect that the net benefit of utilizing a forecasting service would be nil. It is only if foreign exchange markets fail to reflect all available information, or if governments systematically intervene in the markets, that there may be benefits from the use of forecasts.

There are two basic techniques used to forecast exchange rates, which may be distinguished by the types of information sets used to generate the forecast. The first type is based upon the use of the past price movements to generate forecasts of future price movements. These techniques include chartism and momentum analysis. A second type is based upon the use of economic data (e.g. balance of payments) to generate forecasts of future exchange rates. This data may be integrated within an economic model or, alternatively, may be analysed by an experienced economist to produce a forecast. Many commercial forecasting services may combine aspects of both approaches. It is extremely difficult to produce conclusions regarding the success of forecasting services, since there is little or no agreement as to what constitutes success. The authors would recommend treating the claims of forecasting services with scepticism, unless the service can demonstrate a consistent record of success and the prospective purchaser has a similar success. *See also* EFFICIENT MARKET HYPOTHESIS.

exchange rate regime. A system or regime under which exchange rates are set. There are a variety of market mechanisms for establishing exchange rates, i.e. the rates for which one currency can be exchanged for other currencies. However, there are two possible extremes, fixed exchange rates and freely floating exchange rates. The existing market arrangements for foreign exchange represent a system which combines aspects of these two extremes.

Floating exchange rates

A system of freely floating exchange rates implies that exchange rates are determined by the demand and supply for foreign currencies. The demand and supply of currencies would be determined by interest rate and inflation rate expectations, as well as economic growth.

Fixed exchange rates

Fixed rate systems imply that governments agree to maintain the exchange at a particular rate vis-à-vis other currencies and to intervene in foreign exchange markets if the rate deviates too far. The European Monetary System and the Bretton Woods agreement are examples of fixed exchange rate regimes.

Under a fixed rate system, internal economic adjustments are necessary to ensure that fixed exchange rates are maintained. For example, a disciple of purchasing power parity may argue that exchange rates reflect inflation differentials. In order to maintain a fixed exchange rate, it would be necessary to ensure that money supply growth and local inflation rates were similar to the rates pertaining internationally. Domestic policy may be autonomous if a country raises foreign debt to bolster reserves. However, this is only a short-term solution as the debt will need to be serviced in the future and hence deplete foreign currency reserves.

The current system

The current system of exchange rate determination is a mixture of fixed and floating rates. The majority of the world's currencies are either pegged to a reserve currency (e.g. the dollar, French franc or sterling) or unit (e.g. the SDR or some independently determined composite currency). Other exchange rates (e.g. dollar, sterling) are freely floating with occasional intervention by the larger developing countries to stabilize the markets.

exchange risk [foreign exchange risk, currency risk]. The risk attaching to fluctuations in exchange rates, which affect the performance of an MNC. The possibility of such fluctuations is known as the MNC's 'exposure to foreign exchange risk'. Usually a three-fold classification is applied to exposure to foreign exchange risk: translation exposure, transaction exposure and economic exposure.

Translation exposure

The possibility that exchange rate changes may adversely affect the balance sheet or the income statement of the MNC. While economists might argue that people are not fooled by accounting numbers, companies (for whatever reasons) do care. Substantial movements in exchange rates may adversely (or favourably) affect the financial statements and this effect is known as translation exposure.

Transaction exposure

When a company exports or imports goods, there will usually be a time lag between receiving/despatching foreign currency denominated invoices and the payment/receipt of cash. During this period, the firm has a transaction exposure, since the translated amount of foreign currency may fluctuate between the invoice date and the payment date. Foreign currency denominated short-term monetary assets and liabilities would constitute one possible measure of exposed assets.

Economic exposure

Economic exposure may be defined as the effects of exchange rate changes upon the cash flows of the MNC. As such, transaction exposure is a subset of economic exposure, whereas translation exposure is an accounting rather than a cash flow concept.

Whilst economic exposure may be defined in terms of cash flows and exchange rate changes, little progress has been made in producing a more operational definition of the concept. However, the competitive impact upon the firm of changes in exchange rates is an example of economic exposure. For example, a UK-based engineering company might be adversely affected by the strength of sterling due to the erosion of competitiveness in export markets and increasing import penetration in the home market. It is this competitive impact which dominates discussions of economic exposure. Moreover, the presence of import penetration in response to a strong domestic currency highlights the possibility of a wholly domestic company without any foreign currency denominated transactions being exposed to exchange risk. For example, a hotel in the centre of London which depends upon American tourists may find that its revenues are correlated with changes in the dollar exchange rate.

exchange risk management.

Managing transaction exposure

Transaction exposures (arising from, for example, a foreign currency denominated receivable) may be immunized or hedged by the use of either external techniques (adopting positions in financial markets) or internal techniques (modifications to exposures within the firm).

External techniques

The classic external techniques are the use of forward contracts, or the use of foreign currency borrowing or lending. As such, they amount to techniques for altering the denomination of monetary assets and liabilities. Other techniques might include the use of currency swaps, futures and options. Exporters should also examine the availability of government insurance schemes to protect against currency fluctuations.

Suppose that the AB company expects to receive $200,000 from an export contract in one year. The current exchange rate is $2/£ and is expected to be either $2 or $2.4 at the end of the year. The interest rate in the UK is currently 10 per cent, and in the USA, the interest rate is 21 per cent. The 12-month forward rate is $2.2.

Clearly the company has a transaction exposure and its sterling receipts at the year end will be either £100,000 (if the exchange rate is $2) or £83,333 (if the exchange rate is $2.4).

The firm could consider selling the proceeds of the export contract in a forward market. This would result in a certain receipt of £91,000 (200,000/2.2) at the year end. This procedure is known as hedging foreign exchange risks. There is now no risk associated with the dollar receivable since there is an offsetting position in the forward market.

Rather than using a forward contract, the company could utilize a money market hedge to cover the exposure. A money market hedge involves a number of steps:

1 Borrow dollars now and repay the loan with the proceeds of the export contract. In our example, the company could borrow $165,290 now. Given the US interest rate is 21 per cent, interest of $34,710 will be payable at the year end, plus the principal of $165,290. This amounts to $200,000 to repay borrowings; the same amount as the export contract.
2 Convert the dollar borrowings to sterling. This will result in an immediate sterling cash inflow of £82,645.
3 Invest the sterling amount for one year at an interest rate of 10 per

cent. The proceeds of the investment will amount to £82,645 principal plus £8,255 interest, or £90,900.

The reader will note that the firm should, in principle, be indifferent between a forward market and a money market hedge. This indifference arises since according to the interest rate parity theorem, forward rates reflect international interest rate differentials. In practice, firms may prefer to use forward contracts since they may not have access to favourable borrowing and lending rates in international markets. Moreover, the use of foreign currency debt may result in less favourable balance sheet ratios.

Internal techniques

Internal techniques include the use of netting or matching, leading or lagging, and shifting exchange risk to customers or suppliers. They are classified as internal techniques since they do not utilize external financial markets.

There are two types of risk shifting:

1 Insist on all invoices for purchases and sales being invoiced in domestic currency. For example, a UK company selling to the USA might invoice in sterling rather than dollars.
2 Link invoice prices directly to exchange rates. In this instance a US customer would recieve a dollar invoice, but would be expected to pay (receive) a surcharge (subsidy) based upon movements in the sterling–dollar exchange rate between the invoice and payment dates.

The effectiveness of risk shifting techniques will depend to a large extent upon the monopolistic power of the firm in product and factor markets. In extremely competitive markets, a firm may adversely affect its competitive position by insisting upon domestic currency transactions.

A potential compromise is risk sharing. This may be particularly appropriate for long-term contracts. Essentially, the price is fixed provided exchange rates stay within a limited range. However, should exchange rates stray outside this range, then the buyer and the seller agree to some apportionment of the gain or loss.

Managing economic exposure

Most of the techniques suggested for the management of the effects of exchange rate changes upon competitive position are operational rather than financial. The strategies consist of attempting to decrease the exposure of products to price competition from overseas producers, while increasing the opportunities to alter sourcing and production locations in order to minimize costs.

For example, Catcars produces luxury automobiles in the UK for export to the USA. Fluctuations in the dollar–sterling exchange rate are likely to alter profitability dramatically. The company might attempt to emphasize the exclusivity and uniqueness of the Catcar, or move production to the USA in order to ensure a matching between the cost base and the revenue base.

expatriate. A manager or other employee who is a foreign citizen in the country where he or she is working. While expatriates are usually posted for short-term periods, some stay on and become quasi-citizens e.g. many Hong Kong expatriates are known as 'Hong Kong belongers'.

experience curve. The relationship between accumulated production and unit manufacturing costs. First observed by the Boston Consulting Group, the experience curve is now an important element in modern manufacturing management. For many large corporations, unit costs decrease by between 5 per cent and 30 per cent with each doubling of accumulated production. Cost reductions arise from economies of scale, the familiarity of workers with the manufacturing process, lower materials costs per unit of output, lower wastage and the more effective redesign of products. The significance for multinationals of maintaining or expanding market share is thereby confirmed. Exploiting the experience curve is a defence against competitors and a barrier to entry for newcomers. The global integration of production facilitated by an information network enables multinationals to move down the experience curve and thus achieve worldwide cost savings.

export consortium. The voluntary cooperation of a number of non-competing manufacturers in order to promote exports by generating savings in the development of expertise for dealing in certain types of products and with certain groups of countries of special concern to the members of the consortium. Export consortia carry out much of the relevant administrative work involved with exports and also conduct export market assessments.

Export Credit Guarantee Department (ECGD) [UK], *see* EXPORT CREDIT INSURANCE.

export credit insurance. A form of insurance that covers the credit risks associated with exporting: such credit risks include the possibility of

non-payment by the importer arising from either default or pro-
crastination, actions by the government in the importer's country
which leads to non-payment, or other risks including war.

Usually, export credit insurance is offered by government-
sponsored agencies (e.g. the Export Credit Guarantee Department
(ECGD) in the UK and the Foreign Credit Insurance Association
(FCIA) in the USA) in order to encourage exports. A fee is normally
charged to the exporter for the insurance. Essentially, export credit
insurance offers protection against bad debts and the presence of this
insurance is helpful when seeking export finance from commercial
banks, and should decrease the cost of the finance.

Export credit insurance may also be available for the medium- or
longer-term credit risks associated with the export of big ticket items
under long-term contracts.

export licence. An instrument used by government to control the export of
certain goods, such as arms, art treasures and other items of national
importance.

export processing zone (EPZ). Despite the growth of factory automation,
some industries (e.g. textiles and electronics, especially) still use some
very labour-intensive processes. Securing cheap labour is thus
critical, and clearly therefore, developing countries would be the
obvious choice for performing labour-intensive tasks. Multinationals,
though, often manufacture key components in developed countries
and the normal costs of shipping these to LDCs may reduce the
attraction of locating an assembly plant in an LDC. However, poorer
nations require foreign exchange and job-creating projects. Thus
many of them, especially those in South-east Asia and Central and
South America, have established export processing zones, small
areas, with excellent infrastructure, into which companies can import
goods for use in the production of exports without having to pay any
import duty. Mexico, for example, has created numerous EPZs along
the US border, and multinationals from many countries have located
in them in order to avail themselves of such a low-cost location in
close proximity to the US market. High-tech firms in Silicon Valley
can thus ship components to the 'maquiladores' (assembly) plants in
Mexico's EPZs and then re-import the finished product. When
Mexico introduced its Border Industrialization Programme in 1965,
there were 12 plants in the area employing fewer than 4,000 workers.
Just over 20 years later, there were more than 1,000 plants employing
almost half a million workers.

In terms of generating employment, the EPZs worldwide have

been successful, though young, unskilled, female workers account for the vast majority of the workforce in EPZs. In terms of stimulating the local economy through technology transfer, etc. the benefits of EPZs to the host nation are less apparent, raising the question, are EPZs little more than 'sweatshops in the sun'?

expropriation. An extreme form of political risk, occurring when a host government takes over the property of a foreign investor or multinational with or without compensation. Most expropriations are selective rather than general. To improve the foreign investment climates for their investors a number of countries have established bilateral treaties with foreign governments. These agreements generally provide for home country insurance to investors and an agreement for settlement of payments for compensation on a government-to-government basis. A major problem with these agreements is that they do not normally provide a mechanism for settlement.

Exxon [USA]. The world's largest oil company, and the third-largest industrial corporation with sales in excess of $65bn. It has interests in 80 countries, and its principal activities are concerned with energy. These include the exploration, transportation and sale of crude oil and their other products, manufacture of petroleum products, fabrication of nuclear fuel, and the exploration, mining and sale of coal.

The chemical division alone of Exxon has annual sales of $10bn. It is one of the world's largest suppliers of basic chemicals, the third-largest US chemical company, and is in the world's top 12 chemical groups. During the boom conditions of the late 1980s, plant investment increased from $298m in 1987 to $1bn in 1989. This investment focused on improving and expanding existing capacity, as Exxon believed this to be more prudent than opening new sites.

In 1989 Exxon faced a major crisis when its oil tanker *Valdez*, ran aground, releasing tons of crude oil into the sea, causing an environmental disaster along 364 miles of Alaskan coastline. The clean-up operation involved 10,000 people and 70 aircraft, and Exxon wrote off $850m to cover these costs. Legal liabilities may prove even more expensive, with the oil giant facing more than 150 suits. This incident, like Bhopal, underlines the importance of successful crisis management by large corporations. *See also* SEVEN SISTERS.

F

factoring. Factors are commercial banks or specialized companies which purchase both domestic and foreign currencies receivables from companies in exchange for domestic currency immediately, in return for a fee which may be as high as 4 per cent. These costs may be justified for firms which export occasionally, or for firms which export sporadically to many customers in many countries.

The benefits of factoring will depend upon the extent to which the factor bears the political, foreign exchange and credit risks associated with an export receivable. The factor may also undertake some of the administrative work associated with accounts receivable. Finally, the factor is extending credit to the exporter and, therefore, the fee reflects an interest charge.

FASB, *see* FINANCIAL ACCOUNTING STANDARDS BOARD.

FCIA (Foreign Credit Insurance Association), *see* EXPORT CREDIT IN-SURANCE.

FDI, *see* FOREIGN DIRECT INVESTMENT.

Federal Reserve System [USA]. The central banking system of the USA, established after widespread bank failures, the suspension of gold payments and a depression, caused panic in 1917. The National Monetary Commission produced proposals for banking reform and hence the Federal Reserve System was created. Like other central banking systems it manages the US money supply and helps to resolve potential cash crises within the economy. It also tries to achieve a healthy balance of payments and generally oversee a smoothly running banking system.

Federal Trade Commission (FTC) [USA]. Established in 1915, the Federal Trade Commission is one of two federal government agencies in the USA which are responsible for enforcing the anti-trust laws. The other agency is the Anti-trust Division of the Department of Justice.

Fédération Internationale des Bourses de Valeurs (International Federation of Stock Exchanges). A voluntary association of stock exchanges formed to promote the exchange of information and the coordination of listing requirements internationally.

Ferruzzi [Italy]. Raoul Gardini, chairman of Ferruzzi has transformed this company by a series of acquisitions and elaborate cross-holdings, creating in the process Italy's second-largest private group and one of the 50 largest industrial corporations in the world with sales of $18bn and almost 76,000 employees. The world's largest sugar producer, it farms almost every known crop across 2,500 million acres in every climatic and agricultural environment throughout the world. It is also Europe's leading starch producer.

In 1987, Ferruzzi took control of Montedison, the chemicals company which was then Italy's second-largest private group. The group has acquired a reputation for secrecy though, and Ferruzzi received strong criticism for failing to provide adequate disclosure regarding its restructuring plan for Montedison assets.

Fiat [Italy]. This $35bn conglomerate, Italy's largest private company, operates in 52 countries through 574 subsidiaries and 182 associated companies of which 334 are based in Italy.

Group companies are organized into 14 operating sectors, of which automobiles, the largest, accounts for 58 per cent of total sales. The automobile sector sells cars under four marques: Fiat, Lancia–Autobianchi, Alfa Romeo (acquired in 1987) and Ferrari. In 1988, Fiat sold 2.2m cars, of which more than 2m were sold in Europe. It claims to be the European market leader, with a 15 per cent share. In Italy it is undisputed market leader with 60 per cent of the market, selling more than 1m cars each year. Fiat Auto has 36 plants, 33 of which are in Italy, employing more than 130,000 workers. It has one plant each in Brazil, Portugal and Venezuela. It is likely to diversify its European production base, and the UK would be a strong contender for any major investment. In order to increase overseas sales, licensing agreements have been concluded with America's Chrysler and Japan's Mazda, which will market Alfa Romeo and Lancia respectively in their local markets. Fiat is also expanding into Eastern Europe.

Commercial vehicles operating under the 'Iveco' trademark are the second-largest sector, accounting for almost a fifth of total sales. Iveco ranks as number two in the European market, with 20 per cent of the market.

Fiat is also a leading producer of tractors and construction equipment. In Europe it is market leader with a 17 per cent share for the former, and has almost 9 per cent of the latter market. It is also one of

Europe's top vehicle component manufacturers. Its other activities include: industrial components, production systems, civil engineering, rolling stock and railway systems, telecommunications, financial and real estate services, and publishing and communication, which includes *La Stampa*, Italy's third best-selling national daily newspaper.

This massive conglomerate accounts for 5 per cent of Italy's GDP, 6 per cent of its total exports, and one-third of its R&D by private companies.

Like France's leading car companies, Fiat made an astonishing recovery during the 1980s. The Uno launched in 1983, has become Europe's best-selling small car, and $1.7bn has been invested in launching the Tipo, which Fiat hopes will replace Volkswagen's Golf as Europe's best-selling car.

The 1980s produced disappointments too (e.g. the collapse of the merger between Ford of Europe and Fiat Auto in 1985, and the resignation in 1988 of Vittorio Ghidella, who is credited with masterminding the recovery), but there was also good fortune. In 1986 the Libyan Government sold back its 15.9 per cent stake in Fiat for $3.1bn. This benefited Fiat in that the Libyan connection had become a handicap to the group, especially when seeking to win US defence contracts. The buy-back also allowed Fiat chairman, Giovanni Agnelli, to raise his family's stake in the world's fifteenth-largest industrial company from 31 to 35 per cent. Not surprisingly, the Agnellis rank among the world's richest individuals and families.

finance, see BACK-TO-BACK FINANCING, CREDIT SWAP, DEBT FINANCE, HOT MONEY, INTERNATIONAL FINANCE CORPORATION, LONDON INTER- NATIONAL FINANCIAL FUTURES EXCHANGE, SWIFT.

Financial Accounting Standards Board (FASB) [USA]. The US body which replaced the Accounting Principles Board in 1973 as the body responsible for establishing accounting standards. The FASB is the independent authoritative body for standard setting and its standards are officially recognized by the Securities and Exchange Commission (SEC) as the only standards that satisfy the Federal securities laws, which are probably the most stringent in the world. In practice, the FASB may be overridden by the SEC or Congress, as in the celebrated cases of accounting for the investment tax credit, and oil and gas accounting, when FASB standards were overturned and replaced by more flexible regulations. The FASB is highly regarded for its work on developing a conceptual framework for financial reporting. In more recent years, however, the FASB has come under increasing criticism in connection with the volume and complexity of the accounting standards it has produced.

firm-specific advantage. The internal advantage unique to multi-nationals which gives them a competitive lead over their rivals. Such advantages comprise special know-how or skills which are unavailable or undeveloped in other companies and which in many cases arise from R&D activities leading to new products or processes, new manufacturing systems, or new marketing and distribution systems. The multinational may also have an advantage in terms of its management organization, strategic planning or marketing approach.

Fisher Effect. The Fisher Effect states that interest rates reflect real interest rates and anticipated inflation. The relationship may be expressed as:

$$(1 + i) = (1 + P)(1 + r)$$

where i = the nominal (observed market) interest rate

r = the real rate of interest

P = the anticipated rate of inflation

While it is difficult to establish whether this relationship holds in practice (given that real interest rates are unobservable), it does highlight the importance of inflationary expectations in the formation of market interest rates. *See also* INTERNATIONAL FISHER EFFECT.

flexible manufacturing system (FMS). The use of robots, modular assemblies, computer-assisted controls of materials together with related innovations to speed up the production process and to make it more flexible and efficient. Japanese car makers have used robots to telling effect since the late 1970s in what has been a manufacturing revolution. European car producers are also now investing heavily in automation to compete with Japanese car producers in the EC.

FMS, *see* FLEXIBLE MANUFACTURING SYSTEM.

Ford Motor Company [USA]. The world's second-largest automobile and industrial corporation, with sales in excess of $90bn, has 14 per cent of the world car market, sells more than 4.5m passenger cars a year, and has over 100 plants in 25 countries. Its products are sold in 200 countries, but its main markets are North America and Europe. It has almost 360,000 employees, and 175,000 of these are based overseas. In Europe alone it has 32 plants, of which 21 are in the UK. Its record profits of $5.3bn in 1988 exceed the turnover of America's

H. J. Heinz, the 89th largest US corporation, and France's computer manufacturer, Bull, the 151st largest non-US corporation.

The Ford Escort was the world's best-selling car in every year during the period 1981 to 1988, selling more than 900,000 models each year since 1985, with 1986 being the peak year when 938,000 Escorts were sold worldwide.

Recent attempts to expand by acquisition or merger in the European mass-production car market have failed. First of all, the proposed merger of Ford's European car operations with Fiat Auto collapsed in 1985 when neither party could agree on who should hold the largest stake in the proposed group. Secondly, in early 1986 political pressure forced the UK government to withdraw from the proposed sale of Austin Rover. Thirdly, Fiat overcame Ford to gain control of Alfa Romeo. However, in late 1989 Ford, which already owned Britain's Aston Martin, acquired Jaguar for £1.6bn. In Asia, Ford holds a 25 per cent stake in Japan's Mazda, and 10 per cent in South Korea's Kia Motors.

In 1988 western Europe accounted for almost one-third of the world's total car production (see table 1), and Ford of Europe is aiming to become the lowest-cost car producer in Europe. It is thus striving to reduce design and engineering costs and accelerate product development, and it has reduced the size of the workforce from 122,000 in 1979 to less than 90,000 in 1988. However, to achieve its goal it must introduce more flexible working conditions at its six car assembly plants. In the UK though, the workforce is opposed to these measures. Ford must negotiate with several trade unions, while incoming Japanese producers are signing single-union agreements. In Europe, Ford's plants are dependent on each other to supply parts and components. This integrated production has traditionally been regarded as a source of competitive advantage, but recent events have exposed Ford to the dangers of this system. For example, in 1988 a

Table 1 Geographical distribution of motor vehicle production in 1988

Region	Units (millions)	%
Western Europe	15.4	31.6
Japan	12.7	26.1
USA	11.2	23.0
South Korea	1.1	2.2
Other	8.3	17.1
Total	48.7	100.0

Source: Volkswagen, 1988 Annual Report

national strike at Ford's UK operations soon had a major effect on several plants on the Continent. Faced with the prospects of European production grinding to a standstill, UK management was forced to back down and withdraw the wages and conditions proposals which had provoked industrial action. This example illustrates the fundamental importance of effective human resource management. Shortly after this strike, Ford scrapped plans to proceed with a major electronics investment in Scotland, and transferred Sierra production from Dagenham in England to Genk in Belgium, the country with the world's highest per capita output of automobiles. In 1990 European production was affected by industrial action by skilled workers in the UK.

In addition to cars and commercial vehicles, Ford is also one of the largest manufacturers of tractors, and has diversified, partly by acquisition, into financial services, becoming one of America's largest mortgage companies.

Foreign Corrupt Practices Act [USA]. US legislation passed in 1977 after an SEC investigation discovered that many companies had made irregular payments. Worst offenders were aircraft companies (e.g. Boeing, Lockheed) and other defence-related companies. The Act makes bribery payments to foreign officials illegal. However, there is some vagueness and inconsistency in the law which, for example, suggests that it is legal to make payments to foreign officials to expedite their compliance with local regulations but not to those officials not directly involved in such compliances but who may nevertheless influence such compliances.

Foreign Credit Insurance Association (FCIA), *see* EXPORT CREDIT INSURANCE.

foreign currency translation. In the process of preparing consolidated financial statements it is necessary to translate, or restate, the accounts of foreign subsidiaries and associated corporations denominated in foreign currencies into the home reporting currency. Foreign currency translation is thus a process involving accounting restatements, not the monetary exchange of one currency for another. It constitutes a unique problem of major importance for multinationals.

If MNC disclosures in the home currency are to be interpretable then foreign currency translation must be meaningfully carried out, as it is such an essential part of the system of information processing and communication about the MNC group as a whole. At the level of reports about the individual subsidiary corporation or sub-groups at country level, the problem is, of course, largely removed except to the extent that such corporations themselves have foreign assets and liabilities.

The importance of foreign currency translation and the problems surrounding it have been recognized only relatively recently with the growth of MNCs and the increasing volatility of exchange rates. The major problems arise from accounting for exchange rate changes. Firstly, which rate should be used to translate the financial statements? Secondly, how should any gains and losses, or differences, arising out of the translation be treated? A related problem is whether or not, and if so how, to account for inflation before or after translation?

At present, there is a considerable variety of approaches in evidence and much controversy has been aroused. As regards the exchange rate to be used, the choice is essentially between the historic rate, i.e. the rate applicable when the translation was initially recorded in the accounts, and the current rate, i.e. the market rate applicable to the period for which the financial statements are prepared. A variety of methods have been developed which apply either the historic or current rate to some or all revenues, expenses, assets and liabilities. The major alternatives are the 'temporal' method and the 'closing rate' method. The temporal method applies the current rate to all items measured in current money terms including long-term liabilities, and the historic rate to all items measured in historic terms. The closing rate method, on the other hand, applies the current rate to all items. The effect of this is that all items are thereby exposed to the impact of changes in exchange rates, in contrast to the temporal method where this impact, so far as the financial statements are concerned, is a function of the measurement base used. The fact that items measured at historic cost are translated at historic exchange rates means that changes in exchange rates are effectively ignored by the accounting process. Apart from this, a major problem with the temporal method would seem to be the differential treatment of long-term assets, translated at historic rates, which are often matched by long-term liabilities, but translated at current rates, with apparently misleading effects. Other alternative methods of foreign currency translation include the monetary/non-monetary method, where only monetary items are translated using the current rate, and the current/non-current method, where only current items are translated at the current rate. Accordingly, both of these methods will have differential effects in terms of exchange gains/losses arising.

The controversy over the treatment of any gains and losses arising from exchange rate changes reported by the translation process stems from the question as to whether such gains/losses should be included in earnings/profits, or treated as adjustments only to shareholders' equity. This is complicated by the question of whether and how price changes should be accounted for. Given that there is a relationship between inflation in the home and host country and exchange rates prevailing between them, it would seem that inflation accounting is an integral part of an effective system of foreign currency translation. The use of historic rates may be just as misleading as the use of historic costs and is apparently perpetuated by an unwillingness to recognize the impact of price changes on the one hand and by adherence to the accounting conventions of consistency and prudence on the other.

foreign direct investment (FDI). The establishment of overseas operations by a firm or the expansion of existing overseas operations. In addition to the financial investment involved, these overseas operations require transfers of technology, management skills, production processes and other resources to the host country. Host countries ideally wish to maximize the quality of such transfers, and if they have bargaining power can impose performance requirements on the foreign investor. In many cases though, the host nation requires job-providing investments, and cannot afford to impose onerous requirements on the investor who may threaten to locate elsewhere.

Foreign direct investment can take the form of:

1 a 'greenfield' investment, whereby the investor chooses a new site;
2 the purchase of an existing unused site; or
3 an acquisition, in which an existing business is purchased.

The first two add to employment in the host nation, acquisition involves simply a change in ownership and thus it tends to meet with a hostile reception in the host country.

foreign exchange risk, *see* EXCHANGE RISK.

foreign positioning. The targeting of a product for a specific foreign segment for marketing purposes. A product consists of attributes which compete to a greater or lesser extent with the attributes of other products. Positioning the product is a skilful process of deploying these attributes to their maximum advantage. In the foreign context this becomes more complex. It involves consideration of whether or not and, if so, how to disclose the country of origin. It also

involves the question of balancing international or global standard-
ization against adapting the product to the specific needs of the
foreign market.

Fortune 500. Each year *Fortune* magazine compiles lists of the 500 largest
US corporations, and 500 largest non-US corporations. From these
rankings by sales volume (which have, where necessary, been translated into US dollars), it is possible to identify the world's largest
corporations. Table 1 lists the world's top 100 corporations by turnover based on 1988 sales.

The USA is home to 39 of these companies, followed by Japan with
15, Germany with 12, France with 9, and the UK with 7 (including 2
Anglo-Dutch). In all, 15 countries are represented, including Brazil,
Mexico and Kuwait. Note that Adam Opel, the German *subsidiary* of
General Motors ranks as the world's 93rd largest company with sales
approaching $10bn.

Table 1 also reveals the main activity of these companies. More
than one-third (i.e. 36) of the list comes from just two sectors –
petroleum mining (19) and motor vehicles (17).

franchising. The licensing out of a right to manufacture or retail a good
with an established trademark or to operate a service under a certain
name. The franchise usually comes with knowhow and sometimes
financial support, but it all depends on the terms of the contract. The
franchisee either pays an initial sum or pays royalties on the goods
sold.

Examples of companies which have benefited by using franchising
are:

Food: McDonalds, Wendys, Wimpy, Burger King

Hotels: Holiday Inn, Ramada

Clothes: Benneton, Laura Ashley

The major attraction of franchises to the purchaser is the instant
clientele due to brand loyalty.

FTC, *see* FEDERAL TRADE COMMISSION.

futures. A futures contract is an obligation to deliver a standard amount of
a commodity or financial instrument at a specified price, time and
location. As such, a futures contract is simply a standardized forward
contract which may be traded in an organized market (e.g. IMM or
LIFFE). However, there are some technical differences between a

forward and futures contract, since daily price movements on a futures contract are limited and the holder may be required to finance these price changes throughout the life of the contract. Foreign exchange futures are limited as an exchange risk management device for an MNC for a number of reasons, including:

1 Since the contracts are standardized, it is only possible to purchase contracts for a few maturing dates during the year.
2 MNCs may require extremely large contracts, and there may be insufficient liquidity in futures markets.
3 Trading in futures may be restricted to an 8-hour period, whereas the interbank forward market is a 24-hour market.

However, interest rate and commodity futures may be a useful risk management device, particularly since forward markets in many commodities and financial instruments are simply unavailable. Forward foreign exchange is the exception rather than the rule. *See also* LONDON INTERNATIONAL FINANCIAL FUTURES EXCHANGE.

Table 1 The world's biggest industrial corporations

Rank 1988	1987	Company	Headquarters	Industry	Sales $ millions	Profits $ millions
1	1	General Motors	Detroit	motor vehicles	121,085.4	4,856.3
2	4	Ford Motor	Dearborn, Mich.	motor vehicles	92,445.6	5,300.2
3	3	Exxon	New York	petroleum refining	79,557.0	5,260.0
4	2	Royal Dutch/Shell Group	London/The Hague	petroleum refining	78,381.1	5,238.7
5	5	International Business Machines	Armonk, NY	computers	59,681.0	5,806.0
6	8	Toyota Motor	Toyota City (Japan)	motor vehicles	50,789.9	2,314.6
7	10	General Electric	Fairfield, Conn.	electronics	49,414.0	3,386.0
8	6	Mobil	New York	petroleum refining	48,198.0	2,087.0
9	7	British Petroleum	London	petroleum refining	46,174.0	2,155.3
10	9	IRI	Rome	metals	45,521.5	921.9
11	11	Daimler–Benz	Stuttgart	motor vehicles	41,817.9	953.1
12	16	Hitachi	Tokyo	electronics	41,330.7	989.0
13	21	Chrysler	Highland Park, Mich.	motor vehicles	35,472.7	1,050.2
14	18	Siemens	Munich	electronics	34,129.4	757.0
15	17	Fiat	Turin	motor vehicles	34,039.3	2,324.7
16	19	Matsushita Electric Industrial	Osaka	electronics	33,922.5	1,177.2
17	15	Volkswagen	Wolfsburg (Ger.)	motor vehicles	33,696.2	420.1
18	12	Texaco	White Plains, NY	petroleum refining	33,544.0	1,304.0
19	14	E.I. Du Pont De Nemours	Wilmington, Del.	chemicals	32,514.0	2,190.0
20	20	Unilever	London/Rotterdam	food	30,488.2	1,485.6
21	24	Nissan Motor	Tokyo	motor vehicles	29,097.1	463.0
22	22	Philips' Gloeilampenfabrieken	Eindhoven (Netherlands)	electronics	28,370.5	477.1
23	27	Nestlé	Vevey (Switzerland)	food	27,803.0	1,392.7
24	32	Samsung	Seoul	electronics	27,386.1	464.3
25	25	Renault	Paris	motor vehicles	27,109.7	1,496.7
26	29	Philip Morris	New York	tobacco	25,860.0	2,337.0
27	35	Toshiba	Tokyo	electronics	25,440.8	438.9

28	26	ENI	Rome	petroleum refining	25,226.8	917.3
29	23	Chevron	San Francisco	petroleum refining	25,196.0	1,768.0
30	28	BASF	Ludwigshafen (Ger.)	chemicals	24,960.5	802.2
31	34	Hoechst	Frankfurt	chemicals	23,308.1	1,037.8
32	37	Peugeot	Paris	motor vehicles	23,249.7	1,485.8
33	33	Bayer	Leverkusen (Ger.)	chemicals	23,025.9	1,055.5
34	39	Honda Motor	Tokyo	motor vehicles	22,236.5	819.5
35	30	CGE (Cie Générale d'Électricité)	Paris	scientific and photographic equipment	21,487.5	362.4
36	31	Elf Aquitaine	Paris	petroleum refining	21,175.0	1,209.9
37	36	Amoco	Chicago	petroleum refining	21,150.0	2,063.0
38	38	Imperial Chemical Industries	London	chemicals	20,839.0	1,490.9
39	47	NEC	Tokyo	electronics	19,626.1	183.4
40	41	Occidental Petroleum	Los Angeles	food	19,417.0	302.0
41	42	Procter & Gamble	Cincinnati	soaps, cosmetics	19,336.0	1,020.0
42	•	Ferruzzi Finanziaria	Ravenna	chemicals	18,311.1	425.6
43	40	United Technologies	Hartford	aerospace	18,087.8	659.1
44	43	Atlantic Richfield	Los Angeles	petroleum refining	17,626.0	1,583.0
45	•	Asea Brown Boveri	Zurich	industrial and farm equipment	17,562.0	386.0
46	•	Daewoo	Seoul	electronics	17,251.2	33.3
47	49	Nippon Steel	Tokyo	metals	17,108.9	291.7
48	•	Eastman Kodak	Rochester, NY	scientific and photographic equipment	17,034.0	1,397.0
49	46	Boeing	Seattle	aerospace	16,962.0	614.0
50	44	RJR–Nabisco	Atlanta	food	16,956.0	1,393.0
51	•	Mitsubishi Electric	Tokyo	electronics	16,857.4	160.6
52	•	Thyssen	Duisburg (Ger.)	metals	16,796.0	372.3
53	•	Dow Chemical	Midland, Mich.	chemicals	16,682.0	2,398.0
54	•	Xerox	Stamford, Conn.	scientific and photographic equipment	16,441.0	388.0
55	•	USX	Pittsburgh	petroleum refining	15,792.0	756.0
56	50	Volvo	Göteborg (Sweden)	motor vehicles	15,752.1	807.3
57	•	Robert Bosch	Stuttgart	motor vehicles	15,746.7	282.6
58	48	Tenneco	Houston	industrial and farm equipment	15,707.0	822.0
59	•	Mazda Motor	Hiroshima	motor vehicles	15,150.9	76.4
60	•	McDonnell Douglas	St Louis	aerospace	15,072.0	350.0
61	•	INI	Madrid	metals	14,985.5	268.7

Table 1 cont.

Rank 1988	1987	Company	Headquarters	Industry	Sales $ millions	Profits $ millions
62	45	Petrobrás (Petróleo Brasileiro)	Rio De Janeiro	petroleum refining	14,806.4	765.0
63	•	Fujitsu	Tokyo	computers	14,797.3	304.5
64	•	Mitsubishi Motors	Tokyo	motor vehicles	14,183.3	96.2
65	•	B.A.T. Industries	London	tobacco	14,066.7	1,717.1
66	•	Total	Paris	petroleum refining	13,986.6	248.4
67	•	Mitsubishi Heavy Industries	Tokyo	industrial and farm equipment	13,398.0	221.8
68	•	Usinor	Paris	metals	13,247.1	737.5
69	•	Pemex (Petróleos Mexicanos)	Mexico City	petroleum refining	13,060.0	570.6
70	•	Pepsico	Purchase, NY	beverages	13,007.0	762.2
71	•	Nippon Oil	Tokyo	petroleum refining	12,773.0	167.0
72	•	Thomson	Paris	electronics	12,566.6	201.0
73	•	Westinghouse Electric	Pittsburgh	electronics	12,499.5	822.8
74	•	Kuwait Petroleum	Safat	petroleum refining	12,078.0	435.2
75	•	Ciba–Geigy	Basel	chemicals	12,059.5	905.5
76	•	Electrolux	Stockholm	electronics	12,055.4	342.8
77	•	Rockwell International	El Segundo, Calif.	aerospace	11,946.3	811.9
78	•	Allied-Signal	Morristown, NJ	aerospace	11,909.0	463.0
79	•	BMW (Bayerische Motoren Werke)	Munich	motor vehicles	11,762.5	215.8
80	•	Ruhrkohle	Essen	mining, crude-oil products	11,749.9	(75.5)
81	•	Mannesmann	Dusseldorf	industrial and farm equipment	11,619.9	135.2
82	•	Digital Equipment	Maynard, Mass.	computers	11,475.4	1,305.6
83	•	Phillips Petroleum	Bartlesville, Okla.	petroleum refining	11,304.0	650.0
84	•	Rhône–Poulenc	Paris	chemicals	10,971.3	613.1
85	•	Goodyear Tire & Rubber	Akron	rubber products	10,810.4	350.1
86	•	Lockheed	Calabasas, Calif.	aerospace	10,667.0	624.0
87	•	Minnesota Mining & Mfg	St Paul	scientific and photographic equipment	10,581.0	1,154.0
88	•	Caterpillar	Peoria, Ill.	industrial and farm equipment	10,435.0	616.0

89	•	Sarah Lee	Chicago	food	10,423.8	325.1
90	•	Sony	Tokyo	electronics	10,133.9	265.6
91	•	British Aerospace	London	aerospace	10,044.6	277.9
92	•	Weyerhaeuser	Tacoma	forest products	10,004.2	564.4
93	•	Adam Opel	Rüsselsheim (Ger.)	motor vehicles	9,935.8	287.2
94	•	Unisys	Blue Bell, Pa	computers	9,902.0	680.6
95	•	Hanson	London	food	9,900.4	1,986.8
96	•	Petrofina	Brussels	petroleum refining	9,898.5	549.1
97	•	Saint Gobain	Paris	building materials	9,886.6	679.1
98	•	Indian Oil	Bombay	petroleum refining	9,853.7	316.8
99	•	Hewlett–Packard	Palo Alto, Calif.	computers	9,831.0	816.0
100	•	Aluminium Co. of America	Pittsburgh	metals	9,795.3	861.4
		Totals			2,308,810.8	107,799.6

• not on 1987 list

Source: 'FORTUNE 500', Fortune, 31 July 1989. © 1989 The Time Inc. Magazine Company. All rights reserved.

G

G7, see GROUP OF SEVEN.

G10, see GROUP OF TEN.

G77, see GROUP OF SEVENTY-SEVEN.

GATT, see GENERAL AGREEMENT ON TARIFFS AND TRADE.

GE (General Electric) [USA]. With sales of almost $50bn, this electrical and electronics conglomerate is one of the world's top ten industrial corporations with interests ranging from aircraft engines to broadcasting to financial services. Since 1981 the company has been led by Jack Welch. He has reduced the number of businesses from 100 to 14. Table 1 highlights GE's strength in a dozen of these. Between 1981 and 1989, Welch eliminated 100,000 jobs, cut out management layers

Table 1 How a dozen GE businesses rank

	in the USA	in the world
aircraft engines	first	first
broadcasting (NBC)	first	n.a.
circuit breakers	first tied with Square D and Westinghouse	first tied with Merlin Gerin, Siemens, Westinghouse
defence electronics	second behind GM's Hughes Electronics	second behind GM's Hughes Electronics
electric motors	first	first
engineering plastics	first	first
factory automation	second behind Allen-Bradley	third behind Siemens and Allen-Bradley
industrial and power systems turbines, meters, drive systems, power transmission controls	first	first
lighting	first	second behind Philips
locomotives	first	first tied with GM's Electro-Motive
major appliances	first	second behind Whirlpool tied with Electrolux
medical diagnostic imaging	first	first

Source: *Fortune*, 27 March 1989. © 1989 The Time Inc. Magazine Company. All rights reserved.

in the corporate hierarchy and transferred assets from mature manufacturing businesses to fast-growing, high-technology service sectors. Divestments have brought in $9bn, as consumer electronics and coal mines were sold off, but $16bn has been spent on acquisitions, notably RCA for its broadcasting business and Kidder Peabody, the investment bank.

GEC (General Electric Company) [UK]. This $10bn corporation with 157,000 employees has been transformed under the leadership of (Lord) Arnold Weinstock who became managing director in 1963. In that year, profits amounted to just over £6m, but by 1988 they exceeded £652m. During the 1960s GEC grew quickly by acquisition and merger, but by the early 1970s it was forced to restructure itself with the loss of 70,000 jobs. In 1985–6 its £1.2bn bid for Plessey, the UK electrical company was blocked by the Monopolies and Mergers Commission, but in 1989 it joined forces with Siemens to mount a successful £2bn bid for Plessey. It also formed strategic alliances with France's CGE in power systems, and with America's General Electric in consumer goods and electrical distribution equipment.

GEC operates in more than 10 business areas, of which the four largest are electronic systems, which accounts for almost 30 per cent of total sales, power systems (22 per cent), consumer goods (9 per cent) and telecommunications (8 per cent). Domestic appliances are sold under the Hotpoint and Creda brand names.

Despite acquisitions in the USA in particular, UK production still accounts for almost 70 per cent of total sales. More than one-third of foreign sales are achieved by exporting from the UK.

General Agreement on Tariffs and Trade (GATT). Established in 1947 by 23 founding member nations, the GATT's members now include almost all of the highly developed non-Communist countries, a number of eastern European countries and many of the newly developed and developing countries. The objectives of the GATT are to lower trade barriers and harmonize trade relations between nations. The most important principle of the GATT is non-discrimination, i.e. each country should impose the same tariff rate on all member countries. This is what is known as the 'most favoured nation' rate. There are some important exceptions to this principle. First, groups of countries can join together as customs unions, free trade areas or trading associations which charge lower tariffs between member countries than those imposed on outsiders. Second, special preferences can be retained – but are of diminishing importance as tariffs are reduced. Third, high-income countries can grant general preferential tariffs to lower- and middle-income countries without extending such lower tariffs to higher-income countries. Another major principle of the GATT is tariff binding, by which member countries agree to bind their tariffs at ceiling level, i.e. if a country wants to charge a higher rate it must negotiate to do this in exchange for concessions elsewhere.

The GATT has also served to help avoid trade wars by providing a forum for discussions about the settlement of international trade disputes. When individual countries cannot settle a dispute by negotiation with each other they can appeal to the GATT which sets up a committee of experts to act as arbitrators.

Since its foundation, the GATT has been responsible for a substantial reduction in tariffs especially for manufactured goods. It has not been so successful with agricultural products mainly because they are specially protected in most countries. A major ommission from the GATT remit is the service sector.

General Electric, see GE.

General Electric Company, see GEC.

General Motors (GM) [USA]. This automobile company is the largest industrial corporation in the world. With sales in excess of $120bn, GM's turnover is bigger than the gross national product of Sweden or Switzerland. In 1988 it reported record profits of $4.9bn, $2.7bn of which was derived from overseas operations, and GM Europe reported a profit of $1.8bn, almost as much as the $2.2bn it had lost in the period 1980–6. GM has some 800,000 employees, about the same as the population of Washington DC or Glasgow, Scotland. It has operations in 122 US cities and 43 countries, and produces more than eight million motor vehicles a year, giving it 18.1 per cent of the world market compared to its nearest rivals Ford with six million (13.3 per cent), and Toyota with almost four million (8.2 per cent). GM's activities are worldwide, but mostly concentrated in North America and Europe.

Its main subsidiary companies in Europe are Vauxhall in the UK and Opel in West Germany. It also owns Lotus, the sports car company, and has a 34 per cent stake in Japan's Isuzu. GM has also established joint ventures (e.g. with Toyota and Daewoo Motors).

During the 1980s, GM was radically transformed. In 1980, it lost $760m – its first loss in its 60-year history – and in 1981 Roger Smith was appointed chairman. Smith reorganized GM's five car divisions into two, laid off 250,000 workers, invested $60bn on expansion and upgrading of facilities, and undertook two major acquisitions – $5bn for Hughes Aircraft and $2.55bn to acquire Ross Perot's Electronic Data Systems. Despite these radical moves, in 1985, for the first time since 1924, GM's profits were less than those of Ford, its smaller rival. It is this discrepancy which has led to fierce criticism of Smith, most embarrassingly when it came from Ross Perot. In 1986, Perot agreed to give up his position as GM's largest shareholder and most outspoken director in return for $750m – double the market value of Perot's GM shares. Furthermore, the arrangement included a penalty clause under which Perot must return up to 1 per cent if he publicly criticizes GM.

In 1989, GM acquired a 26.5 per cent stake in Avis Europe, Europe's largest car hire company, and having failed to acquire Jaguar, paid $600m for a 50 per cent stake in the troubled car business of Sweden's Saab–Scania.

geocentric organization. An outward-looking company which believes in a global perspective while at the same time serving national needs. In such cases the need to instil a strong corporate culture becomes very important if communication problems are to be avoided. The usual means of achieving this is by adopting a matrix organizational structure integrating the three dimensions of function, product and region. The matrix structure has some of the benefits of decentralization while also facilitating overall coordination. The main advantage is that there is greater emphasis on markets, competition and local environmental aspects. The main problem with the matrix structure is its complexity. To make it work requires a heavy investment in information systems and management training if the competing demands of functional division, product lines and regions are to be managed successfully.

global strategy. A competitive strategy which develops plans to coordinate and manage the activities of the multinational corporation on a worldwide basis so that it can obtain a competitive advantage relative to its global competitors. According to Michael Porter from the Harvard Business School, the major issues of deciding how to spread the company's activities internationally can be summarized in two key dimensions. The first is the configuration of the company's activities worldwide, i.e. the location(s) where each activity is to be carried out. The second is coordination, which concerns how each of the activities performed in different countries is coordinated. Thus, there are many different kinds of global strategy, depending on a company's choice about configuration and coordination throughout the range of its activities such as operations, marketing and sales, service, R&D and procurement. Accordingly, a global strategy is defined as one where a company 'seeks to gain competitive advantage from its international presence through either a concentrated configuration, coordination among dispersed activities, or both' (*Competition in Global Industries*. Boston, Harvard Business School Press, 1986, p. 29).

GM, see GENERAL MOTORS.

goodwill. The term used to describe the difference between the value placed upon a company and the sum of the values of its individual assets and liabilities as identified and recorded in the accounting system. There are three reasons why this difference exists:

1   the assets are traditionally disclosed in the balance sheet at historic cost rather than current value;

2   in addition to tangible assets disclosed in the balance sheet most firms possess intangible attributes such as: a favourable location, a good reputation, good industrial relations, a skilled workforce, experienced management, etc., which contribute to its success without appearing on the balance sheet; and

3   assets operating together, i.e. synergy, usually have a higher value than the sum of the values of the assets operating separately.

Goodwill only enters the accounting system when one company purchases another company or part of a company, and that portion of the purchase price which exceeds the fair market value of the net assets represents the amount paid for goodwill. As goodwill represents the cost of acquiring (intangible) assets, the accruals concept indicates that the cost should be carried forward and matched against the revenues of periods expected to benefit from the use of those assets. On the other hand, as these benefits are uncertain and the determination of when they arise could cause problems, the prudence convention would appear to suggest that the amount paid for goodwill should be written off immediately. Given this conflict between accounting conventions it is not surprising that a number of proposals for accounting for goodwill have arisen. The EC Fourth Directive requires companies to write off goodwill over a maximum period of five years or over a limited period exceeding five years provided that the period does not exceed the useful economic life of the asset. In the UK, the current standard permits either the immediate write-off of goodwill against reserves, the majority practice, or its amortization over a period not exceeding its useful economic life. In the USA, the FASB requires amortization over a period not exceeding 40 years – a practice said to show US companies in a less favourable light than UK companies, with consequent competitive disadvantage. Given that goodwill usually relates only to a part of a business, and that it is impracticable for the goodwill of the entire entity to be revalued on each balance sheet date, it seems unlikely that the inclusion of any goodwill figure will assist account users. At the same time, the application of arbitrary accounting rules could be misleading.

Goodyear Tire & Rubber Company [USA]. This $11bn corporation was, until 1989, the world's leading manufacturer of tyres and rubber products. It has 77 plants in 27 countries. 86 per cent of total sales are derived from tyres. It also relies heavily on the North American market which accounts for 59 per cent of sales, but only 44 per cent of profits. Its two main rivals, France's Michelin and Japan's Bridgestone have both established a major manufacturing presence in the US. One means of protecting its market share is by developing technologically superior products, and R&D accounts for 3 per cent of revenues.

Like many other US companies that were industry leaders, Goodyear has faced increasingly tough competition in recent years. During the 1970s, longer-lasting radial tyres pioneered by Michelin in 1948 became increasingly popular with motorists, and Goodyear was left behind. Between 1974 and 1984 it spent $3.2bn to retrieve Michelin's temporary technological advantage. At the same time, motorists became more cost-conscious following the dramatic rise in oil prices in 1973. Given that tyres are in the main a purely functional product, the only way to differentiate the product was to manufacture a tyre that was better value and longer lasting than those of competitors. The upshot of these and other factors was a slump in demand and a severe excess-capacity problem. In such a competitive market, producers have been compelled to seek a short-term advantage either through improved productivity which generates further surplus capacity, or through technological innovations which render their products more durable, but in the long term lower demand. Despite such adverse circumstances Goodyear remained profitable throughout the 1980s.

Probably one of the most dramatic events in the company's history came in the autumn of 1986, when it received a hostile $5.3bn takeover bid from Sir James Goldsmith, the Anglo-French financier. He claimed that in its attempts to diversify into aerospace and energy, the company 'had strayed into industries about which it knew nothing, jeopardizing the very heart of its business, competitive position, and the security of all those associated with it'. The then chairman of Goodyear called upon the Reagan administration to impose restrictions on unrestrained takeover activity to protect US companies. He described Goldsmith's actions as 'a form of economic terrorism'. Goodyear's US dealers took out full page newspaper advertisements warning him that 'you may buy this great company – but you will never buy our loyalty'. Goodyear fought off the raider but at a high cost. It paid $619m to buy back Sir James's 11.5 per cent stake, giving him a profit of over $90m.

Grand Metropolitan [UK]. One of Britain's largest companies, this food and drinks and retail group has grown rapidly and is a major force in each of its main business lines. Sales in the UK and Irish Republic still account for the bulk of sales, but a series of international takeovers have reduced the group's dependence on its domestic market. As of 1988, Grand Met's sales amounted to $6bn, and it had 90,000 employees. Grand Met is among the world's eight largest food companies. Its brands include Eden Vale, Green Giant, Munch Bunch and Ski. It is number one in distilled spirits (see **Guinness**, table 1). Its brands include Smirnoff and Popov, the world's most popular vodkas, Croft, the world leader in pale cream sherry, J&B scotch, the world's second best-selling whisky, Malibu, Le Piat d'Or, the most popular table wines exported from France, Metaxa, the world's best-selling brandy in duty-free outlets, and Bailey's Original Irish Cream, the world's top international liqueur, selling more than three million cases a year. Grand Met has one of the largest number of retail outlets of any company in the world (e.g. Berni Inns, Burger King, Peter Dominic off sales). In 1989 it sold Mecca, and William Hill, the bookmakers, to Brent Walker for £690m, and then paid £180m to acquire United Biscuits' fast-food restaurants (i.e. Wimpy, Pizzaland and Perfect Pizza).

During the 1980s the company shifted from its original business of hotels to food and drinks. In 1989 it sold Inter-Continental Hotels, acquired from Pan-Am for $500m in 1981, for $2bn just prior to acquiring Pillsbury, the US food group (Burger King, Doughboy, Green Giant) for $5.8bn. It aims to revive Burger King, a poor second to McDonald's among fast food restaurants, and trim Pillsbury's excessive costs. In the first six months, Grand Met fired some 1,200 people, almost one-third of Pillsbury's managers, saving $60m a year. Five of Pillsbury's 35 US plants were closed, saving around $14m a year. Further rationalization should allow Grand Met to achieve its target of saving $80m a year. It also recouped some of the original purchase price by selling the Steak & Ale/Bennigans chain for $430m.

Group of Seven (G7). The world's seven leading industrial countries, i.e. the USA, Japan, Germany, France, the UK, Italy and Canada, meet periodically to discuss the coordination of economic policy with the primary aim of promoting the stability of exchange rates and the correction of trade and money imbalances. A smaller Group of Five (G5) comprising the G7 countries minus Italy and Canada also meets secretly on occasion to discuss similar matters.

Group of Seventy-even (G77). Formed at the first United Nations Conference on Trade and Development, the organization now has over 100 members. The group is the means by which developing countries seek to promote their economic interests jointly, and to maintain a determined, unified bargaining front in the face of richer countries. The group includes a wide range of countries from the semi-industrialized countries in Latin America, to the extremely poor countries of Africa and Asia.

Group of Ten (G10). An association of countries, also known as the Paris Club, which forms the developed nations' pressure group, lending to the International Monetary Fund. The group comprises the USA, the UK, Germany, France, Italy, Japan, Canada, the Netherlands, Belgium and Sweden.

Guinness [UK]. One of the world's leading drinks groups, and owners of the world's best-selling scotch and gin, Johnnie Walker and Gordon's respectively, it underwent two major transformations during the 1980s under two different chief executives. (See table 1.) In 1981 its market capitalization was £90m, just three million pounds higher than it was in 1961, and the share price had slumped to 49p, reflecting years of stagnant profits. Then Ernest Saunders was appointed chief executive, and he sold off an assembly of unrelated, mainly loss-making businesses which had been acquired. He also rationalized the core businesses, and consolidated the leaner but fitter company's position in its key markets, drinks, and to a lesser extent, retailing. In June 1985, Bell's was acquired for £370m, and less than a year later Guinness paid £2.5bn for Distillers, the world's leading whisky company, raising the market capitalization value of Guinness to more than £3bn. But Saunders had reached the pinnacle of his career for in early 1987 it was revealed that Guinness had allegedly manipulated

Table 1 Top 25 spirit brands worldwide 1989 (millions of 9-litre case shipments)

Rank	Brand	Company	Type	1985	1986	1987	1988	1989E	% change 1988–9E
1	Bacardi	Bacardi & Co. Ltd	rum	18.8	19.1	20.7	21.2	22.0	3.8
2	Smirnoff	Heublein Inc. (IDV/Grand Met)	vodka	13.8	13.9	14.0	14.1	14.8	5.0
3	Ricard	Groupe Pernod Ricard	anis/pastis	7.2	7.2	7.4	7.4	7.4	—
4	Gordon's Gin	United Distillers (Guinness)	gin	7.0	6.7	6.9	6.8	7.3	7.3
5	Johnnie Walker Red	United Distillers (Guinness)	scotch whisky	6.8	6.7	6.3	6.3	6.8	7.9
	TOTAL top 5			53.6	53.6	55.3	55.8	58.3	4.4
6	J&B Rare	IDV (Grand Met)	scotch whisky	4.4	4.6	4.7	5.0	5.3	6.0
7	Ballantine's	HWAV (Allied–Lyons)	scotch whisky	4.2	4.3	4.4	4.8	5.0	4.2
8	Jim Beam	Jim Beam Brands Co. (American Brands)	bourbon	4.8	4.5	4.5	4.7	4.8	2.1
9	Suntory Old	Suntory Ltd	Japanese whisky	5.7	5.5	4.5	4.3	4.4	2.3
10	Seagram's 7 Crown	The Seagram Co. Ltd	American blended whiskey	5.3	4.8	4.6	4.5	4.4	-2.2
	TOTAL top 10			78.0	77.3	78.0	79.1	82.2	3.9
11	Jack Daniel's Black	Brown-Forman Corp.	Tennessee whiskey	3.7	3.8	4.0	4.2	4.4	4.8
12	Presidente	Pedro Domecq SA	brandy	4.1	4.0	4.2	4.2	4.3	2.4
13	Bell's	United Distillers (Guinness)	scotch whisky	3.9	3.9	4.0	4.1	4.1	—
14	Suntory Reserve	Suntory Ltd	Japanese whisky	3.2	3.3	3.3	4.0	4.0	—
15	Popov	Heublein Inc. (IDV/Grand Met)	vodka	3.8	4.0	4.0	4.0	4.0	3.4
	TOTAL top 15			96.7	96.3	97.5	99.6	103.0	3.4

16	José Cuervo	Tequila Cuervo SA (Groupo Cuervo)	tequila	2.0	2.4	2.9	3.5	3.8	8.6
17	Seagram's Gin	The Seagram Co. Ltd	gin	3.4	3.4	3.4	3.6	3.8	5.6
18	DeKuyper	Johs De Kuyper & Zoon BV	liqueur	3.3	4.3	4.1	3.9	3.7	-5.1
19	Larios	Larios SA	gin	4.1	4.1	4.1	3.6	3.7	2.8
20	Dewar's	United Distillers (Guinness)	scotch whisky	3.5	3.5	3.5	3.5	3.7	5.7
	TOTAL top 20			113.0	114.0	115.5	117.7	121.7	3.4
21	Canadian Mist	Brown-Forman Corp.	Canadian whisky	4.3	4.0	3.8	3.7	3.6	-2.7
22	Absolut	V&S Vin & Sprit	vodka	1.4	2.1	2.2	2.9	3.6	24.1
23	Bailey's	IDV (Grand Met)	liqueur	2.4	2.5	2.6	2.9	3.3	13.8
24	Chivas Regal	The Seagram Co. Ltd	scotch whisky	2.5	2.6	2.9	3.0	3.2	6.7
25	Canadian Club	HWAV (Allied–Lyons)	Canadian whisky	3.5	3.2	3.0	3.1	3.1	—
	TOTAL top 25			127.1	128.4	130.0	133.3	138.5	3.9

E – estimated figure
Source: Impact International

its share price during the Distillers takeover bid. Saunders was sacked and along with some other prominent members of the City is facing criminal charges. In 1989 Guinness was instructed by the Takeover Panel to pay £85m in compensation to Distillers shareholders. The Guinness affair is considered one of the worst scandals to have hit the City of London in living memory.

Saunders' successor, Anthony Tennant, has divested retail operations and expanded into luxury goods. Guinness for example has a 24 per cent stake in France's Möet Hennessy Louis Vuitton, renowned for its top-quality luggage, perfume and champagne. In order to protect itself from a hostile takeover bid, Guinness has included a valuation of recently acquired brands on its balance sheet. It has placed a £1bn-plus valuation on them – more than the value of the group's physical assets.

H

Hanson Trust [UK]. Hanson Trust is an acquisitive industrial $10bn conglomerate. It has grown rapidly since its stock market flotation in 1964 to become one of Britain's largest companies. It has enjoyed many years of unbroken earnings per share, dividend and profit growth.

Hanson Trust's main acquisitions in Britain have included Berec (i.e. Ever Ready) (1982), UDS (1983), London Brick (1984), Imperial Group (1986), and Consolidated Gold Fields (1989) for a record £3.5bn. In the USA, Hanson's main acquisitions have been US Industries for $571m (1984), SCM for $930m (1986), and Kidde for $1.6bn (1987).

After an acquisition, Hanson usually recoups much of the original purchase price by well-chosen divestments, and retains those divisions capable of generating profits. This strategy was spectacularly successful in the case of the SCM and Imperial deals. All of Hanson's main acquisitions have been of companies in mature, slow-growth sectors, with undervalued assets.

Hecksher–Ohlin Theorem. A theorem describing a model of world trade based on differing factor endowments and factor cost considerations. Trade between nations takes place because they possess factors of production in different proportions and this leads to differences in the relative costs of production. Nations with a large labour force will have a competitive advantage in labour-intensive industries and will export these goods while importing capital-intensive goods. Countries which are relatively rich in capital will do the opposite. Basic assumptions of the model are that the costs of transportation are nil, that all economies are perfectly competitive, and that there are identical production functions in all nations.

Hirsch Method. A method proposed by Seev Hirsch for choosing between exporting, foreign direct investment or licensing as a means of servicing a foreign market. The method includes an assessment of country-specific costs, i.e. the normal costs of producing goods in the home country and the normal costs of producing goods in the foreign country; and special costs, i.e. export marketing costs, the additional costs of operating in a foreign country especially cultural, environmental and political information costs, and the costs associated with knowledge dissipation from licensing agreements. Exporting, foreign direct investment or licensing will be preferred depending on which mode of entry is the cheapest.

Hoffman La Roche [Switzerland]. With sales of $6bn, it is only half the size of Ciba–Geigy, and is smaller than Sandoz, but La Roche is probably the best known of Switzerland's 'big three' chemical and pharmaceutical companies. It consists of seven divisions, of which the two largest, pharmaceuticals and vitamins, account for almost 70 per cent of total sales. Pharmaceuticals generates just over 40 per cent of total sales, but La Roche slipped from number two in the 1970s to 14th position in pharmaceutical rankings by the late 1980s. This decline reflects falling sales for its two best-ever selling products, the tranquilizers, 'Valium' and 'Librium'. 'Valium's' patent expired in 1986 so it must now compete with cheaper generic drugs, though there is also some concern about the side-effects of these products. In order to find future best-selling drugs, La Roche spends 13–14 per cent of total sales on R&D, and it conducted an R&D audit every second year after 1986 to assess the commercial viability of projects. ICI implemented such a procedure only in 1989.

Geographically, Europe accounts for almost half (i.e. 47 per cent) of total sales – though Switzerland itself provides only 4 per cent, while North America is responsible for almost one-third. La Roche has interests in 52 countries, 109 sales operations, 90 manufacturing plants and 16 R&D centres. Worldwide employment borders on 50,000.

La Roche has faced legal actions in Canada and Europe over unfair practices selling pharmaceuticals, and it was fined by the EC in the 1970s for abusing its dominant position in the vitamins market, where it controlled between 46 and 86 per cent of the market. However, in some underdeveloped countries, the company also provides essential vitamins free or at cost price, and has established its own Sight for Life organization.

In 1987, La Roche bid $4.2bn for Sterling Drug, one of America's largest companies in the over the counter (OTC) drug market. This hostile bid failed when La Roche's chief executive refused to match Eastman Kodak's $5.2bn bid. Since then La Roche's financial structure has been changed to facilitate raising funds on the world's stock markets, and in early 1990, La Roche paid $2.1bn for a 60 per cent stake in Genentech, a US company that ranks as one of the world's leading biotechnology groups.

home country. The country in which a multinational corporation (MNC) has its headquarters. All MNCs have domestic operations and foreign subsidiaries, but maintain a headquarters in the 'home' country (e.g. the USA is the home country of General Motors, Germany of Volkswagen, Japan of Toyota, etc.). Most MNCs are based in developed countries. Thus in 1985 such countries accounted for $693.3bn or 97.2 per cent of total outward stock of FDI.

The USA and the UK are the first- and second-largest home countries respectively, accounting for almost half of the total outward stock of FDI. Indeed, the huge increase in annual outflows of UK FDI during the late 1980s saw the UK replace the USA as the largest home country in terms of outflows rather than stock.

One of the most significant trends during the period 1960–85 has been the emergence of Japan as a significant home nation. In 1988 alone Japanese companies invested $47bn overseas. More recently, the newly industrialized countries, South Korea and Taiwan in particular, have become home nations as domestic pressures (e.g. rising wages, appreciation of currency against the dollar) and abroad (e.g. protectionism) encourage them to locate overseas. Indeed, the prospect of 'Fortress Europe' after 1992 has led to an onslaught of inward investment to the EC by non-EC multinationals.

host country. A country receiving inward investment. During the 1980s the USA became the world's largest host nation as the value of inward investment soared from $16.9bn in 1980 to $58.4bn in 1988.

Competition for mobile investments intensified significantly during the 1980s, and numerous nations relaxed controls on inward FDI. For example, the EC had to impose a ceiling on the level of financial incentives which EC member countries can offer MNCs to secure investments. Nevertheless, some observers remain critical of incentive-bidding to secure investment. In order to avoid any criticism, Toyota declined accepting the incentives to which it was entitled when it announced its £1bn investment in the UK.

Competition to attract FDI is not restricted to the EC. Worldwide, countries are competing to secure FDI. This has entailed relaxing or abolishing controls unattractive to the MNCs. For example in Mexico, the 1973 Law on Foreign Investment limited the maximum foreign shareholdings in Mexican ventures to 49 per cent for particular industries, though IBM, Xerox and Ericsson received exemptions. During the 1980s, in contrast, not only did Mexico establish export processing zones on the US border to woo investors, but in 1989 it opened fresh sectors of the economy to foreign capital and allowed 100 per cent foreign ownership.

hot money. A term used to describe bank deposits and holdings of short-term financial assets which are likely to be transferred from country to country in response to changes or anticipated changes in exchange rates and interest rates. The term is also used in a pejorative sense to suggest that these financial assets may arise from illegal activities (e.g. drug dealing).

HRM, *see* HUMAN RESOURCE MANAGEMENT.

human resource management (HRM). Developing capable staff is a key factor in carrying out a successful global competitive strategy. The multinational must identify the human resources necessary and either develop them within the company or arrange to hire them externally. Staff must be capable within functional or specific areas but also have appropriate experience in the international business environment. Human resource management is an integral part of the process of strategy formulation and implementation in the multinational. An important decision concerns the allocation of home and host country nationals. While the use of home country nationals abroad has the advantage of an orientation towards the parent company there are the disadvantages of cost and the possibility of problems in dealing with foreign workers and trade unions. While the use of host country nationals will tend to overcome these problems there is the danger that there may be a tendency to put local interests first and adhere to local business practices which may not be the most efficient.

Hyundai [South Korea]. Founded in the early 1940s as a truck and motor service business, the Hyundai group is now one of the world's largest conglomerate in terms of sales, and is still controlled by the founder and his family. Group activities range from engineering and construction to motors, shipbuilding, machinery, shipping and finance. The $20bn-plus conglomerate consists of some 27 companies, and among these, Hyundai Motor Company (HMC) has been spectacularly successful.

Founded in 1967, HMC initially simply assembled Cortinas and Granadas from kits shipped from Ford UK under a licensing agreement. Then in 1976 it produced the Pony subcompact car under licence from Japan's Mitsubishi which has a 15 per cent stake in HMC. In 1985 it began exporting to the USA and 168,000 cars were sold, a record for first year car imports into the USA. The following year it opened a manufacturing facility at Bromont in Canada (capacity 100,000 units), which currently supplies Chrysler with 30,000 cars a year for sale in the USA under the Eagle brand.

HMC has increased motor vehicle production from a mere 19,289 units in 1976 to 647,387 in 1988 – 60 per cent of total Korean motor vehicle production. HMC is clearly intent upon emulating the success of the Japanese auto producers. However, South Korean car exports in 1989 were down 40 per cent on 1988's level of 576,000.

I

IASC (International Accounting Standards Committee), *see* INTER-NATIONAL ACCOUNTING STANDARDS.

IBM (International Business Machines) [USA]. 'Big Blue', the world's largest computer company, operating primarily in the field of information processing systems, is the world's fifth-largest industrial corporation. With sales of almost $60bn, almost 60 per cent of which are made overseas, it has 390,000 employees and 40 manufacturing plants, mainly in North America and Europe. The 14 European factories provide 27,000 jobs of IBM's European total of 108,000. In the UK it has two plants and a workforce of almost 19,000. It is Britain's third-largest exporter of manufactured goods with exports worth £2.14bn in 1988.

IBM's dominance of its industry (see table 1) stems from its key ownership-specific advantage, technological leadership and the fact that the company has been able to license technology to domestic and foreign rivals. Some rivals (e.g. Japan's Hitachi and Mitsubishi) obtained IBM technology illegally. In 1982 Hitachi paid $622,000 to obtain stolen information about IBM products. This case of industrial espionage occurred despite the fact that IBM was already spending $50m a year on security measures. In order to protect its technology IBM prefers 100 per cent ownership of any foreign investment. It was forced to leave India when it refused to accept a dilution of control, and only invested in Mexico when it was exempted from the country's foreign investment legislation.

Recent attempts to diversify have failed. For example, it sold Rolm Telecommunications to Siemens only a few years after acquiring the company.

IBRD (International Bank for Reconstruction and Development), *see* WORLD BANK.

ICC, *see* INTERNATIONAL CHAMBER OF COMMERCE.

ICI (Imperial Chemical Industries) [UK]. Britain's largest chemicals group, and the world's fifth-largest, with sales of almost $21bn, ICI has some 130,000 employees, sites in 40 countries, and markets in 150 countries outside the UK. This gives it the widest geographical

Table 1   Top 25 of 1988: Datamation 100

Company	Information technology sales ($m)
IBM	55,002.8
Digital Equipment	12,284.7
Fujitsu	10,999.1
NEC	10,475.7
Unisys	9,100.0
Hitachi	8,247.6
Hewlett–Packard	6,300.0
Siemens	5,951.0
Olivetti	5,427.9
NCR	5,324.0
Groupe Bull	5,296.7
Apple Computer	4,434.1
Toshiba	4,226.6
Matsushita	3,441.0
Canon	3,391.6
Control Data	3,254.3
Wang	3,074.4
Nixdorf Computer	3,044.9
Philips	2,794.6
Xerox	2,650.0
AT&T	2,445.0
STC	2,425.1
Memorex–Telex	2,078.5
Compaq	2,065.6
Nihon Unisys	2,057.7

Conversion: ¥128 = $1
Source: Financial Times

diversity of the world's major chemical groups and this is reflected in the high proportion (75 per cent) of chemical sales to non-UK customers. ICI operates in four industry segments:

consumer and speciality products (pharmaceuticals, paints and other effect products);

industrial products (general chemicals, petrochemicals, plastics, fibres and explosives);

agriculture (agrochemicals, plant breeding, fertilizers and related products);

oil and gas.

The chemical industry consists of speciality products and commodity or bulk chemicals. The former includes relatively high-value, research-intensive materials (e.g. agrochemicals, paints, pharmaceuticals and plastics) which are considered immune from cyclical demand, while bulk chemicals include high-volume plastics, fibres, general industrial chemicals and fertilizers, and demand for these can fluctuate wildly with adverse consequences in a slump for the manufacturers. ICI spent more than $5bn between 1985 and 1989 buying 120 companies, mainly in the speciality sector, including Glidden Paints ($560m) and Stauffer ($1.7bn). Consequently speciality chemicals now account for 60 per cent of sales. However, in the late 1980s demand for bulk chemicals was buoyant and these accounted for 49 per cent of profits.

The Glidden and Stauffer purchases were a direct result of two other US acquisitions by European companies. After buying SCM for $920m, Hanson recouped more than half its costs by selling the Glidden Paints division to ICI for $580m. When ICI bought Stauffer Chemicals in 1987 it became the third owner in as many years. Chesebrough–Pond's had acquired Stauffer for $1.25bn in 1985, but it was subsequently taken over by Unilever which was attracted by the portfolio of skin-care brands. Then Unilever wanted rid of Stauffer, and ICI was prepared to pay the $1.7bn price because it had fallen behind in the agrochemicals sales league when France's Rhône–Poulenc acquired Union Carbide's agrochemical division in 1986 for $575m. As of 30 June 1987, the final move in this intricate 'pass the parcel' was ICI's announcement that it was selling for $625m the speciality chemicals division of recently acquired Stauffer to the Dutch multinational, Akzo. These deals exemplify the complexity of the takeover merry-go-round.

IDA (International Development Association), see WORLD BANK.

IFAC, see INTERNATIONAL FEDERATION OF ACCOUNTANTS.

IFC, see INTERNATIONAL FINANCE CORPORATION.

ILO, see INTERNATIONAL LABOUR OFFICE.

IMF, see INTERNATIONAL MONETARY FUND.

Imperial Chemical Industries, see ICI.

industrial espionage. Stealing corporate secrets is rife in industries where superior technology is critical in establishing and maintaining competitive advantage. One such industry is electronics and the most notorious case of industrial espionage occurred in 1982. Sixteen employees of Hitachi and Mitsubishi were arrested and accused of conspiring to steal trade secrets from IBM. According to the FBI, they paid almost $650,000 to obtain stolen information about IBM products, Hitachi paying $622,000 and Mitsubishi $26,000.

In February 1983, Hitachi pleaded guilty to the charges in San Francisco's US District Court, and under the terms of an agreed plea-bargain, the Japanese company was fined $10,000 and further criminal charges were dropped. Later in the year, in an out-of-court civil suit settlement, Hitachi agreed to comply with a number of undertakings.

Hitachi undertook:

1   to refrain from using stolen secrets and allow IBM to inspect all its new products for five years, to satisfy the US company that its intellectual property was not incorporated in Hitachi's products;
2   to return stolen documents to IBM;
3   to identify those who offered Hitachi IBM secrets;
4   to pay all IBM's legal and other costs, unlikely to be less than several million dollars.

At the time IBM was already spending $50m a year on security measures, and its Information Systems group alone had over 400 people working full-time on security measures.

The West Germans have also had problems with industrial secrets being passed to East Germany. According to one report, East Germany had as many as a thousand economic spies in West Germany, and that their intelligence saved the East Germans $1.7bn a year in R&D.

infant industry. The infant industry argument is that governments should be permitted to protect their infant industries (i.e. those industries with newly established local companies) by restricting trade so that a domestic market can be secured until such time as companies have developed and can protect themselves from established foreign producers. The argument can be extended to justify direct and indirect subsidies especially for exports. Infant industry protection is necessary in order to achieve sufficient economies of scale to compete internationally. Essentially, short-term welfare reduction is exchanged for long-term welfare gains. Historically, the protection of infant industries has been a critical factor for success in countries such as the USA and Japan. However, in small countries such as Australia and Canada the benefits of protection have resulted in a reluctance by infant industries to become efficient and achieve maturity. Without an agreed programme of protection reduction there is considerable pressure on governments to maintain the status quo with consequent welfare losses to the nations concerned.

Interest Rate Parity Theorem (IRPT). The IRPT states that the difference between forward and spot exchange rates reflects international interest rate differentials. The rationale for the theorem is based upon the presence of covered interest arbitrage. In general, it offers a valid explanation of the determination of forward exchange rates, since traders in forward markets use interest differentials to guide their activities. It may, however, break down during periods of extreme turbulence or due to government regulations (e.g. exchange controls) which act as a barrier to arbitrage.

internalization theory. A theory designed to explain multinational enterprise based on the idea that the existence of imperfections in markets may make it less costly, or more profitable, for companies to carry out certain activities and transactions internally rather than to use external market processes. Thus MNCs will be generated whenever there are sufficient market imperfections for internalization to be justified from a cost/benefit perspective.

international accounting standards. Recommendations or guidelines issued by the International Accounting Standards Committee (IASC), established in 1973 by leading professional accountancy organizations in Australia, Canada, France, the Federal Republic of Germany, Ireland, Japan, Mexico, the Netherlands, the UK and the USA. The IASC now has a membership of professional organizations from more than 40 countries, including the founder members who constitute a majority of the governing board and thus retain a significant measure of influence. The stated objectives of the IASC are

(a) to formulate and publish in the public interest accounting standards to be observed in the presentation of financial statements and to promote their world-wide acceptance and observance, and (b) to work generally for the improvement and harmonisation of regulations, accounting standards and procedures relating to the presentation of financial statements.

The main aim of international professional standards in practice would seem to be to achieve a degree of comparability which will help investors in making their decisions while reducing the costs of multinationals in preparing multiple sets of accounts and reports. The IASC also sees itself as playing a role in coordinating and harmonizing the many agencies involved in setting standards for multinationals though its preference is to take over this responsibility from government agencies. The IASC's powers of enforcement are limited as it relies on member organizations to 'use their best endeavours' to follow their standards due to the lack of authority of professional accountancy organizations in many countries, e.g. France, Germany. The IASC is also too ambitious in attempting to prescribe worldwide standards for all corporations in that substantial national environmental differences often exist which call for accounting systems which may be quite different from the Anglo-Saxon stock market oriented approach assumed by the IASC. A better approach may be to focus on multinationals involved in international stock markets.

international auditing. Just as MNCs grew in the 1970s and 1980s so did international auditing firms in response to the worldwide demand for auditing services. At the same time, firms such as Price Waterhouse, Arthur Andersen, Arthur Young, KPMG, Touche Ross, Deloitte Haskins & Sells and Coopers and Lybrand diversified into management consultancy, corporate finance, personnel recruitment and so on. This trend towards providing integrated services has manifested itself in mega-mergers between, for example, Arthur Young and Ernst & Whinney and Touche Ross and Deloitte Haskins & Sells.

International Bank for Reconstruction and Development (IBRD), see WORLD BANK.

International Business Machines, see IBM.

international cash management. Essentially, the centralization of global cash balances of an MNC, as opposed to each foreign subsidiary's managing its own cash balance. The concept is alien to many European MNCs.

While the benefits of centralized cash management in a domestic context have long been recognized, in an international context there are a number of constraints upon international cash management.

1 *Transaction costs*. The costs of transferring cash from one subsidiary to another in a domestic context are relatively low, compared with the costs of transferring cash internationally. The incremental costs might include the additional costs of communicating instructions internationally, gathering information on cash balances, bank charges and the bid–ask spread associated with converting currencies. However, improved information technologies and the availability of international clearing systems has decreased some of these transaction costs in the last few years.

2 *Institutional barriers*. Differing tax systems, exchange controls and, ultimately, blocked funds may impede the transfer of assets and decrease the viability of international cash management.
3 *Local liquidity needs*. Considerable investment in information systems is necessary in order to ensure that the future liquidity needs of the foreign subsidiary are known. There is little value in transferring funds out of a subsidiary, only to transfer them back two days later.
4 *Organizational considerations*. HQ management of local cash balances may be perceived as interfering with local autonomy and local operational decisions.

However, despite these constraints, some companies may benefit substantially from international cash management if it does result in considerably lower global cash balances and the opportunity to pursue superior investment policies with surplus funds. In addition, the decreasing costs of international communication and funds transfer mean that companies should constantly re-evaluate the costs and benefits of international cash management.

International Center for the Settlement of Investment Disputes, *see* WORLD BANK.

International Chamber of Commerce (ICC). An organization of national chambers of commerce established in 1920, with the purpose of exchanging information on matters of international interest. The ICC was one of the first organizations to attempt to introduce a code of conduct for MNCs. The ICC also operates a court of arbitration to resolve commercial disputes, especially between governments and multinationals.

International Development Association (IDA), *see* WORLD BANK.

International Federation of Accountants (IFAC) [USA]. An organization of professional accounting bodies worldwide. It was formed in 1977 to pursue all areas of interest to these bodies including education, ethics, auditing, management accounting and so on, except for international accounting standards, which are set by the International Accounting Standards Committee (IASC). The IFAC and IASC have the same membership and are closely linked by central committees. However, the IASC has complete autonomy in the setting of international accounting standards.

International Federation of Stock Exchanges, *see* FÉDÉRATION INTER-
NATIONALE DES BOURSES DE VALEURS.

International Finance Corporation (IFC) [USA]. The IFC, an affiliate of
the World Bank, was established in Washington in 1956 to promote
the economic growth of its developing member countries through
private-sector investment. It is owned by more than 130 member
countries.

The IFC acts as a multilateral merchant bank by providing and
arranging both debt and equity financing as well as a wide variety of
financial services for its clients. In the year to 30 June 1988, the IFC
achieved record net income of just over $100 million, on an end-year
net worth of $1.3 billion and total assets of $3.4 billion.

The IFC's Capital Markets Department is the focal point of its
efforts to promote the healthy growth of capital markets in its
developing member countries. It operates in four main ways:

1 providing advisory services to assist its developing member
   countries in establishing appropriate legal, regulatory and tax
   frameworks;
2 preparing and publishing the IFC Emerging Markets Data Base, a
   unique source of information on 19 emerging capital markets;
3 investing directly in capital markets institutions such as merchant
   banks, investment management companies, insurance companies,
   venture capital companies, etc.;
4 facilitating access by its clients to the international capital markets
   through pooled investment vehicles such as mutual funds and
   investment trusts, and assisting individual companies to tap these
   markets through debt and equity issues.

See also WORLD BANK.

international Fisher Effect. A theory stating that international interest
differentials reflect expected exchange rate changes. Assuming
interest rate parity holds, it is tantamount to stating that the forward
rate is an unbiased predictor of the future spot rate. Empirical studies
have demonstrated that there are systematic biases associated with
the use of forward rates as a forecasting tool, and this would in turn
suggest that the international Fisher Effect is a crude forecasting tool.
Moreover, an unbiased predictor does not mean that borrowing in
one currency and lending in another is a risk-free investment. It
simply means that such an investment will have a zero expected
value. *See also* FISHER EFFECT.

International Labour Office (ILO) [Switzerland]. This United Nations affiliate, located in Geneva, is composed of government, industry and union representatives. It seeks to improve working conditions, improve employee standards and to encourage economic and social stability. Its research papers concentrate on multinationals and labour-related issues. In 1977 it published its *Tripartite Declaration of Principles Concerning Multinational Enterprises and Social Policy*.

international mergers. Mergers between corporations, or one or more of its business units, with parent company management located in different countries. International mergers have increased with the European 'invasion' of the USA, in particular, and a trend towards product or industrial consolidation and geographical diversification. Japanese multinationals are also becoming more acquisitive as opposed to their former 'greenfield' investment strategy.

During the 1980s there was a huge increase in the number and value of international mergers – see table 1 for details of international mergers in the USA for the period 1985–8.

International Monetary Fund (IMF) [USA]. The IMF was founded under the Bretton Woods agreement of 1944 to supervise and ensure the stability of the foreign exchange market. Amongst its duties are to supervise government intervention and assist governments with temporary balance-of-payments fluctuations. With the advent of floating exchange rates, the oil crisis and the debt crisis, the IMF has become an important source of finance for many developing countries. Frequently the provision of finance may be implicitly linked to reforms of domestic economic policies. *See also* WORLD BANK.

International Organisation of Securities Commissions (IOSCO) [Canada]. The leading international body for securities regulators. Established originally as a forum for South American securities regulators, it has grown to include all the major industrial nations. It now has 50 members including the US Securities and Exchange Commission, the UK Securities and Investments Board, the Securities Bureau of Japan's Finance Ministry, and France's Commission des Opérations de Bourse. A technical committee was established in 1987, with members from countries with the most developed securities industries, i.e. Australia, Canada, France, Germany, Hong Kong, Italy, Japan, the Netherlands, Sweden, Switzerland, the USA and UK, to look into international regulatory problems. A number of working parties are investigating a variety of issues including the definition and maintenance of capital adequacy for multinational securities firms, the exchange of financial data between regulators, multinational share offerings, multiple listings, accounting standards, off-market trading, clearing and settlement and futures markets.

international taxation. The presence of many tax jurisdictions is an important source of both threats and opportunities for the multinational corporation. Tax jurisdictions may differ with respect to the types of tax levied, rules for computing the basis for taxation, the administration of the tax system and the rate of tax charged. By way of example, we shall focus upon corporate income taxation and its implications for MNCs.

Most MNCs are liable to taxation in their home country on all income earned in the home country, which is deemed to include dividends and interest received from foreign subsidiaries and income earned by foreign branches. However, it should be pointed out that in some countries, foreign source income is not subject to taxation. Moreover, foreign subsidiaries will be expected to pay local income taxes in the countries in which they are incorporated. The objectives of international tax planning are to ensure that:

1 tax payments are minimized;
2 the recognition of taxable income is delayed for as long as possible;
3 the recognition of losses is accelerated.

Needless to say, these are fairly general rules and they may conflict with one another (e.g. 1 and 2 if tax rates are expected to increase) and with the goals of the MNC (e.g. being a good corporate citizen). Within this framework, however, we can examine some examples of devices which may be used by MNCs in higher tax countries to further the objectives of international tax planning.

Transfer pricing

The AB company is a UK company which manufactures computers in its Irish subsidiary, and sells them in the UK. Assume that the tax rate in Ireland is 0 per cent and 30 per cent in the UK. Accounting data is supplied in table 1 on p. 122.

By increasing the price at which goods are transferred between Ireland and the UK, the company could ensure that income was eradicated in the UK and that the company pays no taxes. The effects of altering the transfer price are shown in table 2.

However, if the Irish subsidiary pays all its income as a dividend to the UK, then the tactic ceases to be effective, since UK taxes would be

Table 1 Value of United States takeovers by foreign companies, 1985–8

Country	Acquisitions		Acquisitions for which the value is known	Total value of acquisitions for which the value is known	Percentage
	Number		Number	$bn	
		1985			
Canada	52		19	0.6	4
France	24		7	0.2	2
Germany	29		11	1.4	11
Japan	38		24	0.4	3
Netherlands	23		5	0.9	7
Switzerland	23		9	3.4	26
United Kingdom	101		58	4.3	33
Sub-total	290		133	11.2	86
Other	82		36	1.8	14
Total	372		169	13.0	100
		1986			
Canada	57		29	5.5	24
France	20		10	2.5	11
Germany	19		7	1.0	4
Japan	68		46	2.0	9
Netherlands	23		11	1.3	6
Switzerland	18		8	0.5	2
United Kingdom	113		69	7.0	31
Sub-total	318		180	19.8	87
Other	102		44	3.0	13
Total	420		224	22.8	100

1987			
Canada	66	29	1.0	3
France	33	10	1.3	4
Germany	25	9	4.1	12
Japan	97	65	5.3	16
Netherlands	20	7	4.2	12
Switzerland	20	7	1.1	3
United Kingdom	173	92	12.3	36
Sub-total	434	219	29.3	87
Other	113	68	4.5	13
Total	547	287	33.8	100

1988			
Canada	47	23	12.1	26
France	36	19	3.4	7
Germany	28	14	1.6	4
Japan	104	63	9.0	19
Netherlands	13	5	0.5	1
Switzerland	10	4	0.8	2
United Kingdom	159	97	14.6	31
Sub-total	397	225	42.0	90
Other	79	42	4.7	10
Total	476	267	46.7	100

Source: United States, Department of Commerce, International Trade Administration, Office of Trade and Investment Analysis Division, *Foreign Direct Investment in the United States: Completed Transactions 1974–83* (1985), annual reports published in 1986, 1987 and 1988

Table 1

	Income Ireland	Income UK	Income (total)
Sales	200	600	600
Cost of goods sold	−100	−200	−100
Gross profit	100	400	500
Expenses	−50	−250	−300
Pre-tax income	50	150	200
Taxes	0	−45	−45
Income after tax	50	105	155

Table 2

	Income Ireland	Income UK	Income (total)
Sales	350	600	600
Cost of goods sold	−100	−350	−100
Gross profit	250	250	500
Expenses	−50	−250	−300
Pre-tax income	200	0	200
Taxes	0	0	0
Income after tax	200	0	200

payable on the dividend. This in turn highlights the objective of the tactic; it is a device that delays the payment of taxes. Hence, it is a way of obtaining interest-free loans from the tax authorities.

Tax authorities don't wish to wait forever for taxes, so legislation is frequently enacted which permits the authorities to substitute 'arm's-length' prices for 'artificial' prices. The main difficulty which tax authorities must overcome is the establishment of 'arm's-length' prices for which there are no readily observable market prices or data to establish the costs of the products or services transferred. This in turn would suggest that companies engaged in the transfer of commodity-type products across national boundaries will have less opportunity to manipulate transfer prices than a monopoly supplier of intangible services.

The scope for the use of transfer pricing has decreased in recent years due to the increasing sophistication of tax authorities. Apart from the computation of 'arm's-length' prices, recent developments have included increased exchanges of information amongst national tax authorities.

Table 3

	Income Ireland	Income UK	Income (total)
Sales	350	600	600
Cost of goods sold	−100	−350	−100
Gross profit	250	250	500
Expenses	−50	−250	−300
Pre-tax income	200	0	200
Taxes	−60	0	60
Income after tax	140	0	140

Table 4

	Income Ireland	Income Panama	Income UK	Income (total)
Sales	150	350	600	600
Cost of goods sold	−100	−150	−350	−100
Gross profit	50	200	250	500
Expenses	−50	0	−250	−300
Pre-tax income	0	200	0	200
Taxes	0	0	0	0
Income after tax	0	200	0	200

Tax havens

Tax havens are countries that have tax systems which permit the MNC to reduce or defer taxes by channelling income through the country. Returning to our transfer pricing example, assume that Ireland also has a tax rate of 30 per cent; the effects upon table 2 are shown in table 3.

It may be seen that there is no gain from transfer pricing. However, let us assume that we can incorporate a paper subsidiary in Panama which pays no taxes. We could then sell all the computers to the Panamanian subsidiary which in turn would sell them to the UK subsidiary. The effects of this manoeuvre are shown in table 4.

Tax havens do differ and they may be used for many reasons other than transfer pricing. Some tax havens may be particularly suitable for insurance activities, others for shipping activities and others for banking activities. Therefore, it is necessary to know exactly what the MNC wishes to achieve before choosing a haven. Certain havens may be unsuitable due to the lack of global communications facilities, exchange controls, currency instability, political instability, incorporation laws, double taxation agreements (discussed below) and banking facilities.

Many countries have enacted anti-avoidance legislation to ensure that tax revenues are not foregone due to the existence of tax havens. This legislation is aimed particularly at the creation of paper subsidiaries which have been established with the sole intention of avoiding taxes.

Double taxation agreements

Double taxation agreements are treaties between countries which help ensure that income taxed in one country is not taxed in another. The treaties define residence and the way in which income is allocated between the two countries. Another aspect of the treaties is that they set out rates of withholding taxes. Withholding taxes are taxes on overseas remittances which may include dividends, interest royalties and fees. Double taxation agreements help to eliminate or minimize withholding taxes and frequently there will be only a withholding tax on dividends.

The presence of withholding taxes may be critical in the design of the legal form of the MNC, since withholding taxes between countries may differ. For example, A has a subsidiary in country B and the withholding tax between A and B on dividends is 20 per cent. However, the withholding tax on dividends between B and country C, and A and C is zero. Withholding taxes may be minimized by creating a company in C which is the owner of the subsidiary in B. This in turn ensures that dividends may be paid from B to A via C without incurring withholding taxes.

Foreign tax credits

In order to minimize the double taxation of income, tax authorities may permit companies to offset foreign taxes (including withholding taxes) against their local income, where the foreign taxes relate to some portion of that income. This procedure is known as a foreign tax credit. However, it is necessary to examine local legislation, since tax credits may be restricted to the corporate tax rate in the home country. For example, if the home tax rate is 30 per cent and the foreign tax paid is 15 per cent, then it would be necessary to pay 15 per cent tax when the dividends are remitted. However, if the tax paid abroad is 45 per cent, then no tax is payable when the dividends are remitted. This is a serious problem since no credit is obtained in the home country for the additional 15 per cent tax paid overseas. Revenue authorities sometimes allow carry-forwards or carry-backs of these credits. They may also allow the MNC to average the rates paid in different countries and grant credit at the average rate. MNCs may also establish a 'dividend mixer' company in a country with a favourable tax system and a range of appropriate double taxation agreements. Dividends from foreign subsidiaries are routed through the 'dividend mixer' in order to ensure that foreign tax credits are used to the best advantage.

Borrowing strategy

Borrowing in international capital markets is strongly influenced by tax considerations. Firstly, bonds will be more attractive to potential investors if interest is not deducted at source and there are no withholding taxes on the interest. This may dictate the use of overseas vehicles to raise debt which on-lend to the HQ or other foreign subsidiaries.

Secondly, foreign exchange gains and losses arising from the use of foreign currency debt may be treated in a variety of ways by the tax authorities.

1   It is quite possible that gains or losses are not recognized until the gain or loss is realized. If a debt is issued in a weak currency, we would expect that a higher coupon would be payable to ensure that the tax shield arising from debt was maximized.

2   Tax authorities may differ in the way in which they tax gains or losses arising from exchange rate changes. Some of the possibilities are outlined in example 1. It may be noted that issuing debt

---

Example 1   Borrowing strategy

Assume:

Borrow ($)	2,000		
UK interest p.a.	10%		
Exchange rate (S/£)	2		
UK tax rate	40%		

End of period:			
Exchange rate	1.82	2	2.18
US interest rate	0%	10%	20%
Interest charge (£)	0	−100	−183
FX gain/loss (£)	−100	0	83
Pre-tax cost	−100	−100	−100

After-tax cost:			
1 Interest tax deductible	−100	−60	−28
2 FX gain taxed	−100	−60	−60
3 FX gain/loss taxable	−60	−60	−60

in weak currencies will be preferred. However, it should be emphasized that this analysis assumes that the company pays taxes and that interest rate and foreign exchange risk are irrelevant.

international trade unions. There are a number of international trade union confederations which participate at inter-governmental level, such as the International Confederation of Free Trade Unions (ICFTU), World Confederation of Labour (WCL) and the European Trade Union Confederation (ETUC). These confederations represent the national trade unions. In addition, there are international trade union secretariats which focus on a specific industry, e.g. the International Metalworkers Federation, and represent internationally those trade unions involved with the relevant industrial category.

IOSCO, see INTERNATIONAL ORGANISATION OF SECURITIES COMMISSIONS.

IRPT, see INTEREST RATE PARITY THEOREM.

ITT Corporation [USA]. This $20bn corporation was transformed during the 1980s by its chief executive, Rand Araskog, to the extent that services now account for almost 70 per cent of total sales. In contrast, under Harold Geneen, Araskog's predecessor, ITT grew to become a huge industrial conglomerate renowned for its acquisition activity. Sales grew from $766m in 1959 to $17bn in 1979. But ITT had lost its strategic direction. Moreover, the company had become a byword for abuse of corporate power, following its role in the 1973 military coup in Chile.

Under Araskog, ITT reduced its manufacturing base. In 1987 it sold its telecommunications business to France's CGE for $1.5bn, and transferred $800m of its debt to the balance sheet of Alcatel, the joint venture between CGE and ITT in which the US company has a 37 per cent stake. Alcatel ranks behind AT&T as the world's largest telecommunications group with sales in excess of $11bn. It has 120,000 employees, and widely scattered production – by industry standards – in Europe, the USA, Mexico, Taiwan and Australia, though these are being more closely integrated in order to achieve greater scale efficiencies. Alcatel has divested itself of peripheral businesses (e.g. ITT's television business was sold to Nokia).

ITT's business can be divided into products and services. The former, Industrial and Defence Technology, comprises automotive products, electronic components, fluid technology and defence and space equipment. The services division encompasses insurance and financial services, communications operations and information services, and hotels.

ITT Automotive alone has annual sales in excess of $2bn. It pioneered anti-locking brake systems as used by manufacturers such as Ford, GM, Alfa Romeo, Citroën, Saab and Volkswagen. It is the world's largest independent manufacturer of complete braking systems and has produced more than 200 million individual disc brakes.

In services, the Hartford Insurance group ranks as one of the largest in North America, though ITT sold Abbey Life, a leading British life insurance group in the mid-1980s. ITT is also a world leader in telephone-directory compilation. It is the largest producer of 'Yellow Pages' directories outside the USA. ITT's Sheraton Corporation owns, manages or franchises more than 500 hotels, inns and resorts in 62 countries.

J

J-curve. The competitiveness of exports is determined by domestic prices in conjunction with exchange rates. If domestic prices are unchanged then exports will increase only if the exchange rate depreciates. A depreciating currency will encourage exports and deter imports. But there may be a lag to changing the pattern of exports and imports such that there could be an initial deterioration in the balance of payments. This initial deterioration is often referred to as the J-curve.

Japanese-style management. Japanese managers are perceived to have an entirely different approach from western managers. Western managers are characterized as more individualistic in that they compete with each other for advancement to the extent that corporate goals can become obscured. Japanese managers prefer a consensus approach where teamwork skills are emphasized and seniority is more important than individual performance. Friction between management and workers is also minimized. Short-term operating decisions are linked to long-term strategic planning, involving both managers and workers. Production is carefully planned and executed. The attention given to quality borders on the obsessive but with impressive improvement in corporate performance.

JIT, *see* JUST-IN-TIME INVENTORY MANAGEMENT.

joint venture. A partnership involving two or more companies in an enterprise in which each party contributes assets, owns the entity to some degree, and shares the risk. Joint ventures are formed for a number of reasons. Government legislation may prohibit foreign investors from having 100 per cent ownership, and joint ventures with a local partner are a prerequisite of market entry. Thus numerous multinationals have formed partnerships to penetrate markets in eastern Europe, and restrictive countries in Asia and Latin America. A joint venture may also be attractive in order to complement each partner's skills. For example, if a company is strong in production but weak in marketing, it may find a ready partner with the opposite features. Of course, the purpose of joint ventures is to produce mutual benefit(s) to the parties involved. For example, US automobile producers may offer marketing skills to a Japanese partner in exchange for its highly efficient management and production systems. While the formation of joint ventures between US and Japanese firms shows no sign of abating, some argue that US companies have failed to extract the benefits from the partnership, while their Japanese counterparts have been very successful in this respect. In other words, it is argued that US–Japanese joint ventures are precipitating a decline in US competitiveness, rather than protecting it.

junk bond. A device allowing a firm to borrow much more than its credit rating would normally permit. Such loans are clearly high-risk and this is reflected in the high interest charged to borrowers. Junk bonds have been the means of financing a number of spectacular takeover bids including Beatrice Foods, Safeway and RJR–Nabisco.

In the peak year of 1986 junk bonds worth some $40bn were issued in the process of creating a $200bn market. More recently many companies have shied away from these bonds because of the Wall Street scandals associated with them, and a number of serious defaults resulting in considerable nervousness among investors. April 1990, Michael Milkin, of Drexel Burnham Lambert, who pioneered junk bonds, pleaded guilty to six federal offences and agreed to fines of $600m charges, while his former employers had earlier filed for bankruptcy.

just-in-time inventory management. An approach to inventory control developed by the Japanese that controls the inflow and outflow of materials, components and finished goods so that inventory levels are kept to the minimum, i.e. inventory requirements are satisfied 'just in time' (JIT). This eliminates the need for the company to tie up capital in inventory. This potentially very efficient method is now being widely used by western companies. They are discovering though that JIT requires zero defects in components, so JIT enhances quality control as much as inventory control.

K

keiretsu. The Japanese term for a corporate group lacking a holding company – the typical configuration in modern Japanese business. The corporate groups which dominated economic activity in Japan up until the end of the Second World War were known as *zaibatsu*. Although formally dissolved during the Allied occupation of Japan, new groups began to form, and old groups to re-form, in the 1960s and 1970s. The corporate groups in contemporary Japan such as Mitsui, Mitsubishi and Matsushita are known as *keiretsu*, or 'headless combines', which refers to the absence of a holding company or controlling board. The relationships are indicated by cross-holdings of shares. The activities of corporations within the group are influenced by the group's council of presidents who meet regularly to exchange views. The lack of a central holding company and the typically small cross-holdings among corporations within Japanese groups make the relationship between such corporations difficult to assess, especially as there are many other factors involved, including debt relationships, interlocking directorships, interdependencies of raw materials, technology and market outlets, and historical associations.

Komatsu [Japan]. A group of 66 companies in a multitude of businesses; its principal area is construction equipment, accounting for two-thirds of total sales of $6bn. Overseas sales account for one-third of the total but Komatsu is expanding rapidly abroad, establishing a plant in the UK to serve the EC market for hydraulic excavators, acquiring Germany's Hanomag, and establishing a joint venture with Dresser Industries in the USA. Komatsu–Dresser has eight plants, four in the USA, and two each in Canada and Brazil.

Komatsu has 22,000 employees and spends around 3.5 per cent of sales on R&D. It is also intent on diversifying and it aims to expand sales of non-construction equipment to account for at least 50 per cent of total sales, and to double 1988 sales to $12bn by the year 2000. Komatsu is also developing its electronics related business and is making strategic acquisitions to secure leading-edge technology.

L

LAFTA (Latin American Free Trade Association), *see* LATIN AMERICAN INTEGRATION ASSOCIATION.

LAIA, *see* LATIN AMERICAN INTEGRATION ASSOCIATION.

Latin American Free Trade Association, *see* LATIN AMERICAN INTEGRATION ASSOCIATION.

Latin American Integration Association (LAIA) [Uruguay]. Based in Montevideo, LAIA was formed in 1980 as the successor to the moribund Latin American Free Trade Association (LAFTA). Similar to LAFTA, the objective of LAIA is to establish a common market within Latin America.

Law of the Sea Convention. A treaty resulting from a series of conferences held under the auspices of the UN from 1958 dealing with the exploitation of the mineral wealth of the oceans. The Law of the Sea Convention signed in 1982 was significant for establishing the principle that the seabed and its resources were 'the common heritage of mankind' and not subject to national jurisdiction.

leading and lagging. A technique involving retiming transfers of funds in order to take advantage of expected exchange rate changes. For example, if a company expected the French franc to devalue, it might slow down the payment of franc payables and expedite the collection of franc receivables. This would ensure that receivables were not affected by the devaluation and that payables decreased by the amount of the devaluation. The technique may be in breach of local exchange regulations and it also presumes that the company has a modicum of forecasting ability. The technique also assumes that third parties are gullible since it is a zero-sum game. For this reason, it is used most frequently for transactions within companies.

letter of credit. A letter addressed to the seller of goods or services, written and signed by a bank acting on behalf of the buyer, in which the bank promises to pay drafts drawn on itself if the seller conforms to the specific conditions laid down in the letter.

LIBOR, see LONDON INTERBANK OFFERED RATE.

licensing. A type of agreement permitting one firm (the licensee) to use the intellectual property (copyrights, design, patents, technology, trademarks or specific business skills) of another (the licensor) in exchange for compensation (royalty payments). Firms are likely to license-out intellectual property when: other forms of international market entry are impossible or non-viable; R&D costs can be recouped without endangering competitiveness; or rapid market entry is essential. Moreover, licensing can play an essential role in establishing an industry-wide standard – witness the outcome of JVC's willingness to license-out its Video Home System and Sony's initial reluctance, until too late, to do the same with Betamax. Of course, Sony's hesitation was understandable in that it wanted to avoid creating competitors. In 1989 America's Sun Microsystems licensed-out key technology to two Taiwan computer manufacturers (Datatech and Tatung) which allows them to make clones of its workstations. Datatech paid Sun an advance royalty payment of $500,000, but Sun began to use licensing to make its microprocessors the industry standard. For the Taiwanese, licensing-in technology permits them to produce state-of-the-art machines without incurring substantial R&D costs.

lifestyle research. A form of market research (pursued successfully by Japanese companies), which aims to identify future behaviour rather than current consumer preferences. This form of research was pioneered by Sony in the 1950s and resulted in the Japanese company identifying the portable TV market niche after General Electric's use of traditional market research led it to conclude that there was no market demand for such a product.

LIFFE, see LONDON INTERNATIONAL FINANCIAL FUTURES EXCHANGE.

Lomé Convention. An agreement between the European Community countries and a large number of developing countries in Africa, the Caribbean and the Pacific, which was intended to promote economic and social development by giving such countries preferential trading access to the EC together with financial and technical aid.

London Interbank Offered Rate (LIBOR). The interest rate applicable to interbank deposits (i.e. money deposited by one bank in another bank) in London. LIBOR frequently determines the base rate applicable to Eurodollar loans, and the lender pays an interest rate equal to LIBOR plus a spread over LIBOR (depending upon the borrower's credit rating). This spread over the basis (LIBOR) is usually expressed as LIBOR plus a number of basis points. A basis point is 0.01 per cent. Interest payable on the loan (if it is a floating rate loan) is then adjusted to reflect changes in LIBOR.

London International Financial Futures Exchange (LIFFE). The London-based market for financial futures, founded in 1982. Contracts traded include currency and other financial futures. Examples of financial futures include interest rate contracts and stock index futures. Currency options are also traded on LIFFE.

Lucky-Goldstar [South Korea]. The group's origins date to the formation in 1948 of the Lucky Chemical Company which specialized in personal products. By 1958 Lucky dominated the domestic market, and with limited growth opportunities, Goldstar Co. was formed – South Korea's first electronics manufacturer. Since then Lucky–Goldstar has diversified into: energy and resources; construction and engineering; securities, insurance and finance; trade and distribution; and public services and sports. It comprises more than 30 affiliate companies in these businesses. Electronics and energy together account for almost 70 per cent of total sales of this $20bn conglomerate. Goldstar's objective is to become the world's largest consumer and industrial electronics company. Like Samsung, it is expanding overseas, promoting its brand name, and investing heavily in R&D. Of the group's 150,000 employees, 4,500 are engaged in R&D, most of which is performed in Korea itself. Excluding royalty payments for technology, the group spends $550m or 5 per cent of sales on R&D.

M

3M, see MINNESOTA MINING & MANUFACTURING.

management, see EXCHANGE RISK MANAGEMENT, HUMAN RESOURCE MANAGEMENT, JAPANESE-STYLE MANAGEMENT, JUST-IN-TIME INVENTORY MANAGEMENT, MANAGEMENT BUY-OUT, MANAGEMENT CONTRACT.

management buy-out. A situation in which the incumbent management buys out the business with the advantages of job retention, independence and a share in the equity of the company. Management buy-outs usually occur where a division or subsidiary is unprofitable and the owner cannot find an alternative buyer at a higher price. While there are advantages in thus disposing of loss-making activities there is the danger that in declining industries such a course of action will only make things worse for all companies in the sector and do no more than delay ultimate exit. Merchant banks tend to be the promoters of buy-out schemes which usually involve large amounts of debt finance and an equity stake held by outsiders. Pressures to pay back the debt and to realize the value of the investment often lead to the sale of the company within a three- to five-year period, either by takeover or by a sale to the public via a stock market listing. Management buy-outs have become increasingly popular in the USA and UK, and this trend is now spreading to continental Europe.

management contract. A contract for the licensing of managerial expertise. Management contracts enable the multinational to control its knowledge advantage more effectively and, by way of its influence on the management of the foreign company, to obtain other benefits, e.g. as a supplier of raw materials. Further advantages of management contracts include the capacity to control quality and the provision of international experience for the multinational's own managers.

market segmentation. Markets are made up of buyers and market segmentation is a method of grouping together all those individuals with similar characteristics. These characteristics may take the form of needs, wants, age, sex, income, etc., and make up the market segments which allow the company to target specific groups of people. International market segmentation is used to adapt to customer heterogeneity both between and within countries. By differentiating the product between countries and target segments a better match between products and buyers can be achieved.

marketing mix. The mixture of controllable marketing variables that the company uses to pursue projected sales in a target market. There are countless marketing mix elements which can be grouped under four general headings, often referred to as 'the 4Ps': product, price, place and promotion, of, e.g. quality, list price, location and advertising. It is a part of the company's overall marketing strategy to calculate as well as possible the optimal marketing mix. In the international context, the scope and complexity of this task increases with the number of countries involved.

markets, marketing, see ASIACURRENCY MARKET, CHICAGO INTERNATIONAL MONEY MARKET, EFFICIENT MARKET HYPOTHESIS, EUROMARKETS, EUROPEAN COMMUNITY, MARKET SEGMENTATION, MARKETING MIX, SOURCE–MARKET MATRIX.

Matsushita Electric [Japan]. Since its foundation in 1918 by Konosuke Matsushita (1894–1989), it has grown to become the global leader in consumer electronics and one of the world's top 20 industrial corporations. Worldwide employment exceeds 190,000, and its products are sold in 130 countries with foreign sales now accounting for more than 40 per cent of total sales, which exceeded $40bn for the first time in 1989. Overseas production has grown rapidly since it established its first foreign plant in 1961 in Thailand. By the late 1980s it had 69 manufacturing companies and 32 sales and financial subsidiaries in 37 countries oustide Japan, employing some 58,000 people. Between 1986 and 1988 the yen's value appreciated by almost 100 per cent and this accelerated Matsushita's internationalization process. The Americas and Europe are Matsushita's two main markets, accounting for more than 70 per cent of total sales. By products, video equipment is the largest business segment, accounting for almost 30 per cent of total sales, followed by communication and industrial equipment (20 per cent), home appliances (14 per cent), electronic components (13 per cent) and audio equipment (9 per cent).

Matsushita has 30 principal research laboratories and it spends more than $2bn or nearly 6 per cent of total sales on R&D. It holds some 55,000 patents. R&D is concentrated in the seven areas earmarked for special emphasis: information/communication, factory automation, semiconductors, new audio-visual equipment, automotive electronics, housing-related products and integrated air-conditioning systems.

Matsushita's strategy for 1992 was directed by the company's
European regional headquarters in the UK. In 1989 major regional
headquarters functions were shifted from Japan to overseas locations
in North America, Europe and Asia, underpinning Matsushita's
commitment to internationalization.

mercantilism. An early economic philosophy based on the idea that a
country's wealth is dependent on its holdings of gold and other
'treasure'. In order to increase wealth, countries should simply
attempt to export more than they import. This approach was overtaken in the early 1800s by the development of ideas about absolute
advantage (Adam Smith) and comparative advantage (David
Ricardo). Neomercantilism is a term used in more recent times to
describe countries that attempt to maintain a favourable balance of
trade, not to build up gold reserves but to achieve social or political
objectives.

Merck [USA]. The world's largest pharmaceutical company, with sales of
almost $6bn. The fact that Merck has only one drug in the world's top
20 selling drugs (see table 1) is a clear indication that pharmaceuticals
remains one of the world's most fragmented industries. The top 10
companies account for just 26 per cent of the drug sales market, while
Merck holds 4 per cent. Success in this industry demands substantial
and increasing expenditure on R&D (see table 2). In 1979 Glaxo spent
a mere £25m on R&D, ten years later the figure was £300m.
  When in 1981 Glaxo launched Zantac, the world's best-selling
drug, the total cost of bringing Zantac to the market was £25m. Today
the cost for a new drug would be £100m. While developing new
drugs is expensive the rewards are great. In 1987 total drug sales
amounted to $125bn of which the top two drugs alone accounted for
$2.5bn.
  Fragmentation and soaring R&D costs create the possibility and the
incentive for industry restructuring. The first such sign was the
merger between America's SmithKline Beckman and Britain's
Beecham. This deal created the world's second-largest drugs
company with a turnover of $4bn, a salesforce of 6,000, and an R&D
budget of £300m. Within 48 hours of its formation, SmithKline
Beecham was overtaken, when Bristol–Myers and Squibb announced
they too were merging.

merger accounting. A method of accounting for business combinations
based on the dubious assumption that a 'merger' is distinguishable
from an 'acquisition'. It has been suggested that the term 'acquisition'

Table 1 The world's top-selling drugs

Brand name Disorder	Company	Annual sales ($m)
Zantac ulcers	Glaxo[a]	1,479.0
Tagamet ulcers	SmithKline	1,132.0
Tenormin hypertension	ICI	867.0
Capoten hypertension	Squibb	779.0
Vasotec hypertension	Merck	635.0
Adalat angina	Bayer[a]	587.0
Naprosyn arthritis	Syntex	555.7
Voltaren arthritis	Ciba–Geigy	544.1
Feldene arthritis	Pfizer	524.0
Ceclor infections	Eli Lilly	515.0
Cardizem angina	Marion	425.0
Zaditen asthma	Sandoz[a]	390.0
Ventolin asthma	Glaxo	387.7
Inderal hypertension	ICI[a]	376.2
Amoxil infections	Beecham	368.5
Dyazide hypertension	SmithKline	365.0
Kefral respiratory	Shionogi	363.8
Trinovum contraception	Johnson & Johnson	360.0
Krestin cancers	Sankyo	359.1
Claforan infections	Hoechst	358.4
Rocephin infections	Hoffmann La Roche	355.6

[a] Originating company
Source: Flemings Research

Table 2   Expenditure on research (1988)

	Market share %	R&D spend (£m)
Merck	4.2	395
Glaxo	3.0	240
Ciba–Geigy	2.8	275
Hoechst	2.6	350
SmithKline	2.2	165
Pfizer	2.2	225
Lilly	2.1	280
Bayer	2.1	400
Sandoz	2.1	230
American Home	2.1	155

Source: Nomura Research Institute

describes a business combination where one company dominates or controls the other, whereas the term 'merger' describes a confederation or pooling of interests with each company preserving its own identity and autonomy. In practice, however, a 'merger' is highly unlikely as there is invariably a dominant managerial strategy and some perception of synergy which, in effect, results in a transformed or new entity with new economic prospects and new legal relationships.

The use of merger accounting, which is permitted by law and accounting standards in the UK (and required in the USA) where 90 per cent or more of the consideration is in the form of shares, gives rise to substantially different representations of income and financial position compared to acquisition accounting. Under acquisition accounting the acquired company contributes to group profits only subsequent to the combination whereas under merger accounting all of the pre-combination profits in the year of acquisition are included. Furthermore, under acquisition accounting the investment by the holding company is recorded at market value and the assets and liabilities of the acquired company are revalued to 'fair values' at the date of combination, whereas under merger accounting the investment is recorded at nominal value, and assets and liabilities are not revalued. The effect of this difference is that under the acquisition approach profits subsequent to the combination may be decreased by increased depreciation charges relating to revalued assets. Profits may also be decreased by the amortization of goodwill – though immediate write-offs against reserves are encouraged in the UK. The potential for misleading information does not, however, rest entirely with merger accounting. A pessimistic view of asset revaluations coupled with provisions for reorganization and anticipated future losses and the immediate write-off of goodwill against reserves may encourage a preference for acquisition accounting where a choice is available – as is the case in the UK. It would seem that accountants currently prefer to follow rules based on arbitrary criteria reflecting corporate interests than to pursue methods of reporting that reflect the economic substance of business combinations.

mergers, merger policy, see ANTI-TRUST LEGISLATION, INTERNATIONAL MERGERS, MERGER ACCOUNTING, MONOPOLIES AND MERGERS COMMISSION.

Michelin [France]. In the autumn of 1989 this company, Europe's number one tyre producer, agreed to pay $810m to acquire America's Uniroyal–B. F. Goodrich, and to assume $690m of its debt. Thus Michelin finally overtook Goodyear to become the number one in the $41bn tyre industry, which has more than 500,000 employees and 373 plants that are owned by more than 100 private companies and 25 state enterprises in 80 countries on five continents. The industry though has become highly concentrated with the top ten firms holding around 90 per cent of the total global market. The top three firms alone account for almost 60 per cent of the market: Michelin/Uniroyal–Goodrich (24 per cent), Goodyear (19.3 per cent), and Bridgestone/Firestone (15.6 per cent).

Minnesota Mining & Manufacturing (3M) [USA]. This $11bn diversified, technology-based manufacturing company has 83,000 employees, operates in four sectors, has 14 groups and 49 divisions. The industrial and electronics sector accounts for more than one-third of total sales and its array of products include 'Scotchguard' carpet protectors and speciality chemicals. Information and imaging technologies sector, which accounts for more than a quarter of total sales, produces magnetic storage products (i.e. tapes and floppy disks). Life sciences (22 per cent of sales) offers a wide range of products for medical, surgical, orthopaedic, pharmaceutical and dental markets, not to mention materials for traffic signs. It also supplies the world's leading manufacturers of disposable nappies/diapers with adhesive fastening tapes.

The commercial and consumer sector (14 per cent of sales) is the world leader in transparent tape with its 'Scotch' brand, and in repositionable notes with the 'Post-it' brand.

3M products are sold in more than 40 major markets and inter-national sales account for 42 per cent of total sales. It operates in 52 countries and has manufacturing plants in 42 of them. It has 34,000 employees outside the USA. In Europe alone it has 23 plants in 11 countries, 13 R&D centres in 7 countries, and 21,000 employees. Its regional headquarters are in Brussels and in preparation for 1992 3M has moved away from national to pan-European advertising.

The most significant feature of 3M though is its commitment to product development and hence to R&D. A key feature of corporate policy is that in any given year, products launched within the previous five years should account for more than a quarter of total sales. In 1988 almost one-third (i.e. $3bn) of total sales came from such products. Interestingly, R&D expenditure during the five years 1984–8 was also around $3bn, and each year it is normally around 6.5 per cent of total sales – nearly double the average for the 50 largest US industrial corporation. 3M has more than 7,000 scientists and technicians, or 8.5 per cent of the total workforce, engaged in R&D.

MMC, *see* MONOPOLIES AND MERGERS COMMISSION.

momentum analysis, *see* CHARTISM.

Monopolies and Mergers Commission (MMC) [UK]. A government body established in the UK to investigate mergers and takeovers or monopoly situations at the discretion of the Secretary of State for Trade and Industry on the advice of the Director General of the Office of Fair Trading. The commission makes recommendations to the Secretary of State having regard to the public interest. At present, the public interest is defined primarily, but not exclusively, in terms of competition. The commission has no powers of its own to take action in cases where companies are considered to be operating against the public interest.

multinational [transnational] *corporation*. The term 'multinational enterprise', 'multinational company' and 'transnational corporation' are alternatives in use. The multinational corporation is usually defined broadly, e.g. by the UN, to mean a corporation which owns and/or controls economic resources in two or more countries. The multinationality, size and complexity of some of the largest multi-nationals explains why they have often become the object of a wide range of criticism. The existence of business organizations operating in a number of different nation states but with common ownership and/or control provides opportunities for decisions relevant to tax avoidance, the bypassing of national restrictions, the sourcing of production and the choice of areas of expansion and contraction which are not available to domestic corporations. The extent to which these opportunities are actually used and their effect on the welfare of individual nation states or host governments is the central question in the political debates on multinationals.

In the 1970s the attitude of many nations towards multinational corporations tended to be antagonistic. In the more turbulent economic circumstances of the 1980s, relationships became more pragmatic and businesslike as developed and developing countries alike competed intensely with each other for foreign investment. Thus, numerous governments dismantled or relaxed their controls on inward investment by multinationals.

N

NEC (Nippon Electric Company) [Japan]. This $23bn corporation was founded in 1899 under the name Nippon Electric Company, and it was Japan's first joint venture with foreign capital participation. The foreign partner, Western Electric Company of Illinois provided technology and by 1900 NEC was making telephones, and the company motto had been devised. 'Better Products, Better Services'. In 1946 it introduced Japan's first statistical quality-control programme in manufacturing operations, and four years later it launched semiconductor research. Thus, NEC has been a pioneer in Japanese management skills and technological progress. During the 1980s it became the world's leading semiconductor manufacturer (see table 1).

NEC consists of five divisions, the largest being Computers and Industrial Electronic Systems accounting for some 43 per cent of total sales, followed by Communications Systems and Equipment (26 per cent), Electron Devices (19 per cent), Home Electronics Products (7 per cent) and other operations (5 per cent). Geographically, it still relies very heavily on Japan which accounts for three-quarters of total

Table 1 Semiconductors: 1988 world ranking

Company	Rank		1988 revenue ($bn)
	1987	1988	
NEC	1	1	4.53
Toshiba	2	2	4.30
Hitachi	3	3	3.51
Motorola	4	4	3.03
Texas Instruments	5	5	2.74
Fujitsu	6	6	2.36
Intel	10	7	2.35
Mitsubishi	9	8	2.28
Matsushita	11	9	1.88
Philips	7	10	1.76
National	8	11	1.70
SGS–Thomson	13	12	1.22
AMD	12	13	1.10
Sanyo	14	14	1.08
Sharp	18	15	1.04

Source: Dataquest

sales. This concentration is reflected in the distribution of manufacturing capacity. NEC has 54 plants in Japan alone, and overseas it has 25 plants in 12 countries. Worldwide employment exceeds 104,000.

NEC views R&D as 'the key to future growth'. Between 1987 and 1989 it spent 16 per cent of sales each year on R&D, spending more than $9.7bn – $3.6bn of that in 1989 alone. Its main US rivals spend much less on R&D. For example, Texas Instruments, which in 1958 invented integrated circuits which led to the development of microchips, spends less than $500m a year on R&D. Motorola spends less than $700m. For both companies these figures amount to 8 per cent of total sales.

Nestlé [Switzerland]. This $28bn corporation is the world's largest food company (a high proportion of Unilever's sales are of non-food items). Its brands include Nescafé coffee, Libby's fruit juices, Vittel mineral water, Findus frozen foods, and Chambourcy yoghurt. It has also acquired best-selling brands through the purchase of Carnation (1985) for $3bn, Rowntree (1988) for £2.6bn, Italy's Buitoni (1988) for SF1.8bn, and three sweet businesses from RJR–Nabisco (1989) – Baby Ruth, Butterfinger and Pearson – for $370m. In 1989 it formed a joint venture with General Mills of the USA, Cereal Partners Worldwide, to challenge Kellogg's cereals dominance.

Away from foods, it has a 50 per cent stake along with Swissair in Swissotel, an international chain of high-quality hotels. It also owns the Stoffer hotel chain. In pharmaceuticals it is the US market leader in solutions for contact lenses with its Alcon brand. It is also the indirect holder of a minority interest in L'Oréal, the French company which ranks as the joint first (with Unilever) cosmetics company in the world.

It has a total of 428 factories in almost 60 countries, and its products are sold in over 100 countries. Europe, however, still accounts for just under half (i.e. 47 per cent) of total sales, while North America accounts for just over a quarter (i.e. 26.3 per cent). It has 198,000 employees, and all but 7,000 are employed outside Switzerland.

During the 1970s, it achieved notoriety for its marketing practices in selling its powdered baby milk in LDCs. The product was considered inappropriate due to a combination of poor sanitation facilities and the low literacy level of consumers in these countries. Illiterate mothers failed to boil the water as required or prepare baby-bottles according to the stipulated dosage. Nestlé's activities resulted in a number of orchestrated boycotts of Nestlé products in developed countries, especially the USA.

In its 1988 Annual Report, Nestlé reviewed the performance of all eleven of its divisions except one – infant foods and dietetic products. The company's statement in this report regarding the OECD's Guidelines for Multinational Enterprises is also illuminating:

The business policies which the Nestlé Group applies in its home country and abroad are largely in line with the OECD Guidelines. . . . In this annual report the guidelines concerning the disclosure of information have been observed wherever possible.

netting. A valuable international cash management technique for minimizing the bid–ask spreads and other transaction costs associated with intra-group transfers of foreign exchange. Two types of netting may be distinguished: bilateral and multilateral netting.

1 *Bilateral netting*. This technique may be used if two subsidiaries trade in both directions with one another. For example, suppose that the US subsidiary is about to pay $500,000 to the UK subsidiary, and that the UK subsidiary is about to pay $700,000 to the US subsidiary. By netting these payments, the UK subsidiary would simply pay $200,000 to the US subsidiary. If transaction costs are 1 per cent, then the use of netting would result in a saving of $10,000. While this example may sound trivial, it may occur in practice, since many MNCs may have a number of subsidiaries of different divisions operating in a single country.
2 *Multilateral netting*. Multilateral netting (i.e. between a number of countries) is useful if there is a more complex pattern of intra-company transactions.

One might conclude that significant savings will result from the use of netting. However, the use of netting is constrained in a similar way to international cash management. Moreover, there may be additional difficulties associated with netting:

1 Netting may be forbidden by local exchange control regulations.
2 Textbook examples of netting assume that intra-group payments are made at exactly the same point in time. In practice, this may not be the case, and it will be necessary to deploy exchange risk management techniques to alter the timing.
3 Many MNCs may not have significant trade flows in opposite directions between subsidiaries. It may be that trade flows are arranged in a hierarchical manner.

new international economic order. In 1974 the United Nations issued a declaration calling for a new international economic order. This declaration called for measures to redistribute world resources to eliminate the widening gap between the developed and developing countries. Actions to be taken included commodity price stabilization, preferential entry of manufactured exports from developing countries, transfer of technology, more favourable financial arrangements and the regulation of multinationals. Not surprisingly, on account of the conflicts of interest involved, there has been little action taken in practice, much to the disappointment of the developing nations.

newly industrializing country, *see* NIC.

NIC (newly industrializing country). Asia's 'four tigers' (i.e. Hong Kong, Singapore, South Korea and Taiwan), plus Brazil and Mexico, constitute the newly industrializing countries. The Asian countries in particular have recorded spectacular growth rates since the early 1960s when they adopted export-oriented trade strategies. Faced with relatively small domestic markets, they decided to exploit their advantage of cheap labour and concentrate on labour-intensive production for overseas markets. More recently, they have switched to more capital intensive sectors in order to stay abreast of countries with even cheaper labour rates (e.g. Indonesia, Thailand). South Korea and Taiwan have been so successful that their trade surplus position with the USA accounts for a large proportion of the US trade deficit. Between 1985 and 1988 South Korea's total exports doubled from $30.2bn to $60.7bn, and its trade surplus with the US did almost the same, rising from $6.5bn to $8.6bn. During the same period Taiwan's total exports and US trade surplus increased from $30.7bn to $60.5bn, and from $10.6bn to $10.9bn (down from $18.6bn in 1987) respectively. The US trade administration therefore exerted pressure on these countries to appreciate their currencies to make exports less competitive, and the US erected protectionist barriers, as did the EC, against certain goods imported from the 'four tigers'.

In 1989, however, South Korea and Taiwan recorded slower export growth rates. This may reflect a loss of competitiveness but also a shift in international market supply strategies. Companies from these countries (e.g. South Korea's Samsung and Taiwan's Tatung) are establishing manufacturing facilities in key overseas markets (i.e. the USA and EC). The NICs are thus no longer just host nations to inward investment, but the home countries of rapidly growing multinationals.

Nineteen-ninety-two (1992). Nineteen-ninety-two is the date which has been targeted for the completion of the internal market of the

European Community. This internal market is defined by the Single European Act of July 1987 as being 'an area without frontiers in which the free movement of goods, persons, services and capital is ensured in accordance with the provisions of the Treaty'.

While the Rome Treaty of 1957 established the European Community as a major tariff-free area in western Europe, non-tariff barriers have remained, and have been erected, in the form of protective national standards, local regulations, customs procedures and discriminatory public procurement policies.

These barriers have been detrimental to Europe's ability to compete internationally and it was realized that a major and dramatic initiative was necessary. The aim of the 1992 programme, therefore, has been to remove the variety of non-tariff barriers to trade so as to become more efficient internally, thereby being in a better position to compete externally with the USA, Japan and other economic powers. Whether this is a realistic objective is questionable but there is no doubt that much has been achieved to date and that many businesses have been galvanized by '1992' into rethinking their corporate strategy and preparing for changes in, and the development of, international business relationships. '1992' has created fears of a protectionist Europe among non-EC multinationals, and their response has been to establish or expand their EC production bases. Witness in particular the large increase in Japanese investment in the EC.

Nippon Electric Company, *see* NEC.

Nippon Telegraph & Telephone (NTT) [Japan]. Founded in 1952 as a government monopoly to provide telephone services, NTT has now been privatized. In the late 1980s domestic sales still accounted for 80 per cent of total sales, but during the 1990s NTT will launch an onslaught on the world telecommunications market.

A few facts about NTT underline its potential. It is Japan's largest employer, has the largest amount of assets (i.e. $92bn) and in 1988 it reported the largest profits (i.e. $2.1bn). Moreover, it has the highest stock market valuation of any company in the world (i.e. $164bn) – more than the combined worth of IBM ($64.6bn), AT&T ($38.1bn), General Motors ($25.2bn) and Ford ($24bn) (see table 1).

Nissan [Japan]. The world's fourth-largest automobile company derives 98 per cent of its sales of $30bn from its automotive business, but the company is seeking to diversify into aerospace equipment, textile and industrial machinery, and marine products. Since 1972 it has seen its

Table 1   The world's most valuable companies

Rank				Market value $bn
1989	1988			
1	1	Nippon Telegraph & Telephone	Japan	163.86
2	9	Industrial Bank of Japan	Japan	71.59
3	2	Sumitomo Bank	Japan	69.59
4	5	Fuji Bank	Japan	67.08
5	4	Dai-Ichi Kangyo Bank	Japan	66.09
6	3	International Business Machines	USA	64.65
7	10	Mitsubishi Bank	Japan	59.27
8	6	Exxon	USA	54.92
9	7	Tokyo Electric Power	Japan	54.46
10	12	Royal Dutch/Shell Group	Neth.–UK	54.36
11	13	Toyota Motor	Japan	54.17
12	14	General Electric	USA	49.39
13	11	Sanwa Bank	Japan	49.29
14	8	Nomura Securities	Japan	44.44
15	27	Nippon Steel	Japan	41.48
16	21	American Telephone & Telegraph	USA	38.12
17	17	Hitachi Ltd	Japan	35.82
18	15	Matsushita Electric Industrial	Japan	35.70
19	41	Philip Morris	USA	32.14
20	38	Toshiba	Japan	30.91

Source: *Business Week*

domestic market share slip from 34 per cent to 23 per cent in 1988 while Toyota gained market share. In 1987 it made its first ever loss. Abroad, though, Nissan has been much more adventurous than its larger rival. After Honda, it was the second Japanese auto company to establish a manufacturing presence in the USA, and as clear Japanese market leader in western Europe, it was first to open an auto plant in the EC, in north-east England. By the early 1990s Nissan will have the capacity to produce 440,000 vehicles a year at its US operation, and 600,000 vehicles a year in western Europe. Nissan has faced further wrangling between EC member countries on the local content level of cars built in the UK and whether they should be treated as EC built and excluded from existing quotas on Japanese exports to the Community. This increase in capacity plus the opening of Toyota's new plant in England will no doubt see an increase in Japanese car makers' EC market share from the current level of 11 per cent.

In 1989 the United Auto Workers Union staged its first representation vote in a Japanese-owned US car plant. The 2,400 hourly paid workers at Nissan's Smyrna, Tennessee, plant voted by more than two to one against joining the union. In the course of the union drive, the Tennessee government fined Nissan $5,000 for failing to disclose records on work-related injuries.

Nokia [Finland]. Finland's largest industrial company with sales of almost $3bn has manufacturing plants all in Europe. It is the world's largest producer of cellular radio telephones, Europe's third-largest television manufacturer behind Philips and Thomson, and its seventh largest information technology manufacturer. Under Kari Kairamo, who died unexpectedly in 1988, Nokia diversified from its original base in rubber products and paper into electronics. In the 1970s it already produced telecommunications cables and it expanded into communications by acquiring the Mobira mobile radio business in the late 1970s. Success there saw Nokia move into the office computer and electronic-point-of-sale (EPOS) market. In 1984 it entered consumer electronics, acquiring two television companies, Sweden's Luxor and Finland's Salora, later buying France's Oceanic. In 1987 it acquired Germany's Standard Elektrik Lorenz (SEL) from Alcatel, and in 1988 it paid $217m to acquire Ericsson's Information Systems. As a result of these acquisitions electronics accounted for two-thirds of total sales in 1988 compared to 10 per cent in 1980. Nokia's 'buy-and-integrate' strategy has in the past worked well. Kairamo's successor, Simo Vuoriehto remains confident that the major deals concluded in 1987 and 1988 will succeed, despite conceding that the company would have preferred a more leisurely pace for completing its acquisitions.

Acquisition has been accompanied by divestment. Ten smaller, traditional Finnish divisions were sold in the period 1987–9.

non-tariff barrier. In addition to official custom tariffs, international trade can be impeded intentionally or as a by-product of government action. Such barriers include physical barriers (e.g. frontier controls and customs administration), technical barriers (e.g. product standards and specifications) and financial barriers (e.g. different rates of value added tax among EC member countries). By 1992 such barriers will have been removed in the EC.

In recent years, trade relations between certain countries have deteriorated because of the different perspectives of trading partners. For example, a government may claim that it insists on certain product specifications in order to control pollution. In reality, though, the ostensible environmental concern is a means of restricting imports of foreign cars. Potential exporters are thus frustrated by what they perceive as unfair practices.

NTT, *see* NIPPON TELEGRAPH & TELEPHONE.

O

OECD, see ORGANISATION FOR ECONOMIC CO-OPERATION AND DEVELOP-
MENT.

OEM, see ORIGINAL EQUIPMENT MANUFACTURER.

offshore production. Producing goods or components abroad for import
to the domestic market or for the servicing of other markets. This
occurs when the multinational perceives it to be the most profitable
means of exploiting its competitive advantage. It is a commonly used
approach in the electronics industry, and many countries in low
labour cost locations (e.g. Central America and South-east Asia) have
established export processing zones to become attractive bases for
offshore production.

OPEC (Organisation of Petroleum Exporting Countries) [Austria]. A
producers' association or cartel with the objective of stabilizing and
increasing oil prices. OPEC was established in 1961 and is based in
Vienna. Following the Arab–Israeli War in 1973, the Arab oil-
producing countries introduced an oil embargo against a number of
western developed countries resulting in a substantial increase in oil
prices. However, in the early 1980s a situation of over-supply
occurred owing to reduced demand due to an economic recession in
western countries and to the increased use of alternative energy
sources. The development of oil supplies outside OPEC and the
actions of some OPEC members in selling oil at lower prices have also
contributed to substantial price reductions. To be more effective
OPEC would need to agree a system of export quotas which would be
acceptable to all of its members. Such a community of interests would
be difficult to maintain over a period of time and indicates the
problem of organizing a successful producers' association.

OPIC (Overseas Private Investment Corporation) [USA]. A US government corporation that operates as a component of the International
Development Cooperation Agency. OPIC offers insurance for US
investors against political risks, non-convertibility of currency, and
losses arising from war, revolution and so on.

option. A right to trade a commodity or financial instrument on or before a
future date (the expiry date) at a fixed price (the exercise price). An

option differs from a futures or forward contract since the latter represents an obligation to trade.

Two types of option may be distinguished: call options and put options. A call option is a right to buy a security or commodity, while a put option is a right to sell. Options may also be distinguished as either European or American. A European option allows the holder to exercise it on the expiry date, whereas an American option allows the holder to exercise on or before the expiry date.

An example

Assume:

> 30-day forward rate = 35p per DM
> A call option due to expire in 30 days is available with
> an exercise price of 35p

If we purchase either a call option or a forward contract, the value of our position at the end of the month will depend upon the prevailing spot rate. Assume that the spot rate may be either 30p or 40p.

If we had a forward contract to buy D-marks for 35p, then we would stand to gain or lose 5p. If the spot rate is 40p, then we could purchase D-marks under the forward contract at 35p and sell them for 40p. Conversely, if the spot rate is 30p, we lose 5p since we are obliged to purchase a D-mark for 35p which is only worth 30p. The pay-off from holding a forward contract to buy one D-mark is shown in figure 1.

Conversely, if we contract to sell at the forward rate, we will profit if the sterling price of D-marks decreases. This may be seen in figure 2.

Options are extremely useful instruments, since they are a right not an obligation. As they are a right, we can speculate while also insuring ourselves against downside risks. If we hold a call option (a right to buy) with an exercise price of 35p, then we would only exercise the option (i.e. buy foreign currency) if the value of the currency exceeded 35p. If the value of the currency is less than the exercise price, then the option would expire unexercised, since no rational economic actor would exercise a right to lose 5p. The pay-off from purchasing a call option is illustrated in figure 3.

Rather than buying a call, we could buy a put option. In this instance, we have an option to sell foreign currency, and we would only exercise the option if we could purchase the underlying asset more cheaply. Therefore, if the exercise price is greater than the spot rate, we would exercise the option. The pay-off is illustrated in figure 4.

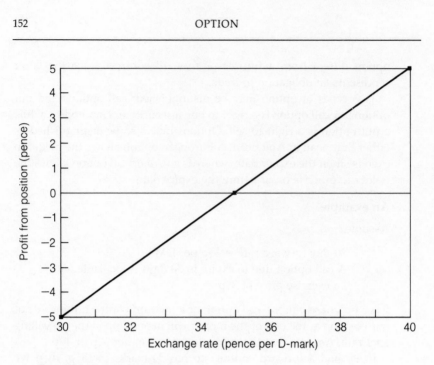

1 Pay-off from forward purchase

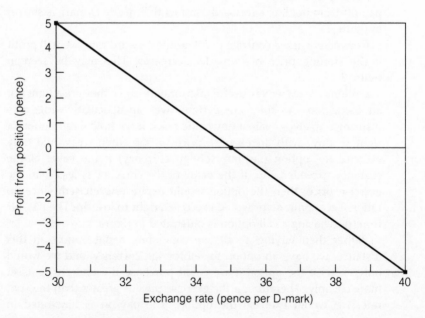

2 Pay-off from forward sale

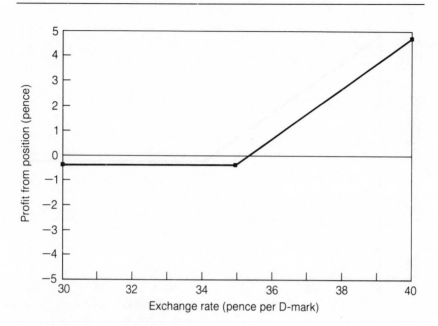

3 Pay-off from buying call option

Moreover, a shrewd speculator might note that if he/she were to purchase both a call and a put, then he/she would always make a profit. This strategy is known as a 'straddle' and is illustrated in figure 5.

But this exposition implies that there is a free lunch available by using options. Speculators will make money so long as there are those who will sell them options. For example, consider the pay-off for someone who writes (sells) a call option. The purchaser of the option will only exercise it if the exercise price is less than the spot rate. The seller of the option will have to purchase currency at the spot rate, in order to sell it at the exercise price and hence will make a loss. The pay-off from writing a call is illustrated in figure 6, and from writing a put in figure 7.

Since the writer of a call will always have an end-of-period pay-off which is less than or equal to zero, we would expect that he/she would insist upon receiving a fee for writing an option. Similarly, we would not be surprised that the purchaser of an option would expect to pay a fee for an instrument which always resulted in a pay-off greater than or equal to zero. This fee is known as an option price, and it is always greater than or equal to zero. The factors which might affect the price of an option are discussed below.

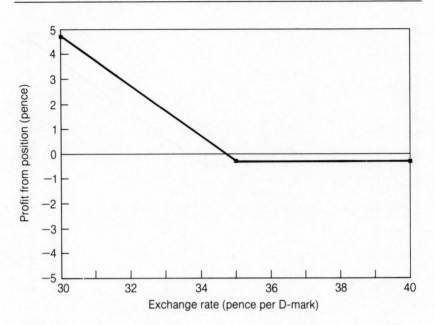

4 Pay-off from buying put option

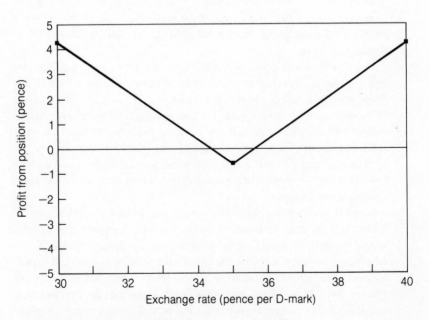

5 Pay-off from buying straddle (buy 1 put and 1 call)

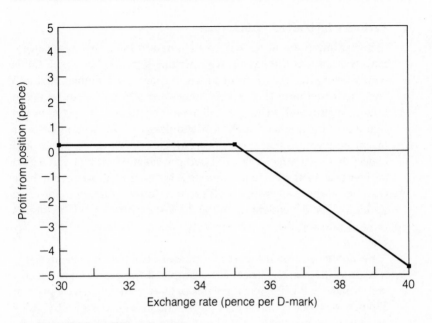

6 Pay-off from selling call option

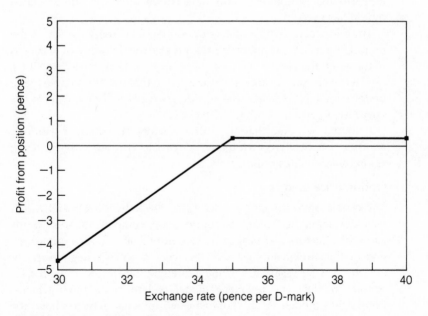

7 Pay-off from selling put option

Factors which affect option prices

The first important factor will be the forward rate. This is so since it may be seen that the pay-off from writing a put and buying a call is equivalent to the pay-off from a forward purchase (combine figures 3 and 7 to form figure 1). Similarly, a forward sale will be equivalent to buying a put and writing a call (combine figures 4 and 6 to get figure 2). In a market which is frictionless (no transaction costs or taxes) and where there are no arbitrage opportunities, we would expect that the current value of buying a call and writing a put would be identical to the current value of a forward contract to purchase currency at the exercise price. This in turn implies that the value of an option will be dependent upon the domestic interest rate, the foreign interest rate and the current spot rate, due to the Interest Rate Parity Theorem.

Secondly, we would expect the value of a call option to be inversely related to the exercise price. For example, if the exercise price is 30p per D-mark, we will make a greater pay-off than an exercise price of 35p per D-mark (see figure 8). Conversely, we would expect the value of a put to be positively related to the exercise price (see figure 9).

Thirdly, the greater the time to expiry, the greater the value of an option. This is evident when one considers that a longer-dated option confers the same rights as a shorter-dated option, except that the longer-dated option may still have value after the shorter-dated option has expired.

The final factor which affects option prices is the volatility of the underlying asset. Surprisingly, the greater the volatility or riskiness of the asset, the greater the value of the option. This arises since, if we hold a call option, we are only interested in the upside potential of the underlying asset. Clearly, the upside potential will be greater if the volatility is greater (see figure 10).

It should be noted that all of these factors may interact with one another and interfere with the *ceteris paribus* (i.e. other things being equal) relationships outlined above.

Option price models

The classic option pricing model is the Black–Scholes model which was developed to value call options on company shares. It incorporates factors identical to those outlined above, with the exception of the foreign interest rate. In order to price foreign currency options, it is necessary to include a foreign interest rate in the Black–Scholes model. The resultant model is known as the Garman–Kohlhagen model. More sophisticated models which allow for stochastic interest rates have also been formulated. Computer

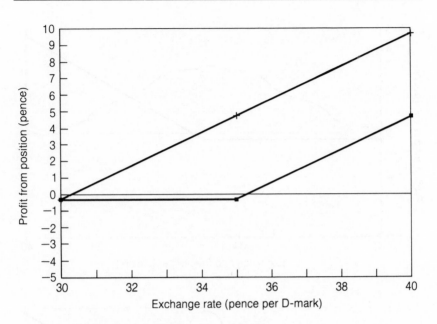

8 Pay-off from calls with different exercise prices

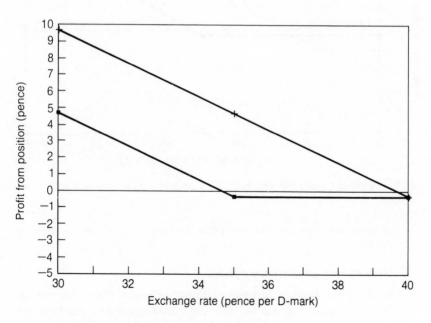

9 Pay-off from puts with different exercise prices

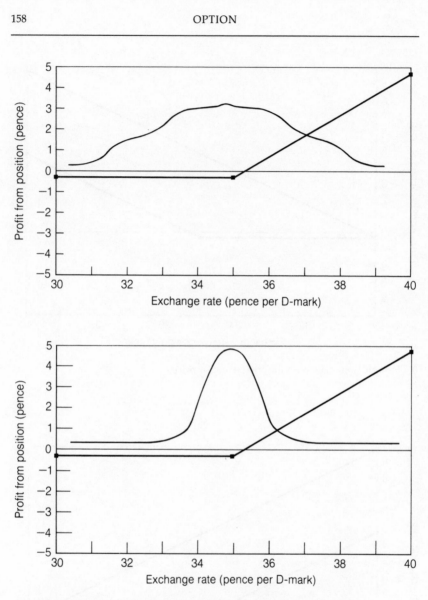

10 Pay-off from buying call option: (a) high volatility; (b) low volatility

programmes are readily available for applying these models in practice.

Uses of foreign currency options

In the 1980s foreign currency options became available from both large, international banks and organized securities markets. In principle, options may be utilized in either of two situations.

Firstly, firms who believe they have superior forecasts of exchange rates, or would like to take advantage of favourable exchange rate changes may use options as a speculative device.

Secondly, firms which have foreign exchange exposures of a contingent nature may consider the use of an option as a hedging device. For example XYZ (a UK company) is tendering for a large dollar-denominated aeroplane contract. Tenders must be submitted three months prior to a decision being reached by the supplier. XYZ might consider the use of a forward contract. However, should the company be unsuccessful, then the firm may have a substantial foreign exchange exposure as it is obliged to sell a quantity of dollars at a predetermined rate. The use of a foreign currency option would ensure that such an undesirable outcome would be impossible.

Organisation for Economic Co-operation and Development (OECD)

[France]. An umbrella organization for intergovernmental cooperation among 24 industrialized countries (see below) on matters pertaining to economic and social policy. Established in 1960, it aims: (1) to promote economic growth, employment and improved standards of living, while maintaining financial stability; and (2) to contribute to the economic expansion of member and non-member nations through multilateral trade.

The members of the OECD are:

Australia	Greece	Norway
Austria	Iceland	Portugal
Belgium	Ireland	Spain
Canada	Italy	Sweden
Denmark	Japan	Switzerland
Germany	Luxembourg	Turkey
Finland	Netherlands	UK
France	New Zealand	USA

The above countries account for only one-fifth of the world's population, but 60 per cent of its industrial output and 70 per cent of its trade. They are seen as members of a 'rich man's club' by the less developed yet heavily populated countries of the South.

With the publication in 1976 of its *Guidelines for Multinational Enterprises*, the OECD became the first international body to approve a document dealing with the conduct of multinational corporations. The guidelines, covering financing, taxation, competition, industrial relations and information disclosure, were issued as part of a package designed to foster a climate favourable to foreign direct investment.

Member governments agreed to recommend these guidelines to multinational corporations but compliance in practice is far from comprehensive.

Organisation of Petroleum Exporting Countries, *see* OPEC.

original equipment manufacturing (OEM). The rapid growth of South Korea and Taiwan is largely due to the large orders which they have secured from original equipment manufacturers (e.g. IBM, Matsushita, Philips). Companies with headquarters in developed countries may subcontract production to firms in the NICs when the latter have a cost advantage in producing a good (e.g. computer terminal, video cassette recorder). Although the good is made by the low-cost producer, it is sold under the brand name of the well established company which can charge a premium because of its brand's reputation (see table 1). Clearly this relationship benefits the firm which farms out production (i.e. the principal), but original equipment manufacturing has long-term disadvantages for the subcontractor, in that profit margins are low, and the emergence of lower-cost rivals can result in the loss of contracts to them. Thus in the electronics industry South Korean and Taiwanese firms, such as Samsung and Acer, are investing heavily to develop their own brand names and technology to improve profits and reduce dependency on foreign rivals for OEM business.

Overseas Private Investment Corporation, *see* OPIC.

Table 1 Illustrative original equipment manufacturing arrangements

Type of product	Industrial country purchaser	Developing country/territory supplier
Fork-lift trucks	Caterpillar (USA)	Daewoo (Republic of Korea)
Small trucks	Fuji Heavy Industries (Japan)	Unidentified firm (Taiwan Province)
Compact cars	Ford (USA)	Kia Industries (Republic of Korea)
	Pontiac (USA)	Daewoo (Republic of Korea)
Microwave ovens	General Electric (USA)	Samsung (Republic of Korea)
Colour television sets	Magnavox (USA)	Goldstar (Republic of Korea)
	General Electric (USA)	Goldstar (Republic of Korea)
Playback-only video casette decks	Cabin Industrial Corp. (USA)	Goldstar (Republic of Korea)
Radio cassette tape recorders	Sanyo (Japan)	Unidentified firm (Malaysia)
Personal computers	Leading Edge (USA)	Daewoo (Republic of Korea)
	Compaq (USA)	Samsung (Republic of Korea)
	Ricoh (Japan)	Unidentified firm (Taiwan Province)
	Unidentified firm (USA)	Hyundai Electronics (Republic of Korea)
Calculators	Casio (Japan)	Several firms in Taiwan Province and Hong Kong
	Sharp (Japan)	
	Canon (Japan)	
	Panasonic (Japan)	
	Casio (Japan)	Unidentified firm (Republic of Korea)
Computer monitors	IBM (USA)	Samsung (Republic of Korea)
	Olivetti (Italy)	Samsung (Republic of Korea)
	AT&T (USA)	Samsung (Republic of Korea)

Table 1 *cont.*

Type of product	Industrial country purchaser	Developing country/territory supplier
Key telephone systems	Vodavi Technology (USA)	Goldstar Telecommunications (Republic of Korea)
Tennis shoes	Nippon Gakki (Japan)	Unidentified firm (Republic of Korea)
Sports shoes	Converse (USA)	HS Corporation (Republic of Korea)
	Nike (USA)	
	Yves Saint Laurent (France)	
Luxury shoes	Yves Saint Laurent (France)	Unidentified firm (Republic of Korea)
Numerically controlled lathes and machining centres	Hitachi Seiki (Japan)	Kia Machinery Industries (Republic of Korea)
Tennis balls	Spalding (USA)	Unidentified firm (Republic of Korea)
Air-conditioner components	Several manufacturers (USA)	Matsushita Compress Plant (Malaysia)
Sanitation fixtures	Toto Ltd (Japan)	PT Surya Toto (Indonesia)

Source: United Nations Centre on Transnational Corporations; *Transnational Corporations in World Development: Trends and Prospects* (New York, United Nations, 1988).

P

Pacific Economic Cooperation Conference, *see* ASIA–PACIFIC ECONOMIC
COOPERATION CONFERENCE.

parallel financing, *see* BACK-TO-BACK FINANCING.

petrodollars. Following the rise in oil prices in October 1973, the OPEC
countries began to accumulate large quantities of foreign currency. A
considerable proportion of this foreign exchange was not converted
into OPEC currencies but used for international portfolio investment.
These stocks of currency are known as petrodollars.

Philip Morris [USA]. Owners of Marlboro, the world's best-selling
cigarette, Philip Morris has invested more than $20bn on acquisitions
to reduce its dependency on tobacco products, for which demand is
waning in the USA and Europe.
　　In diversifying into food and drinks, Philip Morris has grown to
become a $40bn corporation and the world's largest consumer goods
manufacturer with a strong brand portfolio (see example 1). Its
purchases include Miller (1970), the second-largest US brewer,
Seven-Up (1978) – a disappointing purchase and sold in 1986 –
General Foods (1985), best known for its Maxwell House coffee, and
Kraft (1988), with its emphasis on dairy products and strong presence
in overseas markets. Philip Morris borrowed $10bn and paid $13bn
to acquire Kraft.

Philips [Netherlands]. Europe's largest consumer electronics producer has
companies in more than 60 countries and has 310,000 employees.
Consumer electronics is the largest of six divisions, accounting for
more than 30 per cent of total sales of $28bn, which make it among
the world's top 25 companies. The other divisions are lighting,
domestic appliances, professional products and systems, components
and miscellaneous. The major domestic appliance business was spun-
off in 1988 to form a joint venture with Whirlpool of the USA. Philips
holds a 47 per cent stake in the venture which overtook Electrolux to
become market leader in this sector.
　　Geographically, Philips is still very dependent on the European
market which accounts for more than 60 per cent of total sales. It has

Example 1   A sampler of Philip Morris products worldwide

PRODUCTS IN USA

Baked goods
Entenmann's
Freihofer's

Barbecue sauces
Bull's-Eye
Kraft
Thick 'N' Spicy

Beers
Leinenkugel
Löwenbräu
Magnum Malt Liquor
Meister Brau
Miller
Milwaukee's Best

Candy
Kraft

Cereals
Alpha-Bits
Crispy Critters
Croonchy Stars
Fruit & Fibre
Honeycomb
Post
Smurf Magic Berries
Super Golden Crisp

Cigarettes
Benson & Hedges
Cambridge
Marlboro
Merit
Parliament
Players
Virginia Slims

Coffees
Brim
Estate Colombian
General Foods Int.
Kenya AA
Maxwell House
Postum
Sanka
Yuban

Cottage Cheese
Albertson's
Breakstone's
Breyers
Foremost
Jersey Maid
Knudsen
Light 'N' Lively
Sealtest
Westwood

Cream Cheese
Kraft

Desserts
Baker's Fudge-Tastics
Cool Whip
Crystal Light
Jell-O

Dry Desserts
Baker's
Certo
D-Zerta
Dream Whip
Jell-O
Minute
Sure-Jell

Dry Grocery
Country Kitchen
Good Seasons
Log Cabin
Minute Rice
Oven Fry
Ronzoni
Shake 'N' Bake
Stove Top

Frozen Foods
Budget Gourmet
Birds Eye
Kraft Entrees
Lender's Bagels
Ronzoni Entrees
Tombstone

Frozen Products
Breyers
Foremost
Frusen Glädjé
Nice 'N' Light
Sealtest
Stater Bros

Grated & Loaf Cheeses
Kraft
Old English
Velveeta

Milk & Novelties
Carousel
Knudsen
Partytime

Miscellaneous
Claussen Pickles
Kraft Horseradish

Natural Cheeses
Casino
Cracker Barrel

Harvest Moon
Knudsen
Kraft
Select-a-Size

Other Cheeses
Churny
Coon
Elkhorn
Kraft
Light 'N' Lively
Polly-O
Velveeta

Pasta Dinners
Kraft
Velveeta

Processed Meats
Louis Rich
Oscar Mayer

Salad Dressings
J. L. Kraft
Kraft
Miracle Whip
Sauceworks
Seven Seas

Seafood
Louis Kemp

Snacks
Cheez Links
Cheez Whiz
Handi-Snacks
Kraft
Mohawk
Velveeta
Zap-a-Pack Cheez Whiz

Soft Drinks
Country Time
Crystal Light
Kool-Aid
Tang

Speciality Foods
Thomas Garraway

Spreads
Chiffon
Parkay

Spreads & Toppings
Breyers
Kraft

Wines & Coolers
Lindemans
Matilda Bay

Example 1 *cont.*

INTERNATIONAL	Philadelphia Brand	Philadelphia Brand
Asia/Pacific	Post	Riespri
Coon	Sanka	Saimaza
Dairylea	Tang	Schebletten
Fruity		Simmenthal
Kool-Aid	*Europe*	Sottilette
Kraft	Bird's	Susanna
Marim	Dairylea	Tang
Maxim	Gevalia	Tranchettes
Maxwell	Gim	Velveeta
Maxwell House	Golden Churn	Vitalite
Philadelphia Brand	Hag	
Tang	Hollywood	*Latin America*
Vegemite	Invernizzina	Cafe Oro
Canada	Jocca	Cheez Whiz
Baker's	Knack & Back	Consomate
Bird's	Kraft	Facilistas
Chase & Sanborn	Krema	Gourmesa
Cheez Whiz	Kuchenland	Jell-O
Hostess	Mareblu Fish	Kibon
Jell-O	Mato Mato	Kool-Aid
Kool-Aid	Maxpax	Kraft
Kraft	Maxwell	Maxwell House
Maxwell House	Maxwell House	Philadelphia Brand
Mellow Roast	Miracle Whip	Q-Refres-Ko
Minute Rice	Miracoli	Rosa Blanca
Miracle Whip	Mozary	Tang
Parkay	Mr. Brains	Velveeta
	Onko	Ziz
	Osella	

Source: Philip Morris, Annual Report 1988.

made a major acquisition in the USA though, paying $600m for the 42 per cent outstanding stake in North American Philips Corporation.

The consumer-electronics division includes Polygram, the world's third-largest record company, which includes the Deutsche Grammophon, Decca and Philips labels. These hold about 45 per cent of the classical recorded music market. To strengthen its position in popular music, in 1989 it acquired two major independent labels, Island Records ($330m) and A&M ($500m). Bon Jovi, Def Leppard, Dire Straits, Elton John, Brian Ferry, Level 42, Sting and U2 are among the international artists signed to labels owned by Philips.

Consumer electronics, however, is the bête noir of the group, and restructuring has proved necessary as Philips has one of the highest debt ratios (70 per cent) and lowest profit margins (1.8 per cent) in the world electronics industry. In 1988, 16 plants were closed with the loss of 8,500 jobs, and further divestments may prove necessary.

In order to improve corporate control and coordination, Philips is in the process of fundamental reorganization and faces an uncertain future.

political risk. Government intervention in the economy, in both developed and developing countries, increases the risk that multinationals will be subjected to costs or losses arising from government actions such as foreign currency controls, expropriation, changes in tax laws, production controls and pollution controls. There are two basic approaches to measuring political risk: from a country-specific perspective and a firm-specific perspective. The macro perspective attempts to quantify the overall situation in each country. A number of commercial and academic forecasting models are available which normally supply indexes quantifying the level of political risk in each country. In essence, the purpose of these indicators is to measure political stability and to assess likely changes in government which may affect guarantees given to foreign investors. There is little evidence, however, that these indicators are good predictors of political risk. Moreover, not every company in a country is likely to face the same degree of political risk. The micro perspective suggests that company-specific political risk will depend on factors such as industry, size, ownership and technology. Expropriation, for example, seems more likely to occur in the extractive, financial services, and public utility sectors of the economy than in the manufacturing sector. Thus political risk has a different meaning and impact for each company.

polycentric organization. A multinational company which is responsive to the differences and pressures in its many operating environments. A polycentric company is organized by geographical area in a decentralized manner with independent profit centres. The regional manager controls the product lines of the operating companies in a particular geographical area. However, there may be potential for confusion within the organization unless communications are carefully managed as there tends to be little coordination of operations on a worldwide basis.

portfolio diversification. The holding of a variety of securities, usually shares, in order to reduce the variability of returns. Diversification reduces risk when security price movements are not perfectly correlated with one another. The risk that can be eliminated by diversification is known as unsystematic or unique risk whereas the risk that cannot be avoided however much you diversify is known as systematic or market risk, which stems from the existence of economy-wide events which affect all companies. In an international context, it is possible to diversify more widely with consequent additional risk-reduction effects.

Procter & Gamble (P&G) [USA]. Founded in 1837, it has grown to become one of America's top 20 companies with sales of almost $20bn. It is a global leader in detergents, diapers or nappies, and personal products, selling more than 160 brands in 140 countries. Its brands include housecare products such as Ariel, Dash, Fairy Liquid, Flash and Tide; personal products such as Crest toothpaste, Head & Shoulders shampoo, Camay and Zest soaps, Oil of Ulay skincare cream, Pampers disposable nappies and Vicks healthcare products. Promoting such brands is expensive. In 1988 P&G spent £58m on advertising in the UK, more than any other company. In 1978 the largest advertiser (i.e. Rowntree Mackintosh) spent £10.7m (see tables 1–3). In 1988, P&G was the second-largest advertiser in the USA, spending $1.4bn, behind Philip Morris with $1.6bn.

P&G's first overseas plant was in Canada (1915) followed by the UK (1930), Continental Europe (1950s and 1960s) and the Middle East and Japan (1970). It now has 53 plants in the USA and more than 60 overseas, with worldwide employment of 73,000.

During the 1980s, P&G faced a major crisis when the corporate logo was alleged to be a satanic symbol. The company found its products were being boycotted and the logo was removed from all product packaging.

Table 1 Top ten advertisers in the UK, 1978

Company	Spend (£m)	Rank 1978	Rank 1988
Rowntree Mackintosh	10.7	1	16
Cadbury	10.5	2	17
Mars	8.8	3	6
Boots	7.9	4	57
Lever Brothers	7.5	5	11
British Leyland Cars	7.3	6	9[a]
Procter & Gamble	7.2	7	1
Gallaher	6.4	8	13
Brooke Bond Oxo	6.0	9	10
British Railways Board	5.5	10	52

[a] Austin Rover Group only
Source: Media Expenditure Analysis Ltd

Table 2   Top ten advertisers in the UK, 1988

By company	1988 (£m)
Procter & Gamble	58.0
British Telecom	45.6
Kellogg's	41.2
Nestlé	36.1
Pedigree Petfoods	34.5
Mars Confectionery	33.9
Electricity Council	32.9
Vauxhall Motors	32.8
Austin Rover Group	30.9
Brook Bond Batchelors	30.1

Source: Media Expenditure Analysis Ltd

Table 3   Top five advertisers in the USA, 1987

By company	1987 ($bn)
Philip Morris	1.6
Procter & Gamble	1.4
General Motors	1.0
Sears	0.89
RJR–Nabisco	0.84

Source: Advertising Age

product differentiation. A marketing process which establishes a separate identity, and thus a separate market demand, for a firm's product which has several similar competitors. Differentiation may be promoted through the use of brand names, special packaging and extensive advertising (e.g. soap powder).

product life cycle. The product life-cycle theory of international trade and investment, the brain-child of Raymond Vernon of the Harvard Business School, provides a useful explanation of world trade patterns in the 1950s and 1960s. The theory begins with the proposition that new products and processes are developed in response to cost and demand conditions in the innovator's domestic market. Initially, demand is limited and insensitive to price. As demand expands at home and later in foreign markets, the innovating firm exports abroad. Over time, demand expands in all markets and becomes more price-sensitive. At a later stage, product and process technologies become more diffused and production begins abroad. In this stage, production runs are longer and more capital-intensive (to reduce costs). In the final stage, producers abroad are now cost-competitive in the innovator's market and export back to the originating country which becomes a net importer.

By the mid-1970s, however, technological capabilities had increased to the extent that new product and process technologies could be transferred rapidly at relatively low cost outside the innovating country. The movement of many products over the cycle often becomes so rapid that exports from the innovating countries do not occur and imports from abroad, based on lower production costs owing to lower wage costs, soon follows their introduction.

product-line stretching. The development of a line of related products to meet the needs of different customer segments. In the international business context, entry into foreign markets is typically gradual, with product lines ultimately stretched to include a range of products. Japanese car producers, for example, have gradually moved up from small to high-performance vehicles. The benefits of this approach are in the capacity to use the same marketing and distribution channels and in the protection built up against competitors.

product–process matrix. A form of analysing the relationship between stages in a product's life cycle and stages in the processes used to make the product. A matrix analysis of these relationships shows how the multinational can use both its experience and its technology to achieve an optimal balance in terms of adding value to its business segments.

production smoothing. A means by which multinationals avoid periodic under- and over-capacity which can arise owing to fluctuations in demand caused by competition, consumer shifts, government policy and so on.

Protestant work ethic. An approach to work that views it as a means of securing eternal salvation, pursued for its own sake rather than as a means of enjoying consumer goods, leisure and other benefits.

PSA [France]. With sales in excess of $23bn, France's largest private industrial company produces more than two million cars a year, has 158,000 employees, has 150 export markets, and more than 21,000 points of sale worldwide, though France still accounts for 43 per cent of total sales. PSA (i.e. Peugeot and Citroën) is the market leader in

France with 34.2 per cent. In the EC it is number three, behind Volkswagen and Fiat, with 12.9 per cent of the market, and the gap is narrowing. Despite significant increases in production in France and at Ryton in the UK, which assembles more than 80,000 cars a year (31,000 Peugeot '309' and 52,000 Peugeot '405'), annual sales exceed production. But this has not always been the case.

In 1978 it paid $230m to acquire the European operations of Chrysler (which also received a 12.5 per cent stake in the French company) and by 1981 it had excess capacity. Plants were closed in France and abroad (e.g. Linwood, Scotland). Restructuring measures proved unpopular among the workforce, reaching a climax at the Poissy, Paris plant in 1983, when rival factions of the multiracial workforce – armed with guns and slings – confronted each other in the plant. Peugeot was on the verge of bankruptcy, having incurred heavy losses in the five-year period 1980–4. By 1986 though it had recovered and was reporting healthy profits (i.e. $518m). Its share value increased and Chrysler took the opportunity to sell its stake.

Chairman Jacques Calvet plans to make PSA Europe's leading car manufacturer and market leader. Thus in 1989 it launched the '605' model, aimed at the executive car market which accounts for 14 per cent of all new car sales in Europe, but a sector in which the Peugeot group is weak. The '605' is manufactured at Sochaux, France's single largest industrial site, which has a workforce of 23,000. Almost £900m will have been invested in Sochaux by 1994, and the plant should be capable of producing more than 400,000 cars a year. It will produce different models simultaneously on robotized production lines. The plant's production capacity will by then match that of Fiat's Cassino plant, but it will still have 18,000 employees, while the latter has only 7,000.

The Sochaux plant will rely heavily on JIT. It will have 105 suppliers for the '605', 59 of whom will have to deliver components 4–11 times a day. Consequently, component manufacturers are establishing manufacturing or distribution facilities in close proximity to the plant. This example illustrates why there is so much competition among nations and regions to secure local linkages.

Purchasing Power Parity Theorem. A theorem stating that exchange rate changes reflect international inflation differentials. Intuitively, it seems quite plausible that this would be the case if currencies are treated as bundles of purchasing power and it is assumed that the barriers to international trade are immaterial. The absence of barriers to international trade and the presence of arbitrage would ensure that the law of one price holds, and that the same goods cost the same amount in each country. It is also necessary to assume that the weightings used in different national price indices are similar.

In practice, purchasing power parity is unlikely to provide a very accurate explanation or prediction of exchange rate changes for a number of reasons.

1 In practice the law of one price is flagrantly violated due to trade barriers, inefficiencies and government-imposed distortions in national markets, and the presence of non-traded products (e.g. electricity).
2 Consumption tastes vary across countries. It is unlikely that the components of the Portuguese consumer price index would be the same as the Japanese index.
3 Theories of exchange rate determination based upon goods markets are unlikely to be helpful in a world where capital flows outweigh the financial flows attributable to trade.

In conclusion, purchasing power parity may be a useful indicator of the likely direction of exchange rates if inflation differentials are extremely large and capital flows immaterial. However, if inflation differentials are low, capital flows may be a more significant factor in the determination of exchange rates.

Q

quality circle. A philosophy of human resource management developed in the USA in the 1950s but only implemented on a significant scale, and with great success, by the Japanese. In a quality circle, employees become fully involved in the discussion of problems and the formulation of solutions to quality control and other aspects of production management. Success in terms of improving productivity depends on the company's ability to coordinate people in a harmonious environment.

R

reciprocity. With the deregulation of financial markets has come the concern, especially in the European Community, that banks from non-EC countries may have a competitive advantage where a foreign country does not permit equal freedom of access to EC-based banks. Accordingly, the issue of reciprocity has been raised whereby it is proposed that foreign banks will not be permitted to operate in the EC unless reciprocal arrangements apply. This is currently a highly controversial subject and is the subject of negotiation by interested parties, especially the USA and Japan. The issue of reciprocity is now extending into other areas such as merger regulation and practice where it is claimed that companies in some countries, such as the UK and USA, are more open to takeover bids than those, for example, in France, Germany and Japan.

'red' multinational. With radical changes in Eastern Europe, the term is perhaps a misnomer in the 1990s. Previously, it was used to describe state enterprises from socialist countries which had established branches, subsidiaries and affiliates abroad. These overseas operations are virtually all marketing operations to promote exports of goods manufactured in socialist countries.

The changing economic and political environment of eastern Europe will not only entice substantial increases in inward investment, but provide new opportunities for outward investment. In early 1990, Kombinat Polygraph became the first East German company to acquire a US business. In order to expand sales of its printing machinery in the US market, it paid $35m for Royal Zenith, a New York-based trading and marketing firm.

remittance policy. MNCs' policies regarding the remittance of dividends are frequently an area of contention between the headquarters, foreign subsidiaries and host governments. Some of the difficulties associated with the formulation of a remittance policy include:

1   Local funding requirements of the subsidiary and local interest rates, as well as the extent to which the MNC wishes to create an atmosphere of self-reliance and has policies of new investment being funded from local retained earnings and borrowings.

2 Tax considerations may be paramount in determining local
   dividend policies (*see* INTERNATIONAL TAXATION).
3 Local joint-venture partners may wish to have alternative
   dividend policies.

Renault [France]. This, the largest French industrial corporation with sales
of $27bn, is one of the world's top 30 companies. Excluding its
financial activities, it consists of three divisions: automobiles, which
account for more than 76 per cent of total sales, commercial vehicles
(20.5 per cent) and other industrial companies (3 per cent). The car
division also accounts for more than 75 per cent of group employment. In 1988 it produced almost 2m cars and commercial vehicles,
more than half of which were made in France, where it has 29 per
cent of the car market. However, imported cars account for 37 per
cent of the French car market and Renault has been highly critical of
the UK for welcoming Japanese investors such as Toyota, Nissan and
Honda. It is market leader in Spain and Portugal. In Europe, it has
10 per cent of the car market with the Renault 'Super 5' ranking as
Europe's fourth best-selling car with 4 per cent of the market.
Renault, however, fell from being western Europe's market leader in
1982 to sixth position in 1989.

In Latin America, it is market leader in Argentina (33 per cent) and
Colombia (35 per cent). International sales account for 56 per cent of
the car division's total production and 52 per cent of total group sales.

Renault corporation is a candidate for privatization, confirmation
that it has largely recovered from the massive losses incurred
between 1981 and 1986. In 1984 and 1985 it reported losses of $1.4bn
and $1.2bn respectively. In 1987 it made a profit ($614m) the first in
eight years, before reporting a healthy profit of $1.5bn in 1988. But
the group is still burdened with a massive debt of more than $3bn,
and the French government's proposal to write off $1.2bn – an
essential precursor to privatization – was (at the end of 1989)
awaiting approval from the EC Commission which wanted to ensure
that this did not violate competition policy. Renault's difficulties
reflect its unsuccessful internationalization strategy. Its two most
significant international acquisitions, a 20 per cent stake in Volvo Car
Corporation and a 49 per cent stake in American Motors Car
Corporation, were divested, the latter in particular being a con-
spicuous failure.

In 1985 Georges Besse was appointed chairman and given un-
precedented freedom since Renault's nationalization in 1945 and, for
the first time since then, compulsory redundancies were introduced.
Between 1983 and 1988 total employment fell from 221,000 to 180,000,

most jobs being lost in France where the workforce was reduced from 155,500 to 120,000.

In 1986 Georges Besse was assassinated in Paris by Action Directe, and his successor Raymond Lévy has continued to rationalize operations and to reduce Renault's break-even point in Europe from 2m cars to 1.2m cars a year.

Improving competitiveness has also demanded a rethink of human resource management. Thus, Renault is devoting more resources to training, and in 1988 it introduced a profit-sharing scheme for employees. Its renaissance has also allowed Renault to return in 1989 to Formula 1 racing, providing engines for the Williams–Renault Team, after its financial difficulties had forced it to withdraw. Its recovery has also enabled it to increase R&D expenditure, up 22 per cent in 1988 to more than $700m or almost 3 per cent of total sales. In 1990, Renault and Volvo agreed to a partial merger of interests.

Rhône–Poulenc [France]. With sales of $11bn this is one of the world's top corporations and its ninth largest chemical company. It consists of five sectors: chemicals, which account for 44 per cent of total sales, health (24 per cent), agrochemical (15 per cent), fibres (15 per cent), and others (2 per cent). Although it is established in 140 countries, more than half of the group's 80,000-strong workforce is based in France; international sales (including exports from France) account for more than 70 per cent of total sales. Its objective is to rank among the five world leaders in each of its activities and to be amongst the top ten pharmaceutical companies.

In order to achieve this objective it is committed to international acquisitions in order to 'seize every opportunity to rapidly increase our shares of world markets'. In 1986, Rhône–Poulenc paid $576m to acquire the agricultural chemicals division of Union Carbide. In 1987, FF4.7bn was spent on acquisitions, the largest being the basic chemicals unit of Stauffer Chemical Company from ICI for $520m. In 1988, 11 new businesses were acquired for almost FF2.8bn. These deals saw its US sales rise from $380m or 3 per cent of group sales in 1986 to $1.4bn or 12 per cent of group sales in 1988. In 1989 it spent more than FF10bn on acquisitions, paying £518m for RTZ's chemicals business, and $480m for the speciality chemicals business of GAF of the USA. The following year, it completed its largest ever acquisition, paying $3.2bn for the Rorer Group, a leading US drug maker.

Rhône–Poulenc is investing heavily to become one of the world's top five chemical companies. During the late 1980s, its R&D costs and capital expenditure to upgrade plants, increase capacity, protect the environment and so on, amounted to 6 and 9 per cent of total sales respectively each year. At the same time, the state-owned group has divested peripheral or unprofitable businesses.

RJR–Nabisco [USA]. One of the world's leading consumer products companies, and one of the top 20 US corporations, is the result of the 1985 acquisition by R. J. Reynolds, the tobacco giant (with brands such as Camel, Salem and Winston), of Nabisco Brands, the world's largest biscuit company (with brands such as Oreo cookies, Jacobs biscuits, Ritz crackers). The newly formed group's principal operating units were R. J. Reynolds Tobacco Co., Nabisco Brands, Del Monte Tropical Fruit Co., and Heublein, its drinks business. The $4.2bn acquisition created a company with 120,000 employees, 260 plants in 40 countries, marketing in 160 countries. Each day consumers were buying 80 million packages of the company's products. RJR–Nabisco owns 200 brands in 39 product categories. Contrary to the normal pattern in takeovers, the chief executive of the target company (Nabisco), Ross Johnson, was appointed chief executive of the newly created enterprise. He decided the company should streamline its activities and Heublein was sold for $1.2bn to Britain's Grand Metropolitan.

In 1988, Johnson attempted a controversial management buy-out of RJR–Nabisco. The proposed deal would have made Johnson very rich and he featured in *Time* magazine's cover story, 'A Game of Greed'. The board of RJR eventually agreed to be taken over by Kohlberg Kravis Roberts (KKR), the leveraged buy-out firm, even though KKR's bid of $25.08bn was $620m less than Johnson's. This is by far the largest-ever leveraged buy-out.

Having assumed a record level of debt at a high interest rate to finance the buy-out, KKR has had to abandon risky investments and generate cash. Thus, Premier, the 'smokeless' cigarette, was withdrawn after just five months. With costs amounting to $500m, Premier must rank as one of the most expensive failures of a new product. KKR has recovered around $5.3bn from asset sales, including its European biscuit/snack business to BSN for $2.5bn, and its Del Monte fresh-fruit operations to Polly Peck of the UK for $890m. The Del Monte canned foods business was sold in 1990 for a further $1.5bn.

Rockwell International [USA]. Among America's 30 largest companies, this $120bn conglomerate is involved mainly in the aerospace–electronics industry. Almost 50 per cent of total sales are to one customer – the US government. The Department of Defense alone accounts for almost one third of total sales. Aerospace products, including the Space Shuttle, account for one-third of total sales and electronics account for almost 40 per cent. By country, Rockwell relies on the USA for almost 90 per cent of total sales.

S

Saatchi & Saatchi [UK]. Since its foundation in 1970, and flotation in 1975, it has grown to become, until recently, the world's top advertising agency, and among the top five in public relations, design, sales promotion and direct marketing. The company once planned to become a global business-services conglomerate, but its diversification into management consultancy met with little success and perhaps led to a reappraisal of corporate strategy, despite the huge growth in demand for business services. Worldwide advertising expenditure has doubled in the 1980s from $95.3bn to $195.2bn in 1987. Worldwide consulting fees have more than quadrupled during the same period from $37.5bn to $234.4bn. Little wonder then that takeover activity has been so frenetic in the service sector as firms jostle for this expanding and booming business.

Saatchi's growth has been based largely on acquisitions at home and abroad. It has more than 14,000 employees in almost 60 countries, and its clients include half of the world's 500 largest corporations. It represents 70 clients in five or more countries or sectors.

Saatchi believes the business environment of the late twentieth century demands that companies adopt 'the economic logic of the global approach'. It applies this philosophy in its advertising. For example, it uses the same message worldwide to sell Procter & Gamble's disposable nappies, Pampers. It points to the boom in transnational media as evidence of the age of globalization (e.g. *Dallas* is watched in 95 countries; 10 million European homes in 13 nations receive Sky Channel).

After a decade of expansion and diversification the 1990s are likely to see Saatchi concentrate on its core business, advertising.

Saint Gobain [France]. Founded in 1665 in order to supply glass for the Versailles Palace, then under construction, it ranks today beside Britain's Pilkington Brothers, as the world's leading glass company. This $10bn group with 85,000 employees has more than 200 plants in 19 countries, and is among the world's 100 largest industrial corporations. It is involved in light business lines. The largest flat glass accounts for 20 per cent of sales, followed by insulation (18 per cent) and containers (13 per cent). Geographically, the group is very dependent on Europe which accounts for 80 per cent of sales. It has placed special emphasis on boosting market share in Europe, acquiring stakes or full control of companies in Belgium (St Roche), France (Essilor), Spain (Corina) and Sweden (Gulfiber). It has also taken full control of Certain–Teed in the USA, bringing expenditure on acquisitions in 1986 and 1987 to around S2bn.

Between 1981 and 1986, Saint Gobain was state-owned, and the socialist government had a major say in group strategy. It had diversified into computers and electronics, acquiring large stakes in the French company Bull and Olivetti. The government disapproved and the company was told to sell these stakes.

Saint Gobain was the first privatization in France, and current chairman Jean-Louis Beffa can, unlike his predecessor, make key decisions without political interference.

Samsung [South Korea]. Founded in 1938 as a trading firm by the late Lee Byung-Chull, it has grown to become a giant group of 38 companies with sales approaching S28bn. This Korean conglomerate ranks among the top 15 non-US industrial corporations and among the top 30 worldwide. During its 50-year history the company has diversified from low-tech, labour-intensive industries (e.g. textiles) into high-tech sectors such as electronics, aerospace and genetic engineering.

Samsung Electronics Co. was founded in 1969 and the company grew rapidly, aided by cheap labour and imported technology from Japanese rivals. The bulk of production was exported mainly to the USA. Furthermore, the bulk of these sales was on an OEM basis for US department stores and Japanese rivals. In 1983, 60 per cent of Samsung's electronics sales were on an OEM basis. Progress has been made though, and by 1988, 60 per cent of sales were under Samsung's own brand name. Samsung is determined to become one of the major forces in the global electronics industry. It is thus devoting substantial sums to R&D in order to reduce its reliance on licensed foreign technology. At the same time, creating a global brand name requires heavy expenditure on marketing.

Samsung has also been forced to adjust its international market supply strategy. Pressures at home (rising labour costs and the appreciation of the won) combined with protectionism in key markets (the USA and the EC) have led Samsung to establish production facilities in lower-cost Asian countries and in the West. While these have been greenfield investments, it may not be long before Samsung acquires a well-established consumer electronics business. Such a deal could provide an established brand name, technology and a global production and distribution network.

SBU, *see* STRATEGIC BUSINESS UNIT.

SEC, *see* SECURITIES AND EXCHANGE COMMISSION.

Securities and Exchange Commission (SEC) [USA]. Created by an Act of Congress in 1934, the Securities and Exchange Commission is primarily responsible for the administration of various laws intended to regulate the securities markets and to enhance proper financial reporting and disclosure by stock exchange listed companies for the protection of investors.

Securities and Investment Board [UK]. A private organization to which the government has delegated its powers to regulate and supervise the financial services industry under the Financial Services Act of 1986, for the protection of investors.

securitization. The substitution by corporate borrowers of negotiable securities issued in public capital markets for non-marketable loans from financial intermediaries (e.g. banks). This process is also known as disintermediation. Examples of the process include the use of commercial paper rather than short-term loans from banks and the development of floating rate notes (FRNs) for medium-term borrowings.

This development has been attributed to a variety of factors including:

1 The deregulation of financial markets and the decreased costs of using financial markets.
2 The increased costs of bank borrowing and the fact that some large corporations may have better credit ratings than banks.
3 Improvements in technology which have decreased the costs of evaluating credit worthiness.

Security for Worldwide Interbank Financial Telecommunications, *see* SWIFT.

segmental reporting. With increasing diversification, either by line of business or geographical area, has come the practice of reporting on the various activities or segments of a multinational's business. Consolidated information has become increasingly opaque along with the complexity of business, hence the pressure for more disaggregated or segmental reporting. While most developed countries require companies to provide a minimum amount of segmental information, many multinationals voluntarily disclose information, both quantitative and qualitative, in response primarily to international capital market pressures.

seven sisters. The seven major integrated oil companies which once dominated the world oil business. The seven companies – five American (Exxon, Gulf, Mobil, Chevron and Texaco), one British (BP), one Anglo-Dutch (Shell) – were characterized by their world-wide integration, controlling not only their own production but also transportation, distribution and marketing (see table 1). In 1984 Chevron acquired Gulf, reminiscent of Agatha Christie's *Ten Little Indians*?

Table 1   Major oil takeovers

Deal	Date	Price ($bn)
Du Pont buys Conoco	1981	7.5
USX buys Marathon	1982	6.3
Occidental buys Cities Service	1982	4.1
Phillips buys General American	1983	1.2
Texaco buys Getty Oil	1984	9.9
Chevron buys Gulf	1984	13.2
Mobil buys Superior Oil	1984	5.8
Royal Dutch/Shell buys minority of Shell Oil	1985	5.2
BP buys remainder of Standard	1987	7.8
BP buys Britoil	1988	4.1

Source: Press reports; *Acquisitions Monthly*

Siemens [Germany]. This electrical and electronics giant is one of the world's top 20 largest industrial corporations in terms of sales (in excess of $34bn) and number of employees. Excluding Italy's state-owned IRI, it has more employees than any other European company (see table 1).

In October 1989, Siemens completed a radical reorganization of its corporate structure, having outgrown the previous one implemented in 1969. Seven large operating groups were replaced by 15 units and two independent businesses (see figure 1). This reorganization aimed to accelerate decision-making by removing layers from the managerial hierarchy.

Siemens is concentrating on becoming a global player in electronics, including factory automation, information processing and telecommunications. However, a similar objective is shared by other

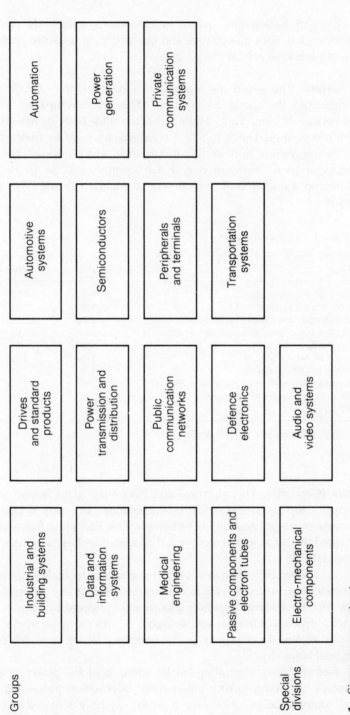

1 Siemens group structure
Source: Siemens

Table 1 Europe's ten largest employers, 1988

Company	Country	Employees
IRI	Italy	417,826
Siemens	FRG	353,000
Daimler–Benz	FRG	338,749
Philips	Netherlands	310,258
Unilever	UK–Netherlands	291,000
Fiat	Italy	277,353
Volkswagen	FRG	252,066
CGE	France	204,100
Nestlé	Switzerland	197,722
Renault	France	181,715

Source: *Fortune*, August 1989

giants, and they have concluded major acquisitions to consolidate their position. Siemens, however, has responded, spending $2bn on acquisitions in 1988. It acquired Bendix Electronics, IN2 – a French computer manufacturer – and Rolm, the telecommunications company which IBM had acquired only years earlier.

In 1989 it joined forces with Britain's GEC to mount a successful £2bn hostile bid for Plessey, the UK electronics firm. In 1990 it acquired the ailing German computer company, Nixdorf. The deal, approved by Germany's Cartel Office, made Siemens second only to IBM in Europe's computer markets.

In 1988 it spent DM11.7bn – around £4bn – on capital investments and R&D – more than any other industrial company in Europe.

Siemens is a truly international group with 173 plants in 35 countries, and under joint venture agreements it has 58 other factories in 26 countries. It operates in 122 countries and it has 130,000 employees outside Germany, 7,000 of whom are engaged in R&D. Despite its extensive international operations, Germany accounts for more than half of total sales, and the rest of Europe another 25 per cent. North America accounts for less than 10 per cent. Siemens is thus seeking to expand in this critical market.

SITC, see STANDARD INTERNATIONAL TRADE CLASSIFICATION.

social charter. The creation of a single market for the EC in 1992 provides business with numerous opportunities. Jacques Delors, the President of the EC, is keen to inject a 'social dimension' into 1992. His social charter seeks to establish an equal playing field in the EC in respect of workers' rights and terms of employment. The charter would establish a minimum wage level, holiday entitlement and health and safety standards, as well as impose a ceiling on the weekly hours which employees may work. As one would expect, trades unions in the EC support Mr Delors' proposals, but employers' groups and certain governments, including the UK especially, appear opposed to the charter.

Sogo Shosha [Japan]. The success of the current champion exporters, the Japanese, is partly attributable to the Sogo Shosha, which consists of nine large general trading companies (GTCs) – Mitsubishi, Mitsui, C Itoh, Marubeni, Sumitomo, Nissho–Iwai, Kanematsu–Gosha, Toyo Menka, Nichiman – but sometimes six smaller companies (Chori, Itoman, Kinsho–Mataicho, Nozaki, Okura, and Toshoku).

Other countries have also established GTCs in the hope that they can emulate the achievements of Japan's Sogo Shosha. The South Koreans have been particularly successful since first establishing such companies in 1975. Korea has eight GTCs – Hyundai, Samsung, Daewoo, Lucky–Goldstar, Sunkyong, Ssangyong, Hyosung and Koti (Korean Trading International Incorporation – an affiliate of the Korea Trade Promotion Corporation).

These Japanese and Korean GTCs are engaged in importing, exporting, countertrade, investing and manufacturing. Their vast size allows them to benefit from economies of scale, and with operations worldwide they can collect, analyse and act upon their massive store of marketing information.

Sony [Japan]. This innovative consumer electronics company – it pioneered the Walkman in 1979 among many other firsts – is best known for its video equipment, audio equipment and televisions, which represent three divisions that account for more than 70 per cent of total sales of $11bn. Its two other divisions are Other Products (i.e. semiconductors, computers and peripherals, telecommunications equipment) and Record Business. In 1987, Sony diversified into software when it paid $2bn in cash for CBS records, the world's largest record label with artistes such as Michael Jackson, George Michael and Bruce Springsteen. Sony also has the world's largest compact disc production capacity with plants in three countries, Japan, Austria, and the USA.

In 1989, in the largest ever Japanese takeover of a US business – as of the end of 1989 – it paid $3.4bn for Columbia Pictures Entertainment, one of America's big-screen film studios. It also assumed $1.4bn of Columbia's debt, and agreed to pay $200m for the services of two of Hollywood's top producers whose hits include *Batman* and

Rain Man. The acquisition gives Sony control of the world's largest film library, as well as two television production companies, and 820 screens in 220 US cinemas.

Outside Japan, Sony has subsidiaries and affiliated companies in 26 countries and manufacturing plants in 15 of these, of which Europe accounts for six, Asia five, and the Americas four. With eight plants in the EC and one in Austria, Sony is well positioned for 1992 and in 1986 it created a regional headquarters for Europe at Cologne in Germany. Worldwide Sony has almost 90,000 employees.

Each year Sony spends between 6 and 9 per cent of total sales on R&D. In common with other television manufacturers it is determined to be at the forefront in developing high definition television (HDTV). In 1989 it thus opened its Advanced Video Technology Centre in the USA, evidence that globalization extends beyond simple manufacturing to R&D.

The Sony Walkman Story

In late 1978 Sony began investigating the possibility of producing a small stereo cassette player with lightweight headphones. At the time its hand-held cassette players did not allow stereo playback and its headphones were large and heavy. Nevertheless Chairman Akio Morita set a firm product launch date of 1 July 1979.

Some months later his staff had devised the name for the new product: 'Walkman'. Morita had reservations but a change of name was out of the question as all the packaging and promotional materials had been ordered. In order to promote the novel product and save on a small advertising budget, Sony paid part-time student workers to wear and listen to their Walkmans in busy public places, especially the bustling Ginza section of Tokyo.

In Japan the product was very successful and the sales potential in overseas markets was obvious. However, both Sony Corporation of the USA and Sony UK opposed using the 'Walkman' name. The former proposed 'Soundabout', the latter 'Stowaway', but Morita insisted that they used 'Walkman'.

During the first ten years, Sony made 50 million Walkman, cassette players and the name was entered in the *Oxford English Dictionary*. (*Source*: Sony.)

source–market matrix. A means of analysing the relationship between the supply of products and the demand for the products in the multinational's various markets. The aim of constructing a matrix is to help the multinational plan its production management owing to the fact that production and logistical costs will vary. In this way, excess production, leading to a build-up of inventory costs, can be avoided and also underproduction which can lead to out-of-stock situations.

sovereign risk. The possibility that a government may exercise its sovereign power and refuse to repay loans to foreign lenders. Alternatively a government might prevent local firms from honouring their international debts. Country risk is a related concept. As such it is the risk of default by a sovereign nation. The advent of the international debt problem has led to sovereign risk becoming a critical issue in international lending.

Standard International Trade Classification (SITC). A system for classifying commodities, products or services for the purposes of compiling and analysing trade statistics. First drawn up by the United Nations in 1950 it is periodically revised to incorporate appropriate changes in the constituents and groupings.

Stiftung. A legal form of organization, something akin to a trust, in the principality of Liechtenstein in continental Europe, which has become popular for personal tax haven purposes. Its advantages are that anonymity can be preserved and regulation is minimal.

strategic business unit (SBU). Strategic management is often implemented through the multinational's strategic business units (SBUs). These consist of a product line or group of similar lines with similar advantages in technological, manufacturing or marketing terms and with a well-defined market and competitors. The multinational will have a number of SBUs and will need to decide how best to incorporate and coordinate the strengths of the SBUs into its overall strategy.

strategic intent. As a counter to strategies based on imitation, which abet the process of competitive decline, G. Hamel and C. K. Prahalad (Harvard Business Review, May–June 1989) argue that 'strategic intent' captures the essence of winning battles for global leadership. It is based on the vision of a desired leadership position and criteria the organization should use to chart progress towards that goal. While 'strategic intent' is stable over time it permits flexibility of operation, motivates people more effectively, and is a better guide to resource allocation. Examples of this in action are Canon compared to Xerox; and Komatsu compared to Caterpillar.

strategy, *see* COMPETITIVE STRATEGY, CORPORATE DIVERSIFICATION,

CORPORATE STRATEGY, EXCHANGE RATE, GLOBAL STRATEGY, HUMAN
RESOURCE MANAGEMENT, STRATEGIC INTENT.

subsidiary company. A company which is controlled by another
company, usually, but not necessarily, by share ownership. A subsidiary is usually included for reporting purposes in the consolidated
accounts of the MNC.

sunrise industry. An industry which is growing rapidly and which offers
opportunities to investors, because of consumer demand, technological changes, environmental circumstances and so on. Examples
are electronics, health care, leisure. These can be contrasted with
declining or 'sunset' industries such as shipbuilding.

swaps. Swaps have become increasingly popular in the past few years, and
many bond issues are now swap-related. The most common types are
interest rate swaps and currency swaps.

Interest rate swaps

An agreement between two parties to exchange interest payments on
an agreed notional amount for a particular maturity. The important
point is that it is a notional amount, so the principal is not exchanged.
The exchange of interest payments may be:

1 *Coupon swap*: the parties to the transaction exchange fixed for
   floating rate coupons.
2 *Basis swap*: the parties exchange coupons based upon e.g. LIBOR
   for coupons based upon e.g. 90-day treasury bills.

Clearly, there are many variations upon these themes; however, they
are used by corporations to manage interest rate risk. For example, a
savings and loan (similar to a building society in the UK) may have
assets consisting of fixed interest rate mortgages and liabilities which
are based upon floating rates. If the current interest rate exceeds the
rate associated with the mortgages, then the mortgage portfolio will
become unprofitable. In order to avoid this eventuality, the savings
and loan might consider swapping its fixed rate assets for floating
rate assets.

Currency swaps

Currency swaps involve swapping two different currencies and
repaying the amounts according to some predetermined rule. This
rule may reflect interest differentials and anticipated changes in the
underlying principal.

If the interest payments are fixed rates, then the payments will be similar to those associated with a series of spot and forward contracts. A currency swap differs from a parallel loan insofar as the principal is unlikely to appear on the company's balance sheet since it is not a loan.

In a frictionless capital market, we would expect that swaps would not occur. However, in practice, firms may have a comparative advantage in certain segments of the debt market, and a swap represents a way of capitalizing upon these distortions.

For example, a US firm may have ready access to fixed rate markets while a UK firm may have ready access to floating rate markets. There may be some scope for the firms to swap their obligations in order to alter exposure to interest rate risk. Usually, banks will mediate between the two counterparties. And the gains from the swap will be divided between the bank and the two counterparties.

SWIFT (Security for Worldwide Interbank Financial Telecommunications). A computer network dedicated to supporting the electronic transfer of funds internationally between over 900 member banks worldwide.

syndicated loan. Many large companies and countries may wish to borrow large tranches of debt and a single bank may be reluctant to lend such a large amount of money to a single firm. This would arise either because of limits upon the size of loans, or because the bank wished to diversify its credit risks. Syndication involves a single bank (a lead bank) approaching a number of other banks to form a syndicate. The members of the syndicate then advance a proportion of the loan to the lead bank's customer. The lead bank obtains the largest fee since it is required to find participants in the syndicate and has given a commitment to the customer to lend money. In some cases the lead bank may also involve some managing banks who also commit themselves at the outset, before the participants are approached.

Increasingly, syndication is becoming less attractive to large MNCs, since it is quite possible that a large MNC may have a better credit rating than a bank. This in turn has led to companies issuing debt in the Euromarkets, and banks advising on and underwriting the issue.

T

takeover bid. A bid by a company or individual to take over the control and management of another company. The bid may take the form of an offer of cash or of shares in the bidding company, where the offer is made by a company. The bid may also be in the form of a combination of cash and shares, or shares with a cash alternative. The 1980s was the decade of the mega-bid made possible by the ready availability of loan finance especially in the form of 'junk bonds'. See table 1 for details of the world's largest takeover bids to date.

tariff. Taxes levied on imports to a country are called tariffs or import duties. They may be *ad valorem* in which case they may be decreased by the use of transfer pricing (unless there are standard prices available for the goods), or they may be a fixed amount per unit imported. As such, they are a barrier to trade since they discourage the local purchase of imports. The advent of GATT and free trade agreements amongst countries (e.g. the EC, EFTA) has increased the importance of non-tariff barriers. These may range from quotas to esoteric health regulations. *See also* AD VALOREM DUTY, NON-TARIFF BARRIER.

taxation, taxes, *see* AD VALOREM DUTY, ANTI-DUMPING DUTY, DEBT FINANCE, INTERNATIONAL TAXATION, UNITARY TAXATION, VALUE ADDED TAX, WITHHOLDING TAX.

technical analysis, *see* CHARTISM.

technology transfer. Modern technology involves not only formulae, machines and products but also salesmen, production workers, management, finance and ongoing research and development. The value of technology lies in the package of expertise surrounding a specific product or process. The transfer of such technology by multinationals is a complex and controversial process and often subject to government regulation. Home governments may be concerned about the export of technology which may result in job losses. Host governments, on the other hand, will pressure multinationals to locate research and development activity abroad but at the same time may be concerned about possible inhibitions to the development of local firms. Multinationals want to protect their rights in technology and tend to do so by transferring it through their own internal markets

Table 1 The world's largest takeover bids

Target	Target activity	Bidder	Bidder activity	Value (£bn)	Date
RJR–Nabisco	tobacco and food	KKR	leveraged buyout	14.3	1988
B.A.T.	tobacco and food	Hoylake	leveraged buyout	13.0	1989
Gulf Corp.	oil and gas	Standard Oil	oil and gas	9.1	1984
Warner Comm.	films and television	Time	publishing	8.2	1989
Time	publishing	Paramount	holding company	7.8	1989
Getty Oil	oil and gas	Texaco	oil and gas	7.6	1984
Kraft	food	Philip Morris	tobacco and food	7.5	1988
Hospital Corp. of America	health care	American Hospital Supply	health care	5.3	1985
Nabisco	food and packaging	R.J. Reynolds	tobacco	4.9	1985
Beecham	pharmaceuticals	SmithKline	pharmaceuticals	4.5	1989
Cons Gold	mining finance	Hanson	holding company	3.5	1989

Source: Acquisitions Monthly

rather than exploiting their advantage in the external market which is in general not capable of dealing with such a complex package. Attempts by host governments to regulate the technology-transfer process are unlikely to be successful when the power of multinationals involves the crucial interaction between technology, capital and management.

Theory Z. A theory that corporate success depends upon a company's ability to coordinate and motivate people rather than the ability to develop technology to improve productivity.

Thomson [France]. This $13bn corporation consists of two core businesses of roughly equal size, electronics and defence systems (Thomson–CSF) and consumer electronics (Thomson Consumer Electronics). In contrast, in 1982 when Alain Gomez was appointed chief executive, Thomson had 23 basic businesses, many of which were loss-makers. Most of these have been divested and the funds used to consolidate core activities. Consequently, Thomson–CSF (60 per cent owned by Thomson) is the second-largest defence electronics corporation in the world, Thomson Consumer Electronics (TCE) is the world's fourth-largest consumer electronics business, and SGS–Thomson is Europe's second-largest manufacturer of semiconductors, and twelfth-largest worldwide. The Thomson group operates 155 plants, technical centres, etc. of which 65 are located outside France, in 50 countries. It has almost 104,000 employees of whom 48 per cent are employed overseas. Europe remains Thomson's largest market, accounting for just over 50 per cent of total sales.

Despite the success of Japanese giants and other Asian producers, Thomson is investing heavily in expanding its consumer electronics business. TCE is the largest consumer electronics company in the USA, following its acquisition of General Electric's RCA business in 1987. It is US market leader in televisions, video cassette recorders (VCRs) and audio equipment. In Europe it has acquired Telefunken from Germany's AEG, and Ferguson from Britain's Thorn–EMI, and is now number two in televisions and VCRs. TCE has 43 plants in 16 countries, and 8 R&D centres in the USA, Europe and Asia. It has more than 52,000 employees, 92 per cent of whom are based outside France. But TCE also relies on international subcontractors. VCRs for the US market are obtained from Asian producers.

The key to success for TCE and Thomson's CSF is technology, and semiconductors in particular. Thus in 1987 Thomson merged its chip business with Italy's SGS to form Europe's second-largest semi-conductor company. In 1987 SGS–Thomson lost $131m, but five plant closures and job losses helped it return a modest profit (S2.2m) in 1988. In order to grow rapidly, SGS–Thomson will have to reduce its dependence on the European market which accounts for 58 per cent of its sales. Europe though holds just 18 per cent of the world market, as against the USA's 30 per cent and Japan's 40 per cent.

Three M (3M), *see* MINNESOTA MINING & MANUFACTURING.

Toyota [Japan]. In 1960 it ranked as the world's 14th-largest car producer, and was the sole Japanese representative in the top 15. It is now the clear number three and has been joined by five other Japanese producers. Japan's 11 auto producers now account for almost 30 per cent of the world's total car production.

Toyota 7,000 sales outlets in more than 150 countries sold almost 3,900,000 vehicles in 1988. In Japan alone it sold more than 2m vehicles, the first company to achieve this, and one-third of the 6m vehicles sold by Japan's 11 auto producers in Japan.

In 1988 almost 46 per cent of Toyota's Japanese car production of 894,000 units was exported. It has 87,000 employees, and plants in 21 countries.

In North America Toyota sells around 1m vehicles a year and in order to serve this market it now produces 50,000 Corollas each year at its Ontario, Canada plant; 200,000 Camrys at its Kentucky plant; and 150,000 Corollas at its California plant which is a 50–50 joint venture with GM, and which also produces the Chevrolet Nova. Similarly, with its annual sales approaching 500,000 units in Europe, a new plant is under construction at Burnaston in the UK. When complete, it will produce 200,000 cars each year and the engines for these vehicles will be supplied from an equally new £140m facility in Wales. Toyota also has a minority stake in a plant in Portugal which assembles a number of Toyota commercial vehicles. In Australasia, it has a stake in plants producing Toyota vehicles in seven countries.

Toyota is very sensitive to 'local circumstances and values' and its main US and UK plants aim to maximize local content. Moreover, Toyota declined the public grants it was entitled to when it established its UK plants.

Renowned for its conservative management methods, in 1989 Toyota announced a radical restructuring of its personnel and management systems in order to 'streamline decision-making . . . and enhance organisational flexibility'. In a significant departure from Japanese culture, employees are now evaluated more on performance than on age or rank. Deferential titles for senior management have been dropped, and instead all are now referred to by the suffix 'san' (i.e. Mr or Ms).

trademark. A sign or mark of identification to distinguish a company's products from those of its competitors. Trademark legislation is designed to provide legal protection of trademarks so as to preserve fair competition, to ensure quality and identification for the consumer. The registration of trademarks is not compulsory but is often advantageous to companies as a means of differentiating products and encouraging consumer loyalty.

transfer pricing. Prices set by multinationals in respect of internal transactions between its business units in different countries. The internalization of transactions means that prices are explicitly determined within the organization (subject to the effectiveness of external constraints) rather than by the market. In many cases there may be no arms-length or market price equivalent. Transfer pricing may be used to minimize global taxation, by shifting profits to lower tax jurisdictions or to get around exchange controls. However, the potential for this is limited by governmental monitoring and control. Transfer pricing also poses problems when it comes to evaluating the business and managerial performance of its strategic business units. Transfer-pricing decisions may adversely affect the motivation of managers while minimizing taxation. Accordingly, different transfer prices may be appropriate for different purposes. *See* INTERNATIONAL TAXATION.

transnational corporation, *see* MULTINATIONAL CORPORATION.

Triad. Kenichae Ohmae, management consultant and author of *Triad Power*, warns companies that the key corporate battlefield is the Triad, namely the American, European and Japanese markets. In order to succeed, firms must strive to establish a presence or ties in each market; hence the upsurge in transnational alliances, international joint ventures and takeovers. Ohmae stresses that cooperation will benefit Japanese and western companies alike, but some western academics have reviewed such alliances and concluded that the benefits invariably flow in one direction, from west to east. While the academic debate rages, industrialists seem more convinced by Ohmae's thesis, judging by the steady formation of strategic partnerships.

turn-key project. A project in which the multinational constructs a factory or facility and trains the personnel necessary to run it so that the facility is ready to be turned on or commence operation when the project is completed. Effectively, the project involves the sale of a fully operational facility.

U

UN, see UNITED NATIONS.

UNCTAD, see UNITED NATIONS CONFERENCE ON TRADE AND DEVELOPMENT.

UNICE (Union [Confederation] of Industries of the European Community) [Switzerland]. The business lobby or employers' counterpart to the European Trade Union Confederation.

Unilever [UK–Netherlands]. Formed in 1930, the world's largest personal products company, and one of the largest food companies, consists of Unilever NV, with headquarters in Rotterdam, and Unilever PLC, based in London. Unilever has a three-man chief executive known as the Special Committee and identical boards. Unilever's core activities are detergents, food, agri-business, personal products and speciality chemicals. It has 291,000 employees and is active in 75 countries with manufacturing plants in most of them. Its sales of almost $30bn are derived mainly from Europe (60 per cent) and North America (20 per cent). Despite its size, the name Unilever is relatively unknown among consumers, but British consumers in particular will be surprised at how many Unilever products they use regularly.

Since 1983, Unilever has implemented a radical acquisition and disposal programme in order to consolidate its core businesses. Between June 1983 and August 1989, Unilever concluded around 120 acquisitions worth £6.1bn, of which the most important were Britain's Brooke Bond (beverages) and America's Chesebrough–Ponds (personal products) and Shedds (edible fats). During the same period, around 100 divestments worth £2.3bn were made. In 1989, Unilever made another substantial acquisition with the purchase of Fabergé and Elizabeth Arden. The $1.55bn deal made Unilever equal first with L'Oréal of France in the world's cosmetics league, having previously paid $306m for Calvin Klein cosmetics.

In order to maintain its position of leadership in its main business, Unilever will no doubt continue to undertake many acquisitions, some of which will be very large. At the same time, the company will continue to invest in R&D. In 1988, 2 per cent of sales (£360m) was expended on R&D, almost half of which was allocated to its four central laboratories (two in the UK, one in the Netherlands, one in the USA).

Example 1   A sample of Unilever's brands

Foods: Batchelors soup, Bird's Eye frozen foods, Brooke Bond and
  Lipton teas, Oxo cubes, Ragu spaghetti sauce, Walls ice-cream,
  John West canned fish
Soaps: Shield, Lux, Lifebuoy, Knight's Castille, Pears
Detergents: Persil, Surf, Comfort, Jif, Vim, Frish, Domestos
Personal products: Mentadent, Signal, SR and Close Up toothpastes,
  Sunsilk, All Clear and Timotei hair shampoo and conditioner;
  Harmony hairspray; Sure and Lynx anti-perspirant; Impulse
  deodorant, Vaseline
Perfumes and after-shaves: Brut, Chloë, Lagerfeld, Obsession, Passion

---

Union of Industries of the European Community, *see* UNICE.

Unisys [USA]. Formed in June 1986 through the $4.8bn merger of
computer giants Burroughs and Sperry, Unisys is the world's third-
largest computer company with sales of $10bn, and among the
world's top 100 industrial corporations. The name 'Unisys' was
chosen as the best entry in the company-wide competition to devise a
new name for the merged group. Project manager Lee Machen
received his prize of $5,000, and a $20m worldwide advertising
campaign was launched to promote the new corporate identity.
  Mainframes and peripherals account for almost one-third of total
sales, but this segment of the computer industry faces a major shake-
out and Unisys may have to reduce employment from the current
level of more than 90,000.
  Unisys has 75 plants, many of which are abroad, mainly in the UK,
Canada, France, Germany, Brazil and Australia. Foreign sales
account for 46 per cent of the total.

unitary taxation. Given the opportunities for MNCs to decrease income in
high tax jurisdictions, an alternative technique for calculating taxable
income is known as unitary taxation whereby tax is levied on a
proportion of the MNC's worldwide income irrespective of the profit
or loss reported in any particular country or region.

Example

Suppose that Dodger Corporation operates in two states Hitaxes and
Lotaxes, and that tax rates are 50 per cent and 10 per cent respectively. Moreover, assume that 90 per cent of the company's manufac-

turing takes place in Hitaxes and that 80 per cent of sales are in Hitaxes. Tax planners at Dodger have ensured that 90 per cent of income arises in Lotaxes in order to minimize the company's tax liability. The government of Hitaxes might consider the introduction of a unitary taxation system which is based upon a proportion of worldwide income for the company, rather than income arising in Hitaxes alone. To determine the appropriate proportion of worldwide income, they might consider using a weighted average of the proportion of local manufacturing and local sales. This would result in 85 per cent of Dodger's total income being subject to taxes in Hitaxes.

The use of this method was operated, but subsequently withdrawn, by a number of states, notably California, in the USA in the 1970s and 1980s, with resultant friction between the US and other governments.

United Nations (UN) [Switzerland, USA]. A multilateral organization that deals with social, economic and political issues. With a membership of over 150 nations it now tends to be dominated by the developing countries. The Charter of the United Nations was signed on 26 June 1945. The purposes of the UN concern security, justice, welfare and human rights. The UN aims to settle disputes without using force. It meets once a year in the form of the General Assembly. There is also the Security Council which meets when any action is being considered. Any one of the permanent members of the Security Council (including the USA, USSR, France and the UK) has the power of veto over any intervention involving the use of force. Another major organ of the UN is the Economic and Social Council which carries out its broad humanitarian policy through the coordination of a number of organizations including the UN Conference on Trade and Development (UNCTAD), the General Agreement on Tariffs and Trade (GATT), the World Bank, the International Monetary Fund (IMF) and the Commission on Transnational Corporations (UNCTC). *See also* UNITED NATIONS COMMISSION ON TRANSNATIONAL CORPORATIONS, UNITED NATIONS CONFERENCE ON TRADE AND DEVELOPMENT.

United Nations Commission on Transnational Corporations (UNCTC) [USA]. A body established by the United Nations in the early 1970s to help ensure effective international arrangements for the operations of transnational (or multinational) corporations and to improve international understanding of the nature and impact of their activities. The commission has established an information centre on transnational corporations and has conducted enquiries into a number of issues including transfer pricing, taxation and international standards of accounting and reporting.

United Nations Conference on Trade and Development (UNCTAD) [USA]. The first conference was held in 1964 and was subsequently established as a permanent UN organization with conferences held on a regular basis. There is now a membership of 136 countries. The motivation for the conference is the concern by developing countries to obtain trade concessions, such as preferential tariffs and commodity agreements, from the developed countries as well as any other actions which will promote their development, e.g. the transfer of technology.

V

value added statement. A financial statement used in corporate reporting. It shows the results of operations attributable to all participants, apart from suppliers, and the distribution of the surplus thus created to shareholders (or investors), employees, lenders and governments (in the form of taxation). This can be contrasted with the conventional income statement or profit and loss account which shows results primarily from the perspective of the shareholders. The term 'value added' is used to indicate value added by the efforts of the corporation to that value brought in from outside. Thus 'value added' may be taken to represent, in monetary terms and for a particular period, the 'net output' of a corporation, i.e. the difference between the total value of its output and the value of the corresponding inputs (materials and services) obtained from other corporations.

value added tax (VAT). A popular form of indirect taxation in western Europe and some Latin American countries. Essentially it is a sales tax which is collected at each stage of production rather than at the point of retail sale. The tax is levied upon the value added at each stage of production. The nature of the tax is illustrated below.

Example

A vineyard owner produces one ton of grapes per annum at $15 per ton. The VAT rate is 10 per cent and he invoices a wine company for $16.50 and pays $1.50 to the revenue authorities. The wine company manufactures wine, bottles it and sells it to a retailer for $60 plus 10 per cent VAT. The wine company then pays VAT to the revenue authorities of $4.50 ($6 tax collected −$1.50 tax paid). The retailer then sells the wine to consumers for $90 plus 10 per cent VAT. The retailer then pays VAT to the revenue authorities of $3 ($9 − $6). These steps are outlined in table 1, and the reader should note that

Table 1 VAT on wine batch

	Revenue net of VAT	Value added	VAT @ 10%	Cumulative VAT
Vineyard	15	15	1.5	1.5
Wine Co.	60	45	4.5	6
Retailer	90	30	3	9

the amount of tax collected is identical to the application of a 10 per cent sales tax at point of retail sale.

VAT rates can be as high as 25 per cent in some EC countries, and normally the rates vary depending upon whether goods are luxury or essential items. Some products may be exempt from VAT in certain countries.

Appropriate planning for VAT is most important, since it will have significant cash-flow implications. Essentially, one should ensure that the recognition of VAT paid on inputs is accelerated and that the recognition of VAT collected on sales is postponed. In an international context, the need for planning becomes even more critical since VAT is not collected on exports but is levied on imports. Moreover, a number of European countries now collect VAT at the point of import, as distinct from the point of invoice. The international dimension becomes more complex when one recognizes the possibility of varying rates of VAT and the definition of goods subject to higher and lower rates differing from country to country.

VAT, *see* VALUE ADDED TAX.

vertical integration. A form of management organization whereby a multinational controls its sources of supply or raw materials, the facilities to manufacture its goods, and the means of distribution and sale to the markets in which it operates. Increased control of resources, production and markets improves coordination which reduces transaction costs (involving supply uncertainties, logistics and search costs) and increases profits. Oil companies are a case in point where there are four stages of vertical integration – extraction, transportation, refining and distribution. Host governments are, however, sensitive to the power that vertically integrated multinationals can wield with consequent high potential for conflict.

Volkswagen [Germany]. This $30bn corporation sold 2.8m motor vehicles in 1988, making it Europe's leading automobile company and number five in the world. Foreign sales account for 42 per cent of total sales, overseas production accounts for 40.5 per cent of total production, and 87,000 of the group's 252,000 strong workforce are based abroad.

In Germany, it (including Audi) has eight plants, the largest being at corporate headquarters in Wolfsburg, which alone employs 63,500 employees and is the world's largest interconnected automobile plant 'under one roof'. Each working day it produces 3,500 vehicles from the Golf and Jetta ranges, and 500 Polos. The logistics involved are awesome. Each day 16 trains deliver sheet iron, tyres and parts produced in other group factories. Similarly, 14 trains leave the plant with supplies of materials and parts for other factories in the group, while 15 others, each with 200–250 cars, depart the plant to deliver completed vehicles to their destination. Such is the scale of the Wolfsburg plant that it includes 72 kilometres (45 miles) of railway sidings, and a network of roads of equal distance.

Volkswagen has a total of 3,000 industrial robots – most of them made by the company itself – in operation at its German plants. It regards Hall 54 at Wolfsburg, where the Golf is produced, as 'the motor industry's most automated production facility', with assembly being totally mechanized. Overall, though, the smaller Emden plant, which produces the Passat and has 10,000 employees, has 609 robots in use, compared to Wolfsburg's 564.

Outside Germany, Volkswagen's main European production activities are in Spain where it has four plants following the 1986 acquisition of the debt-ridden, loss-making, state-owned SEAT. In 1988 SEAT made a profit for the first time in 11 years, and output rose to 433,482 vehicles, making it the largest vehicle producer in Spain, which now ranks as Europe's fourth-largest car manufacturer (after Germany, France and Italy), and sixth in the world. Volkswagen also has a wholly owned plant in Belgium and a minority stake in Tvornica Automobila Sarajevo (Yugoslavia). In 1988 Volkswagen ceased all production in the USA, leading to expansion at its Mexican plant, which produced 60,000 cars in 1988. The Mexican plant now supplies the market in North America. In South America, Volkswagen has a 51 per cent stake in Autolatina, a joint venture with Ford, which has manufacturing facilities in Argentina and Brazil capable of producing more than 500,000 cars a year.

In China, its joint venture, Shanghai Volkswagen Automotive Co. (formed 1985), produces fewer than 20,000 vehicles a year. Volkswagen also has a licensing agreement with Nissan which permits the Japanese company to produce the Santana at its Zama, Tokyo plant.

Volkswagen's activities are now centred on vehicle production, after a disappointing venture into office equipment. In 1986 it sold Triumph–Adler to Olivetti for $490m. This deal also gave it a 5 per cent stake in the Italian company, one of Europe's leading manufacturers of office automation and data-processing equipment.

In 1988 the German government sold its 20 per cent holding in Volkswagen. During that year, its 50th anniversary, Volkswagen was the victim of a major foreign exchange fraud.

Volvo [Sweden]. Scandinavia's largest industrial company is a $16bn diversified corporation. Its turnover is around 11 per cent of Sweden's GNP and it also accounts for more than 10 per cent of manufacturing employment in Sweden where 55,000 of its total workforce of 79,000 is employed. It has 54 subsidiaries in 18 countries, though Scandinavia accounts for 25 per cent of total sales. Sales of cars, trucks and buses account for just over 50 per cent of total sales. It produces some 400,000 cars a year, mainly at three plants in Sweden and at its Borne factory in the Netherlands. These are sold mainly in the USA, the UK and Sweden itself. In order to boost fleet car sales, Volvo has acquired a 20 per cent stake in the parent company of Hertz Corporation, the world's largest car rental organization. However, excess industry capacity in western Europe has proven a powerful motive for Volvo to seek a partner for its car operations, with Renault a likely suitor.

In trucks, Volvo is the world's number two, after Daimler–Benz which sells under the Mercedes and Freightliner names. It produces some 60,000 trucks a year in seven countries and it has strengthened its US business by forming a joint venture with General Motors. In buses too, Volvo is a major player and it has consolidated its presence by acquiring Britain's Leyland Bus, manufacturer of the famous red double deckers used by London Transport.

In order to remain competitive, Volvo remains committed to R&D which accounts for more than 5 per cent of total sales. The company is also renowned for its attempts at job enrichment and decentralized decision-making. There are just over 100 staff employed at head-quarters, making it one of the smallest head offices of a major multi-national in the world.

In late 1989, Volvo abandoned its diversification strategy, exchanging its pharmaceuticals and food interests for a 42 per cent stake in Procordia, a holding company owned by the Swedish government. In 1990, it entered into a partial merger arrangement with Renault.

W

Westinghouse [USA]. The principal markets of this $13bn diversified corporation, with 120,000 employees, include electronics and energy and utility systems among others. It consists of 21 operating business units and 57 plants and offices, providing almost 17,000 jobs in 15 countries. Foreign subsidiary sales, however, are less than half of those to the corporation's largest single customer, the US government and its agencies, which accounts for more than a fifth of total sales.

whistle-blowing. A classic case of 'whistle-blowing', that is, informing the appropriate regulatory authorities of anti-social behaviour, is that of Stanley Adams and Hoffmann La Roche. In the early 1970s, while an executive with Hoffmann La Roche, the Swiss pharmaceutical giant, Adams became disillusioned with his employer's sales policy which included illegal market sharing and price fixing. Before resigning to emigrate to Italy, but after receiving a guarantee from the EC that his identity would not be disclosed, Adams provided the EC Commission with internal documentation as evidence of these misdemeanours. He resigned from La Roche and left Switzerland to run a pig farm in Italy. Unknown to Adams the EC failed to conceal its informant's identity from La Roche, and when he next returned to Switzerland, two years later, he was arrested and imprisoned. The Swiss authorities informed his wife that he faced a lengthy prison sentence, and she took her own life. Adams later jumped bail and fled Switzerland. La Roche was eventually fined £750,000 by the EC Commission which subsequently paid Adams £800,000 in compensation.

withholding tax. A tax levied by governments on dividends or interest paid to foreign investors. While domestic investors can offset such a tax against their personal tax liabilities this is not possible in the case of foreign investors assessed to tax under a different regime. However, double taxation agreements often exist to ensure that the investor is not penalized for investing abroad.

World Bank (IBRD) [Switzerland, USA]. The World Bank consists of a group of three agencies which are a part of the United Nations. The three agencies are the International Bank for Reconstruction and

Development (IBRD) or World Bank, the International Finance Corporation (IFC) and the International Development Association (IDA). The International Center for the Settlement of Investment Disputes operates under the auspices of the World Bank.

1 The World Bank was founded (along with the IMF) at the Bretton Woods Conference in 1944. It lends money to countries at or around market rates for infrastructural projects (e.g. roads, dams, generators) which are likely to show a positive rate of return. More recently, loans have been made to alleviate balance of payments problems. The World Bank insists upon government guarantees for loans.

2 The IFC provides risk capital (loans and equity) to the private sector in developing countries without government guarantees. It is therefore interested in projects which are likely to be profitable.

3 The IDA (founded in 1960) lends money for development projects which are unlikely to offer a commercial rate of return but do offer considerable benefits to the developing country. Loans are expected to be guaranteed by the host government, but the debt service costs are likely to be well below prevailing market rates (e.g. interest-free).

world product mandate. A charter given by a multinational to one of its foreign subsidiaries to develop, produce and market a new product line for the global market. Host nations are keen to attract multinational involvement on this basis and will usually provide incentives. However, most multinationals are wary of such agreements on the grounds of the risk of dissipating their knowledge advantage and the problems of managing parent–subsidiary relationships.

X

X-efficiency. A term coined to describe the efficiency with which management allocates and controls resources within a company. This can be contrasted with allocative efficiency in the context of an economy taken as a whole. The X-efficiency company uses its management skills to the best advantage. It is generally accepted that X-efficiency is greater the more competitive the market.

Xerox [USA]. Despite intense competition from Japanese producers (e.g. Canon, Ricoh, Toshiba, Minolta), Xerox continues to hold 30 to 40 per cent of total world photocopier revenues of approximately $40bn, including sales, service, rentals and supplies. Xerox has manufacturing plants, 100,000 employees, and its products are sold world-wide. During the 1960s Xerox grew rapidly and in 1969 it diversified into computers, paying $900m in stock for Scientific Data Systems. Within six years the deal had gone sour and SDS was closed and written off.

In the meantime, Xerox's patents had expired and the photocopier market was swamped by basic Japanese models. Xerox's three-pronged response was to meet the Japanese challenge in photocopiers and to diversify into high-tech office workstations and financial services. Production costs and the retail price of its photocopiers were slashed by 50 per cent, boosting sales and regaining market share. Xerox has adopted just-in-time component supply, automated assembly, improved quality, but above all product development has been accelerated as the firm invested more than $3bn in R&D during the 1980s. The move into document processing workstations has been unsuccessful, but the foray into financial services has been highly successful. In 1983 it bought Crum and Forster, a property–casualty insurer, and it has since added two investment banks. Xerox Financial Services now accounts for 50 per cent of Xerox's earnings.

Z

zaibatsu, *see* KEIRETSU.

BUSINESS INFORMATION SOURCES: A SELECTED BIBLIOGRAPHY

SOURCE MATERIALS

General

Anbar Abstracts, UK, Anbar Publications (updated quarterly).
   In five sections: Accounting and Data Processing Abstracts; Marketing and Distribution Abstracts; Personnel and Training Abstracts; Top Management Abstracts; Work Study plus O&M Abstracts. Abstracts of articles from up to 250 periodicals, arranged and indexed in a subject coded sequence.

Business Periodicals Index, USA, H. W. Wilson (updated monthly with annual cumulation).
   International coverage, with strong US emphasis. All aspects of business and commerce are covered, with references taken from over 250 journals. Arranged by subject with an index listing articles by company name.

Company Information Directory, UK, Euromonitor Publications Ltd, Business Line Series, 1987.
   Directory of major international databases providing company information. All listed databases are accessible from UK hosts.

EIU Country Reporting Service, Economist Intelligence Unit.
   This service is based on two series: Country Profiles, covering 165 individual countries in an annual volume, and Country Reports which are issued quarterly. Both series provide an analysis of the political and economic situation in each country covered.

Europa World Yearbook, UK, Europa Publications Ltd, 1989 (updated annually).
   This yearbook, published in two volumes contains detailed descriptions of each country and its history, together with information on the economic situation, political situation and other relevant information. Listings of governments, trade organizations and chambers of commerce are also provided for each of the listed countries.

Index of Conference Proceedings Received, UK, British Library (monthly).
   Lists all conference papers from UK and international conferences and symposia which are held by the British Library.

OECD Economic Surveys, UK, HMSO (updated annually).
   This series of individual surveys provides detailed information on each of the OECD member countries, including statistical and trade data and general background information on each country.

On-line Business Sourcebook, UK, Headland Press Ltd, 1986.
   Directory of on-line databases covering general business topics, in addition to company information databases.

Pan-European Associations: a Directory of Multinational Organizations in Europe, Henderson, C. A. P. (ed.), UK, CBD Research, 1983.
   Directory of organizations with branches in other European countries.

Reports Index, UK, Business Surveys Ltd (updated bi-monthly).

Contains information on articles related to business and commerce which appear in a variety of publications including market research reports.

Research Index, UK, Business Surveys Ltd (updated monthly).

Indexes articles relating to business which appear in over 100 UK newspapers and periodicals. All articles are indexed twice: by subject and by company. Cumulations of each section are produced, viz. subject index cumulates into Research Index Industries Amalgamation (quarterly), and the companies section becomes Research Index Companies Amalgamation (monthly, with cumulations three times per year).

SCIMP: European Index of Management Periodicals, Manchester Business School (updated monthly: cumulated three per year).

Contains references taken from over 150 journals. Articles are indexed by author, subject and company, and are listed in subject groupings.

Directories

Current Asian and Australasian Directories: a Guide to Directories Published in or Relating to all Countries in Asia, Australasia and Oceania, Anderson, I. G. (ed.), UK, CBD Research, 1st edn, 1978 (irregular).

This publication provides a list of directories published in or relating to Asia and Australia.

Current British Directories: a Guide to Directories Published in the British Isles, Henderson, C. A. P. (ed.), UK, CBD Research, 11th edn, 1988.

A comprehensive listing of directories produced in or relating to the UK, covers all type of trade, commercial and professional directories.

Current European Directories: a Guide to International, National, City and Specialized Directories and Similar Reference Works for all Countries of Europe Excluding Great Britain and Ireland, Henderson, G. P. (ed.), 2nd edn, 1981 (irregular).

Provides information on the major directories produced in or pertaining to Europe.

Directory of Directories, Marlow, C. A. (ed.), USA, Gale Research, 6th edn, 1988.

Predominantly American in scope, this two-volume work lists directories on all topics, including business, trade and commerce.

Guide to American Directories, Klein, B. (ed.), USA, B. Klein Publishing, 11th edn, 1988.

Provides a comprehensive listing of directories published in or pertaining to the USA.

The Top 3,000 Directories and Annuals 1987–88, UK, Alan Armstrong & Associates, 1988.

Provides information on the main directories and annuals. Predominantly British in scope. New edition due 1991.

Trade Directories of the World, USA, Croner Publications, 1987.

Provides information on classified trade directories worldwide.

Company and general financial information

Africa

Worldtrade Africa Business Directory, UK, Owen's Worldtrade Ltd, 1988.
Provides detailed company information arranged geographically, covering most African countries. Also includes general information on banking, finance, industry and tourism in the countries covered.

Asia

Asia's 7,500 Largest Companies, UK, ELC International, 1989 (updated annually).
Provides company information on the largest Asian corporations ranked by turnover.

Australia and the Far East

Australian Key Business Directory, UK Dun & Bradstreet International, 1989 (updated annually).
Provides company information on around 18,000 Australian companies ranked by number of employees, in two volumes. Vol. 1 includes companies with over 50 employees; vol. 2 covers companies with 20–49 employees.
Japan Company Handbook: First Section Firms, Japan, Tokyo Shinposha Ltd, (The Oriental Economist).
Japan Company Handbook: Second Section Firms, Japan, Tokyo Shinposha Ltd, (The Oriental Economist).
Provides detailed company and financial information on the major industrial firms in Japan.
Jobsons Yearbook of Public Companies, UK Dun & Bradstreet International, 1989 (updated annually).
Provides company information on over 15,000 companies in Australia and New Zealand.
Major Companies of the Far East 1989–90, Carr, J. (ed.), USA, Graham & Trotman/Kluwer, 1989.
Two-volume compilation on over 15,000 companies in Japan and the Far East.

Europe

Belgium and Luxembourg's 3,000 Largest Companies, UK, Dun & Bradstreet International, 1989.
Company information on the largest companies in the Benelux countries. Information includes details on company activity, assets, employees, profit and turnover.
Continental Europe, Ireland & U.K. Market Guide, UK, Dun & Bradstreet International, 1989 (updated annually).
An alphabetical listing of over 26,000 firms, with details of main sphere of activity, and brief notes on financial status.

Europe's 15,000 Largest Companies, UK, ELC International, 1988.
  Contains information on a selection of companies in the major countries of
  Europe. Includes Europe's 500 largest companies, industrials, trading and
  service companies, plus the largest companies in the 14 countries covered by
  the directory.

Extel European Companies Service, UK, Extel Financial Ltd, (card service updated
  weekly).
  Provides regularly updated information on the financial status of approx. 740
  companies, from 15 countries providing information on dividends, interim
  financial results together with information on the activities and structure of
  the company. Historical information in the form of ten years' profit-and-loss
  accounts and three years' balance sheets are also provided.

Kompass Directories Europe, UK, Kompass Publishers, 1989 (directories updated
  annually for each of the following European countries: Belgium, Denmark,
  Germany, France, Holland, Ireland, Italy, Luxembourg, Norway, Spain,
  Sweden and Switzerland).
  European Kompass directories contain product and service information. Also
  includes share capital and turnover information.

Major Companies of Europe 1989–90, USA, Graham & Trotman, (in three vols
  updated annually: vol. 1 – EC countries; vol. 2 – UK; vol. 3 – non-EC
  countries).
  Information on over 5,500 companies in Europe including name and address
  of company, major activity, trade names, directors and principal shareholders. Also includes financial information for the latest two years on
  profits, dividends, sales, share capital and earnings per share.
  Provides financial and company information on the largest Danish, Nor-
  wegian and Swedish companies ranked by turnover.

Who Owns Whom, Continental Europe, UK, Dun & Bradstreet International, 1989
  (updated annually).
  In two volumes: vol. 1 lists over 8,000 parent companies in 15 European
  countries, and details their foreign and domestic subsidiaries whilst vol. 2
  gives an alphabetical listing of all subsidiaries and associated companies cited
  in vol. 1.

Middle East

Major Companies of the Arab World 1989–90, USA, Graham & Trotman/Kluwer
  Publications, 7th edn, 1989.
  Provides company and financial information on the top companies in the
  Arab world.

UK

Bank Register, UK, Euromoney Publications, 1989 (updated annually).
  International directory, provides information on national and international
  banks arranged alphabetically by home country, including details of senior
  management, balance sheet information and information on subsidiaries.

Britain's Privately Owned Companies: the Top 2,000, UK, Jordan & Sons Ltd, 1989 (updated annually).

Provides information on the top 2,000 privately owned companies ranked by annual sales turnover, giving details of company name, address, activity assets and liabilities, pre-tax profit. Tables show leading companies in terms of exports, size and profitability.

Britain's Privately Owned Companies: the Next 2,000, UK, Jordan & Sons Ltd, 1989.

This volume contains similar information on UK companies ranked 3,000–4,000.

Britain's Top 1,000 Foreign-Owned Companies, UK, Jordan and Sons Ltd, 1989.

Provides information on companies registered on the UK Stock Exchange which have more than 50 per cent of their share capital in the hands of foreign-owned corporations. Companies are ranked by sales volume, and details of company name, address, activity, parent/holding company are provided. Other financial information includes assets, liabilities and pre-tax profit.

Crawford's Directory of City Connections, UK, Economist Publications Ltd, 1989.

Provides information on financial, stockbroking, investment and public relations advisors, etc. to major public and private companies in the UK. Also lists the individual advisors with a list of their clients.

Directory of City Business Services, Moody, M. (ed.), UK, Woodhead–Faulkner, 1990 (updated every two years).

Contains information on the names, addresses, telephone numbers of banks, investment trusts, unit trusts, stockbrokers, building societies, insurance companies and brokers, accountants, actuaries and allied financial services available in the City of London.

Directory of Directors, UK, Thomas Skinner Directories, 1988 (in two vols updated annually).

Provides information on directors of UK public and private companies. Arranged alphabetically by director's name – information includes all companies with which each director is connected. Vol. 2 includes financial information on the companies identified.

Extel Handbook of Market Leaders, UK, Extel Financial Ltd (updated every six months).

Contains information on all companies listed on the FT Actuaries All-Share index. Includes basic company information and main activities, and includes two years' balance sheets, three years' dividends and five years' profit-and-loss data and ordinary share record.

Extel UK Listed Companies Service, UK, Extel Financial Ltd (daily card service).

Contains information on 3,000 companies listed on the UK and Irish Stock Exchanges, including basic company information with a brief history of the company. Potted financial information on share prices, dividends, together with four-year consolidated balance sheet, summary of chairman's annual statements and a review of company activities, and five years' profit-and-loss accounts.

Growth Companies Register, UK, Growth Data Services Ltd, 1989 (updated annually).

Information on 2,000 privately owned companies with minimum profits of £50,000. Includes information on the company, name, address, main area of activity and includes a financial history for the previous three years including details of capital employed, return on capital, profits, profit margins, sales, etc.

Hambro Company Guide, UK, Hemmington–Scott Publishing Ltd (updated quarterly).

Contains information on all UK companies listed on the Stock Exchange or who trade in the Unlisted Securities Market, Third Market or Over-The-Counter Market. Provides basic company information plus five years' profit-and-loss accounts.

I.C.C. Datacards, UK, Inter Company Comparisons Ltd.

Provides financial information on UK limited companies together with a four-year analysis of the major business ratios.

Jordans Regional Surveys, UK, Jordan & Sons Ltd.

Provides information on major companies in a series of regional directories. Information includes company details, profit-and-loss accounts and brief financial summary for each company.

Kelly's Business Directory 1990, UK, Kelly's Directories, 1989.

Provides information on over 90,000 companies in the UK. Designed as a buyer's guide, companies are listed under subject headings. Contains relevant company information.

Key British Enterprises, UK, Dun & Bradstreet, 1989 (in three vols, updated annually with optional updates).

Contains detailed information on the top 25,000 companies in the UK. Arranged by company name, cross-referenced indices provide access by means of product group, business activity and geographical location. 1990 edition expanded to cover top 50,000 companies.

Kompass United Kingdom, UK, Kompass Publishers 1989 (in three vols, updated annually).

Information covers products and services, company information and financial information. Provides full details of company name, address, telephone/telex, company registration no., names of subsidiary companies, directors, bank, activity and type of goods manufactured (if applicable), in a geographical listing of companies. Three years' profit-and-loss account information is included in the financial volume, together with turnover, fixed assets, current assets, current liabilities, shareholders' funds.

McCarthys's UK Quoted Company Service, UK, McCarthy Information Ltd (updated weekly).

Card service provides extracts from recent press coverage of individual companies including news on all aspects of company activities. Items are abstracted from 20 leading newspapers from the UK and overseas.

McCarthy's UK Unquoted Company Service, UK, McCarthy Information Ltd (updated weekly).

Card service providing similar information to the Quoted Company Service, dealing with over 7,000 private companies.

Profit Growth 1,000, UK, I.C.C. Information Group Ltd, 1989.

Provides information on the 1,000 companies in the UK with the highest profit growth rate. Also includes company and financial information.

Sales Growth 1,000, UK, I.C.C. Information Group Ltd, 1989.

Provides information on the 1,000 companies in the UK with the fastest growth in sales. Also includes company and financial information.

Stock Exchange Official Yearbook 1989–90, UK, Macmillan Publishing, 1990, (updated annually).

Provides details of companies whose shares are quoted on the UK Stock Exchange. Information includes full details of the company, names of directors and details of subsidiary companies, a brief history of the company and a summary of the balance sheet, current cost account and capital structure of each company.

Times 1,000: Leading Companies in Britain and Overseas 1989–90, Allan, M. (ed.), Times Books Ltd, 1990 (updated annually).

Contains information on the top 1,000 UK companies ranked by turnover. Includes details on activity, export turnover, capital employed, profit and number of employees. Also includes an alphabetical listing of company addresses.

UK Trade Names, UK, Kompass Publishers, 10th edn, 1988.

Provides a means of identifying manufacturers of branded goods by means of an alphabetical index of trade names. Additional index provides a list of companies and their associated trade names. Excludes food, drink, tobacco and pharmaceutical companies.

Unquoted Companies: Financial Profiles of Britain's Top 10,000 Unquoted Companies, UK, Macmillan Publishing, 1989 (updated annually).

Contains detailed financial information on 10,000 companies taken from the latest two years' accounts of unquoted companies with an annual turnover of over £3m.

USM Company Performance: a Comprehensive Analysis of the Company and Sector Performance on the Unlisted Securities Market, UK, I.C.C. Information Group, 3rd edn, 1989 (updated irregularly).

Contains information on all companies trading on the USM market. Contains company information and financial profiles on individual companies, and also industry sector information including ratio tables and graphs.

Who Owns Whom: United Kingdom and the Republic of Ireland, UK, Dun & Bradstreet, 1989 (in two vols, updated annually).

Contains a list of all UK and Republic of Ireland registered parent companies together with their subsidiaries. Vol. 2 contains an alphabetical index of subsidiaries identifying their parent company.

USA and Canada

Anglo-American Trade Directory, UK, American Chamber of Commerce, 1989 (updated annually).

Contains information on UK and US organizations with transatlantic trade links, includes details of main activity of the companies and type of trade links currently engaged in.

Canadian Key Business Directory, UK, Dun & Bradstreet, 1990 (updated annually).

Contains information on larger Canadian companies.

Dun's Business Rankings, USA, Dun's Marketing Service (updated annually).

Contains information on over 7,500 US companies. Lists company, financial and sales information for the top companies ranked by industry and geographical location.

Extel North American Company Service, UK, Extel Financial Ltd (updated weekly).

Card service providing details on over 450 major companies listed on US and Canadian stock exchanges. Information coverage similar to UK service.

Fraser's Canadian Trade Directory, Canada, Fraser's Trade Directories (updated annually).

A classified listing of product manufacturers. Provides brief company details and includes a trade names index.

MacRae's Blue Book, USA, MacRae's Blue Book Inc., (updated annually).

An industrial buyers' guide providing details of over 60,000 US manufacturing companies. Includes company details, and lists sales offices and distributors. Also contains trade name and product indices.

Major Companies of the USA 1989–90, Wilson, A., and R. Whiteside (eds), USA, Graham & Trotman/Kluwer, 1989 (updated annually).

Contains information on over 4,000 US companies. Includes company details, and financial information for the past two years.

Standard and Poors' Corporation Records, USA, Standard & Poors (updated bimonthly).

Contains information on over 8,000 US companies including company history and financial data.

Standard and Poors' Register of Corporations, Directors and Executives, USA, Standard & Poors (in three vols: annual and cumulative supplements (updated annually).

Contains information on over 45,000 US companies. Vol. 1. provides an alphabetical listing of companies with details of their activities and sales figures. Vol. 2 provides details of over 70,000 executives. Vol. 3 indexes companies by SIC classification, location and corporate grouping.

Thomas Register of American Manufacturers, USA, Thomas Publishing Co. (in 17 vols, updated annually).

Contains information on over 123,000 companies. Includes product catalogues, trade names and industry classifications.

Ward's Business Directory, USA, Information Access Company (in three volumes, updated annually).
Provides company, sales and employee information for largest US companies, major private and international companies operating in the USA.
Who Owns Whom: North America, UK, Dun and Bradstreet, 1989 (updated annually).
Contains listings of US and Canadian parent companies, giving details of over 60,000 foreign and domestic subsidiaries.

Marketing information

FINDEX: the Directory of Market Research Reports, Studies and Surveys, USA, FIND/SVP.
Covers US market reports and surveys.
International Directory of Published Market Research, UK, British Overseas Trade Board, 13th edn, 1989 (annual).
Annual listing of international market research reports and findings.
Marketing Surveys Index, UK, MSI/Institute of Marketing (monthly).
Contains information on recently published reports, and includes some stockbrokers' reports.
World Sources of Market Information, Blauvelt, and E. J. Durlacher (eds), UK, Gower Publishing Co. (three vols, Asia/Pacific, Africa/Middle East, Europe; irregular).

Sector reports

I.C.C. Business Ratios. UK, I.C.C. Information Group (updated annually).
This series consists of reports which analyse the performance of 50–120 leading companies within each of 198 industry sectors. The individual reports provide company data sheets giving summary financial figures. Also includes financial ratios.
I.C.C. Financial Surveys, UK, I.C.C. Information Group (updated annually).
This series consists of 160 individual reports on various industry sectors, classified by SIC classification. Information given on individual companies within each sector and includes assets, liabilities, profits and two years' turnover figures.
Jordans Industry Sector Surveys, UK, Jordan Information Services.
Provides detailed surveys of the major UK business sectors. Full details are provided for all companies included in each sector including a financial summary of the latest three years' accounts. Each report also includes a detailed summary of the current state of the industry, and prospects for future developments, and provides comparative performance tables.

Business periodicals

Asia Pacific Journal of Management, Singapore, School of Management, National University of Singapore (three times per year).

The Australian Journal of Management, Australia, Australian Graduate School of Management, University of New South Wales (twice per year).

The Banker, UK, Financial Times Business Information (monthly).

California Management Review, USA, University of California (three times per year).

Columbia Journal of World Business, USA, Columbia Business School, Columbia University (quarterly).

The Economist, UK, Economist Publications (weekly).

Euromoney, UK, Euromoney Publications plc (monthly).

European Journal of Marketing, UK, MCB University Press (quarterly).

European Management Journal, UK, Basil Blackwell for the European School of Management/Glasgow Business School (quarterly).

Forbes, USA, Forbes Inc. (fortnightly).

Fortune, USA, Time Inc., New York (fortnightly).

Harvard Business Review, USA, Harvard Univ. Press, Boston (bi-monthly).

Journal of Accountancy, USA, American Institute of Certified Public Accountants (monthly).

Journal of Banking and Finance, Netherlands, Elsevier/North-Holland (quarterly).

Journal of Business Finance and Accounting, UK, Basil Blackwell (quarterly).

Journal of International Business Studies, USA, Academy of International Business (quarterly).

Journal of International Financial Management and Accounting, UK, Basil Blackwell (quarterly).

Management International Review, Germany, Gabler Verlag (quarterly).

Management Today, UK, Management Publications Ltd (monthly).

On-Line information sources

European databases

European Kompass On-line, Host: Koda On-line.
  Contains regularly updated details on over 300,000 companies in 12 European countries.

Financial Times Company Information, Host: Datastar (updated daily – two-day time lag).
  Includes all articles dealing with individual companies appearing in the London and Frankfurt editions of the *Financial Times*.

Hoppenstedt Austria, Host: Datastar (updated annually).
  Contains descriptions of Austrian companies having over 200 employees or a turnover of over 100 million Austrian schillings. Includes company and financial information.

Hoppenstedt Germany, Host: Datastar & Dialog (updated six-monthly).
  Contains details of over 36,000 West German companies with over 20 employees of annual turnover in excess of DM2m. Includes company and financial information.

Hoppenstedt Netherlands, Host: Datastar (updated annually).
Contains company and financial information on over 20,000 Dutch companies.

PTS Prompt, Hosts: Datastar, Dialog.
Contains abstracts of articles containing company, production and market information from newspapers, periodicals, trade journals, government and special reports worldwide.

Japanese databases

Nomura Research Institute (NRI/E), Host: Wharton Econometric Forecasting.
Contains details, in English, of financial, macroeconomic and industrial data on Japan.

North American databases

Disclosure Financials, Host: Dialog, BRS (updated weekly).
Contains detailed financial information on over 10,000 US companies. Information includes activities, directors, employees, five years' annual income statements and balance sheets, price and earnings information, financial ratios.

Disclosure Management, Host: Dialog.
Contains management information on over 10,000 US companies.

Dun's Market Identifier, Host: Dialog, Pergamon Infoline.
Contains credit reports on over 2 million privately owned US companies.

PTS Annual Report Abstracts, Host: Dialog, DataStar, BRS.
Produced by Predicasts, covers information on over 3,000 public companies.

UK databases

Accountancy and Tax Database, Host: Textline (updated weekly).
Full text database of major British accounting journals.

CSO Databank, Host: CSI–Wharton EFA Ltd.
Contains information on all aspects of the UK economy from statistics compiled by the Central Statistics Office and Bank of England in the form of time series of monthly, quarterly and annual statistics including national accounts, balance of payments and financial statistics.

Dun's Marketing Online, Host: Pergamon Infoline.
Provides information on over 400,000 UK companies including employees, directors and financial information.

I.C.C. Directory of Companies, Host: Datastar, Dialog, I.C.C. Viewdata (updated weekly).
Contains company and financial information on over 1 million companies in the UK. Includes information on companies dissolved since 1968. Additional information is given for up to 90,000 significant public and private companies in the form of Financial Datasheets which include activities, directors, profit and loss accounts, balance sheets and business ratios.

Company Profile Host: Infocheck Ltd.

Contains information on UK limited companies based on information from Companies Registration Office and the financial and business press.

Datastream Company Accounts, Host: Datastream (updated weekly).

Contains data extracted from company annual reports. Covers quoted and unquoted UK companies, US, Canadian, French and German quoted companies. Information includes company profiles, profit-and-loss accounts, balance sheets and ratio analysis. Due to the complexity and flexibility of datastream programs, this database allows users to combine data from a variety of datastream files in order to construct accounting ratios and to effect comparisons of accounting data.

Exstat. Host: ADP, DRI, Finsbury Data Services.

Contains information on over 4,000 companies in the UK, Europe, Australia and Japan. Provides current and historical financial data with up to 13 years' data available.

Financial Times Company Abstracts, Host: Dialog.

Provides information on over 30,000 companies worldwide. Coverage from 1981.

I.C.C. Financial Datasheets, Host: I.C.C. Viewdata, Dialog.

Provides financial information on over 100,000 UK-registered companies including financial history, accounts, etc.

Infocheck, Host: Telecom Gold, Prestel.

Provides basic company information on over 1 million companies, together with more detailed financial information on up to 200,000 of these.

Jordans, Host: Pergamon Infoline, Jordans Viewdata Services (updated weekly).

Contains information on UK-registered companies taken from Companies Registration Office. Information includes company and financial details, e.g. profit-and-loss accounts and balance sheets.

Key British Enterprises, Host: Pergamon Infoline (updated monthly).

Contains details on the top 20,000 UK companies ranked by turnover. Information includes sales, turnover, exports, directors and employee numbers.

Kompass On-line, Host: Reed Information Services, Dialog.

Provides directory-type information on both UK companies and European Kompass On-line. The UK companies file includes data from Kompass, Kelly's and various other directories covering over 1 million companies. Information includes products and services, directors and executives, and selected financial data. Information can be accessed by individual records or by product, location or size of company. The European Kompass file contains details on over 300,000 European companies, giving company information, directors and nature of products or services.

McCarthy Online, Host: Profile Information.

Database covering information from newspapers and periodicals. Divided into two sections: press cuttings service and company fact sheets. Press cuttings service provides access to information from international sources. Company fact sheets provide detailed information on companies.

Management Analysis and Information Database (MAID), Host: Maid Systems Ltd.
 Contains full-text marketing reports from a variety of internationally
 renowned printed sources, and a daily news service of indexed materials
 from over 600 international sources.

Mergers and Acquisitions Database, Host: Infocheck Ltd.
 Database covering mergers and acquisitions since 1979. Divided into three
 sections: Europe, UK, USA, although the latter has the fullest coverage to
 date.

PTS F & S, Host: Predicasts Inc.
 Selected coverage of US business, financial and trade journals, based on
 Predicasts' printed information sources. Increasing coverage of European
 sources.

PTS Prompt, Host: Predicasts Europe.
 International coverage of business information abstracted from newspapers,
 trade journals and other special reports. Also includes a Business International Series of newsletters and reports.

Profile Information, Host: Profile Information.
 Contains full-text information from newspapers, periodicals and media
 services worldwide.

Textline, Host: Finsbury Data Services.
 Contains both abstracts and full-text information from over 1,000 international sources, with records commencing in 1980. Subject coverage
 includes company and market information, products and services, and
 economic and political news.

Who Owns Whom, Host: Pergamon Infoline, (updated monthly).
 Contains information on parent–subsidiary groups worldwide.

Business statistics

UK

Annual Abstract of Statistics, UK, HMSO.
 Contains information on all aspects of economic and social trends in the UK
 including agriculture, industrial production, balance of payments, etc. Over
 400 tables give figures for 11 years with some monthly and quarterly figures
 included.

Economic Trends, UK, HMSO (updated monthly).
 Contains information on the economic situation in the UK by means of charts
 and tables. Information includes statistical data and key economic indicators.
 Balance of payments information and details of the national accounts appear
 quarterly.

Financial Statistics, UK, HMSO (updated monthly).
 Detailed analysis of UK financial and monetary statistics, including national
 accounts, Public Sector Borrowing Requirements, government expenditure
 and interest rates.

HMSO Business Monitors, UK, HMSO (updated quarterly).
 A series of reports concerning production and trade statistics covering the

complete range of products and services identified by the Standard Industrial Classification. In three sections: Production Monitors (PQ Series) – containing 160 individual industry sectors (also includes Monthly Production Monitors (PM Series), Annual Census of Production Monitors and Occasional Production Monitors); Service and Distribution Monitors provide information on short-term trends in the service and distribution industries; and Miscellaneous Monitors which include topics such as current cost accounting, company finance, and mergers and acquisitions.

Monthly Digest of Statistics, UK, HMSO (updated monthly).
The monthly supplement to the Annual Abstract of Statistics, providing updated information for the major tables. Most information covers monthly and quarterly tabulations for at least two years.

Overseas Trade Statistics of the United Kingdom, UK, HMSO (updated monthly with annual cumulation).
Provides detailed figures of imports and exports. Information is arranged by total figures for each month and for the year to date, area and country for each month and for the year to date, and commodity.

Sources of Unofficial UK Statistics, compiled by David Mort and Leona Siddall, UK, Gower, 1986.
Lists over 1,000 statistical sources from a variety of non-government sources including academic institutions, banks and trade unions.

A Survey of United Kingdom Non-Official Statistical Sources and their role in Business Information, UK, Leona Siddall, University of Warwick Library, 1984.

International

Business Conditions Digest, USA, Bureau of Economic Analysis (updated monthly).
Provides economic and trade statistics for the USA.

Business Statistics, USA, Bureau of Economic Analysis (updated six-monthly).
Provides statistical information on the business environment in the USA.

Main Economic Indicators, France, OECD (updated monthly).
Provides detailed information on the economies of all OECD member countries with tables covering national accounts, industrial production, labour, prices, finance, interest rates and trade.

Statistics America, UK, CBD Research Ltd.
Provides information on sources of US statistics including publisher and contents for each statistical source listed.

Statistics Asia and Australia, UK, CBD Research Ltd.
Provides information on statistical sources for each country.

Statistics Europe, UK, CBD Research Ltd.
Provides bibliographical information on sources of statistics for each European country.